P9-CND-051

STRESS LESS

DON COLBERT, MD

SILOAM
A STRANG COMPANY

Most STRANG COMMUNICATIONS/CHARISMA HOUSE/SILOAM products are available at special quantity discounts for bulk purchase for sales promotions, premiums, fund-raising, and educational needs. For details, write Strang Communications/Charisma House/Siloam, 600 Rinehart Road, Lake Mary, Florida 32746, or telephone (407) 333-0600.

STRESS LESS by Don Colbert, MD
Published by Siloam
A Strang Company
600 Rinehart Road
Lake Mary, Florida 32746
www.siloam.com

This book or parts thereof may not be reproduced in any form, stored in a retrieval system, or transmitted in any form by any means—electronic, mechanical, photocopy, recording, or otherwise—without prior written permission of the publisher, except as provided by United States of America copyright law.

Unless otherwise noted, all Scripture quotations are from the New King James Version of the Bible. Copyright © 1979, 1980, 1982 by Thomas Nelson, Inc., publishers. Used by permission.

Scripture quotations marked AMP are from the Amplified Bible. Old Testament copyright © 1965, 1987 by the Zondervan Corporation. The Amplified New Testament copyright © 1954, 1958, 1987 by the Lockman Foundation. Used by permission.

Scripture quotations marked KJV are from the King James Version of the Bible.

Scripture quotations marked NIV are from the Holy Bible, New International Version. Copyright © 1973, 1978, 1984, International Bible Society. Used by permission.

Scripture quotations marked NLT are from the Holy Bible, New Living Translation, copyright © 1996. Used by permission of Tyndale House Publishers, Inc., Wheaton, IL 60189.

All rights reserved.

Cover design by DogEared Design/Kirk DuPonce
Interior design by Terry Clifton

Copyright © 2005 by Don Colbert, MD
All rights reserved

Library of Congress Cataloging-in-Publication Data:
Colbert, Don.
Stress less / Don Colbert.
p. cm.
ISBN 1-59185-611-6 (hardback)
1. Stress (Psychology) 2. Stress management. 37
3. Stress--Religious aspects--Christianity. I. Title.
RA785.C63 2005
155.9'042--dc22
2005005023

Neither the publisher nor the author is engaged in rendering professional advice or services to the individual reader. The ideas, procedures, and suggestions in this book are not intended as a substitute for consulting with your physician. All matters regarding your health require medical supervision. Neither the author nor the publisher shall be liable or responsible for any loss or damage allegedly arising from any information or suggestion in this book.

While the author has made every effort to provide accurate telephone numbers and Internet addresses at the time of publication, neither the publisher nor the author assumes any responsibility for errors or for changes that occur after publication.

People and incidents in this book are composites created by the author from his experiences in private practice. Names and details of the stories have been changed, and any similarity between the names and stories of individuals described in this book to individuals known to readers is purely coincidental.

05 06 07 08 09 — 987654321
Printed in the United States of America

Dedication

I would like to dedicate this book to my fellow physicians and colleagues. Ask any physician why he or she chose to practice medicine, and the majority of them will tell you that they had a sincere desire to make a difference in the world one patient at a time. Perhaps the Hippocratic Oath intrigued them: "First do no harm." Most physicians genuinely want to help heal people.

The life of a physician is extremely stressful. Many new physicians aren't aware just how stressful a life in medicine will be. But they soon find out as the tremendous stress and pressures of the health-care industry bear down upon them, rendering many physicians frustrated, exhausted, anxious, overwhelmed, and literally stressed out!

There are outside stressors adding to the burden for physicians, such as the insurance industries with their Preferred Provider Organizations (PPOs) and Healthcare Maintenance Organizations (HMOs), which sign over hundreds of patients to manage yet offer very little compensation for the physician's services.

Governmentally run health-care plans such as Medicare and Medicaid implement rules and regulations for treating their patients that make rendering good quality medical care incredibly difficult and even more stressful. Each year these plans seem to find new ways to further cut physician reimbursement or deny important preventative screenings and procedures.

Physicians can't just focus on patient care anymore. Medical practitioners are under siege by governmental agencies like OSHA, CLIA, AHCA, and other organizations that require the physician to strictly adhere to their rules and regulations, thus making solo practitioners struggle to maintain a thriving medical practice.

Malpractice insurance has become a major concern. Physicians are finding it increasingly more difficult to find, maintain, and afford malpractice insurance. Today's society seems to be focusing more on "litigation" in the medical field. Attorneys have taken to the airwaves advertising on television in an attempt to find more physicians to sue. Physicians are feeling the "squeeze" from all sides. It's similar to a fat tuna swimming in a tank full of sharks. Malpractice rates are skyrocketing and forcing many physicians to close their doors.

Cutbacks in insurance reimbursements have caused physicians to see more patients and work longer hours. As a result, they spend less quality time with their own families. This lack of time spent with loved ones often contributes to divorce, rebellious children, drug and alcohol consumption, and eventually real health issues for the physician himself.

Our physicians are our healers, and we must protect them from burnout and an early demise. I pray that this book helps my colleagues as well as others who are suffering from the dangerous effects of stress.

Acknowledgments

There are so many people who work behind the scenes on all my projects. I simply assume that they realize how important each and every one of them is to me. However, I would like to take a moment to express my sincere thanks to those people who have blessed my life and let them know how important they are to me.

First, I would like to thank Stephen Strang, Bert Ghezzi, Jeff Gerke, Deborah Moss, and the whole Siloam family for believing in me and my work and for helping me to bring it to fruition.

I wish to acknowledge my office staff who work in the trenches with me every day, lending their expertise and invaluable support: Amy Russo, Sherry Kaiser, Ana Rivera, Jennifer Weaver, Birgita Kerns, Taylor McClure, and Debbie Day. You have my sincere appreciation and thanks!

A special note of appreciation goes to Erin Leigh O'Donnell, Jan Dargatz, and Kay Webb for their assistance in this publication.

I offer my heartfelt thanks to my wife, Mary, who has supported me throughout this endeavor.

Contents

1

I Am a Physician Who HAS Healed Myself

I have had my share of stress. Perhaps even more than my "share."

In my third year of medical school, while running a 3-mile run in 95-degree weather, with almost 100 percent humidity, I suffered a massive heat stroke. My body temperature reached 108 degrees Fahrenheit.

I was rushed to a hospital emergency room where I received intravenous fluids. My leg muscles were literally bursting, however—the medical condition is called rhabdomyolysis. I watched as my legs withered before my eyes. The pain was excruciating.

I was hospitalized for two to three weeks so I could receive massive amounts of intravenous fluids and be monitored for kidney failure. I began urinating coffee-colored urine from the muscle breakdown, and I was so weak that I eventually was forced to use a wheelchair.

Rather than improving, my condition grew worse as my leg muscles continued to deteriorate in spite of all the treatments. A surgeon was called in to perform a muscle biopsy. This revealed extensive muscle necrosis—in other words, muscle cell death. I was told I would probably never walk again. By this time, my arms actually appeared larger than my legs.

I felt under extreme stress. I had missed more than a month of medical school, and now I was being told I would probably never walk again!

I needed a miracle, and I received one. After a couple of months of rest and a lot of prayer, I was able to walk again. Miraculously I regained the strength as well as the size of my leg muscles.

As a result of missing so much school, I had a significant amount of makeup work to do. Medical school is difficult enough without falling a month behind. Again, prayer and God's wisdom about how best to use my time and focus my studies pulled me through.

After I graduated from medical school, I began my internship and residency at Florida Hospital in Orlando, Florida, in the specialty of family medicine. I was on call every fourth night and usually did not sleep while on call. The stress of a resident's schedule and the demands of the work—which often are stressful to the point that many medical school graduates burn out during this period—were compounded by the birth of our son, Kyle. I pressed on, however!

In my second year of residency I worked part time or "moonlighted" in emergency rooms one to two weekends a month. One emergency room had a forty-eight-hour shift over the weekend. That was a particularly rough job since I got no sleep all weekend and then had to be present bright and early for my training as a resident on Monday morning.

After residency I opened a solo private practice in family medicine. I worked five days a week and took "beeper call" every night for years. I did not take a vacation for ten years. Many nights I was awakened from a sound sleep by patients who called with rather minor problems, such as constipation or insomnia. One couple actually phoned to ask me to give them some marriage counseling by phone at four o'clock in the morning!

The stress of this pace eventually took its toll on my body, as well as on my mind and emotions. One morning I awakened with intense itching and a rash on my legs. I applied hydrocortisone cream, but the rash and itching worsened and spread to my knees, arms, elbows, and hands. I thought I might have contracted scabies from a patient I had seen recently. I applied Kwell lotion from my chin down, but the rash and itching grew worse. Finally I consulted a dermatologist—a friend of mine—and he diagnosed me as having psoriasis, but not the typical psoriasis with plaques and silvery scales. He prescribed cold tar creams that caused me to smell like kerosene and stained my clothes and sheets yellow orange. The rash and itching persisted.

Many of my patients took one look at my skin and asked me about my "problem." They no doubt feared I was contagious!

Eventually, through detoxification procedures and nutritional supplementation, the psoriasis cleared up, but I began to notice that it would flare up again every time I was severely stressed.

The stress of excessive work—not only the long hours and pressures associated with medicine, but also too many nights on call without any breaks—caused me to feel extremely fatigued, and my immune system became compromised. I developed recurrent sinus infections and took antibiotics frequently to treat the sinusitis. Then I developed severe irritable bowel syndrome, with abdominal pain, bloating, and episodes of diarrhea. The tremendous fatigue led to short-term memory loss. To top it all off, I continued to feel overwhelmed emotionally by the debt I had incurred in opening up a solo private practice while paying off medical-school loans. Like many physicians, I also feared potential lawsuits and found the rising costs of malpractice insurance to be a staggering financial burden. In other words, I was also suffering from anxiety.

All of these factors seemed to influence one another to create something of a downward spiral—the fatigue grew worse; my immune system was further weakened; and the chronic sinusitis, psoriasis, and irritable bowel syndrome were aggravated. The more I suffered from infections and irritable bowel syndrome, the more fatigue I felt and the weaker my immune system became. I was trapped! I was a medical doctor, but I was sick—I was literally stewing in my own juices and saw no way out of my stress.

I remember what a psychiatry professor—a former dermatologist—shared during a lecture in medical school. In his previous practice, he treated many patients who had suffered with psoriasis. I was curious as to why he no longer practiced as a dermatologist but instead chose psychiatry, and his answer surprised me. He told me that treating so many people suffering from skin disorders led him to the conclusion that people were actually "weeping through their skin." That is what prompted him to go back to residency training in psychiatry. He knew the skin disorder was just a superficial sign of a much deeper problem.

That should have been the time when things hit bottom...but no. I compounded my own stress by writing books and facing publisher deadlines. By then my son had become a teenager and went through a rebellious stage. I spent many sleepless nights in prayer for him.

Do I know about stress? Indeed, I do.

I had to learn to deal with stress—not in theory, but in order to survive. The information you will read in this book is what I applied to my own life. It literally saved me from mental, emotional, and physical illness, and probably an early death. What I share with you in this book I have applied to my own life. I continue to live by these principles, which I have also taught to countless other people. I count it a privilege to share these truths with you.

If I could find a way out of my own stress, I have no doubt that you can, too! I believe in a brighter, healthier future for you.

One Nation, Under Stress

We have a stress epidemic in our nation.

The majority of Americans very likely have excessive stress in their lives, and reports of stress seem to indicate that the percentage of Americans each year who feel under "a great deal of stress" is rising.

Did you know that 75 to 90 percent of all visits to a primary care physician's office are related to stress disorders? That's according to the American Institute of Stress.

What is driving us to the shelves of a pharmacy? Feelings of stress. Americans are consuming five billion tranquilizers, five billion barbiturates, three billion amphetamines, and sixteen tons of aspirin every year.[1] Much of this "medicine" is being taken to help alleviate stress or the resulting headaches and pain associated with stress!

The stress-management industry is flourishing. Many people are taking short courses or reading books to learn techniques for stress management such as time-management skills, coping mechanisms, relaxation techniques, and other strategies. Some stress-management courses offer instruction that is action oriented—confronting problems head-on, thus changing one's perception or environment. Other courses offer emotional skills, which allow a person to change his or her perception of a circumstance but not actually change the circumstance. Still other stress-management courses offer coping or acceptance skills to help a person accept inevitable stress in a healthier way. This latter approach is often easier said than done. Accepting things that cannot be changed is often difficult when a person is feeling overwhelmed or frustrated.

Sadly, our children are not immune to stress. The American Academy of Pediatrics estimated in the year 2000 that one in five children in the United States had psychosocial problems related to stress—this was up from one in fourteen children in 1979.

We are at epidemic levels of depression, anxiety, eating disorders, obesity, type 2 diabetes, heart disease, hypertension, sexual dysfunction, sleep disorders (especially insomnia), osteoporosis, alcoholism, road rage and other forms of violent behavior, PMS, and headaches—and at the root of most of these diseases and ailments we find excessive stress!

Instead of treating the root cause of these ailments, however, many physicians are treating the symptoms. Prescriptions for antidepressants or antistress medications such as Prozac, Zoloft, Paxil, and Lexapro are at an all-time high. These drugs, however, do not prevent stress. There are serious doubts about their ability to treat stress in the long run. Furthermore, many medications used to treat stress are addictive, which may mean they are even more stress producing with prolonged use.

This book is about how stress manifests itself in the body, the root causes of stress, and the ways in which we might reduce stress. It is aimed at helping you deal with the root cause of what ails you.

WHAT IS STRESS, AND WHERE DOES IT COME FROM?

We have a common phrase in our culture: "I'm stressed out!" But what does that really mean? Does it mean to be overwhelmed for a day or two by too much to do in too little time? Does it mean that the person is in panic mode while facing a pressing deadline? Does it mean that the person has had so much stress for so long that there are no physical or emotional reserves left from which to draw strength and energy?

In my opinion, stress is the pressures of life and how one perceives, believes, reacts, and copes with these pressures. All forms of stress, however, produce a very well-documented physical reaction in the body. The actual definition from Webster's is "a physical, chemical, or emotional factor that causes bodily or mental tension and may be a factor in disease causation." The body's stress response involves more than fourteen hundred known physical and chemical reactions involving more than thirty different hormones and neurotransmitters. Excessive release of "stress hormones" damages cells, tissues, and organs.

For most people, the daily stress hassles are the most damaging to the body. Internalizing stress creates something of a steady drip, drip, drip of stress hormones into the person's tissues, including the brain. The little stressors add up over time and can do far more damage than an occasional negative event that might produce a more massive stress reaction.

MAJOR CATEGORIES OF STRESS PRODUCERS

The potential sources of stress are endless and everywhere. Anything that might rob us of our peace and joy, and eventually compromise our health, might be considered a source of stress. One researcher broke down sources of stress into *major life stressors* and *daily life stressors.* The top causes for stress were identified for each category, as shown below:[2]

Major life stressors (chronic)

- Divorce
- Death of a family member
- Prolonged illness
- Poverty
- Unhappiness in the workplace

Daily life stressors (acute)

- Traffic jams
- Paying bills
- Family tension
- Noise

- Crowds
- Sleep disturbance
- Isolation
- Hunger
- Danger

FOUR CATEGORIES OF STRESS

There is another system of classification that may give us a more detailed picture of stress-causing agents. This one places stress into four general categories: physical stress, emotional and mental stress, chemical stress, and thermal stress. Let's take a brief look at each one.

Physical stress

Physical stress often arises from a lack of sleep, overworking, excessive exercise, physical injury or trauma such as a motor vehicle accident, surgery, infections, physical disease, and chronic pain. Chronic infections are especially stressful to the body. Longstanding and frequently recurring bouts of sinusitis, bronchitis, Epstein-Barr virus, prostatitis, and chronic H. pylori gastritis all cause chronic physical stress. The more severe the infection—especially pneumonia or kidney infections—and the longer the infection lasts, the more stress the body experiences.

Major diseases and conditions such as heart disease, diabetes, arthritis, Alzheimer's disease, cancer, asthma, and autoimmune disease generally stimulate a chronic stress response in the body. Certain physiologic changes can add to a person's stress burden—for example, menopause, hormonal imbalance, inadequate nutrition, insomnia, and various factors associated with aging.

Not all conditions or environments produce physical stress to the same degree in each person. A workout at the gym may not produce physical stress for one person, yet produces significant stress for another. Some people thrive on hard manual labor, strenuous sports, and difficult physical challenges such as mountain climbing. Others feel tremendous stress associated with these activities.

Emotional and mental stress

This area of stress is also called psychological stress, and we will use the terms *emotional, mental,* and *psychological* stress interchangeably since there's a great deal of overlap in the medical research when it comes to these terms.

Various emotions such as anger, hostility, depression, anxiety, and fear can cause chronic emotional stress. The same for "mental stress"—the worries and general anxiety that often arise from too much work and too little play, too much debt, marital difficulties, children using drugs or alcohol, and other mental stresses related to one's work, finances, family issues, or school. Mental stress often arises from a feeling of being overwhelmed, losing control, or feeling trapped with no way out. Perfectionists who continually strive to do more and more, and who constantly drive themselves with no real feelings of satisfaction at their own performance, are especially prone to mental stress.

A person's brain interprets whether a situation or interaction is stressful or not. In other words, any condition or circumstance can become stressful if you think it is!

At times, two people may view the same situation and come up with very different conclusions based upon their perceptions. One person's stress may be another person's pleasure. I used to dread public speaking—it caused me a great deal of stress. After speaking, I would be drenched in sweat. My wife, however, seems to thrive on public speaking; therefore, she would volunteer my speaking services frequently!

Many people who suffer from depression, anxiety, frustration, anger, fear, and guilt have habitual distortional thought patterns (more on these later) that lock them into a stress-producing mentality.

Family fights, pressing deadlines, too many commitments, and a too-busy lifestyle can all result in mental and emotional stress.

Chemical stress

Chemical stress comes from excessive use of various substances such as excessive sugar, caffeine, stimulants, alcohol, nicotine (cigarette smoking), and food additives. Chemical stress is also related to substances to which a person may be exposed in the environment: mold, dust, allergens, and toxic chemicals such as diesel exhaust, secondhand cigarette smoke, and pesticides. Various unwanted chemicals in our foods and beverages can cause a chemical burden to the body, such as mercury in fish, cadmium in shellfish, and chemicals such as chlorine in tap water. Mercury in dental amalgams can cause chemical stress. Marijuana is a major chemical stressor to the adrenal glands, possibly owing to marijuana's effects on blood glucose levels. People who smoke marijuana just one time a week for several months are much more prone to signs of significant adrenal fatigue.

Certain environments, such as crowded cities, gridlock traffic patterns, and areas with numerous factories, seem to be loaded with more chemical-related stress sources than others. Not every person responds to these environmental factors in the same way, however. One person might develop allergies, asthma, recurrent infections, severe breathing problems, and adrenal fatigue in a polluted environment; another person might have no obvious physical reactions.

Thermal stress

The final category of stress is related to being exposed to extremes in temperature, either hot or cold, for prolonged periods of time. Individuals who suffer from heat exhaustion, heat stroke, and hypothermia experience severe thermal stress. Thermal stress is actually rare in our culture today since the vast majority of people have heating and air conditioning systems in their homes and cars, but occasionally an athlete will suffer from thermal stress by exercising too much in extreme heat. Hikers, mountain climbers, or boaters may also suffer from hypothermia after getting lost and having inadequate shelter or clothing in extremely cold conditions.

HOW TO KEEP FROM DROWNING IN A SEA OF STRESSORS

Countless people today are drowning in a sea of stressors. Some of the stress sources are ones over which a person has no control. At the other end of the spectrum are stress sources that are of our own making! Between these two extremes are countless stress sources that can be managed and controlled. At the outset of this book, we need to recognize that we each have a tremendous capacity to control the critical factors related to stress:

- We can control our thoughts.
- We can control our social situations—and define or redefine our relationships.
- We can control, to a certain extent, our exposure to chemically polluted environments.

Dr. Albert Ellis, a renowned psychologist and the founder of rational emotive therapy, once said, "The best years of your life are the ones in which you decide the problems are your own. You do not blame them on your mother, the ecology, or the president. You realize that you control your own destiny."[3]

Owning up to the truth that we do have control over significant portions of our life is often the first step toward reducing stress in our lives.

Controlling our own thoughts

We each can transform our thoughts—we can change the way we think. We can "rewire" the thought patterns in our own minds and adopt new thought habits. We can alter our perceptions and reactions so that we are able to flow with a stressful situation, much as a surfer rides a wave and lets the wave carry him toward the beach, in contrast to a swimmer who fights a riptide that seems to suck him back out to sea.

Let me give you an example of this. Since the disastrous events of September 11, 2001, a whole new layer of "stress producers" seems to have been added to our culture. People are concerned about the threat of terrorism, especially people who live in large cities, people who live close to nuclear facilities, and people who perceive that they are more prone to chemical or biological acts of terror. The threat of terrorism has produced longer waits and searches at airports and has resulted in various restrictions or new rules imposed in public buildings and schools.

Much of our response to terrorism, however, is a matter of how we think about terrorism. A person might have a general feeling of a loss of safety or increased vulnerability—these feelings may or may not be related to anything that is real. These feelings are far more likely related to how a person thinks and feels! A long wait in an airport line might be perceived as a minor nuisance by one person, a pressure-filled incident by another person who did not allow enough time before a flight for the more thorough security procedures, an opportunity to talk to new people by yet another person, or a fear-inducing threat factor by a fourth person. The amount of stress produced by the same long line in an airport becomes a matter of how a person perceives and thinks!

Controlling our own social and "chemical" environments

We each have a significant capacity to make our own world. The majority of us can choose where and how we will live—the schedules we will keep, the projects we will take on, the commitments we will make, the housing and neighborhoods in which we will live, and the people with whom we will associate. We can determine the closeness of a relationship. We can choose how we will respond to what others around us say and do.

We generally can't control with whom we will work. One scientific study has concluded that the leading source of stress for adults in our nation is our work. An estimated 60 percent of all absenteeism from work is related to stress.[4]

How much control?

"But," you may be saying, "how much stress can I eliminate from my life through the things I can control?" The answer is, a great deal!

Emotional stress and mental stress cause the same hormonal response in the body as physical, chemical, and thermal stressors. A person who is capable of lowering emotional and mental stress can lower his risk of developing diseases that kill. The flip side of this truth is that people who do not learn to manage their emotional and mental stress often experience higher rates of disease. Consider these research findings:

- A long-term study by Dr. Hans Eysenck and his colleagues at the University of London showed that chronic unmanaged stress—of the emotional and mental variety—was six times more predictive of cancer and heart disease than cigarette smoking, high cholesterol levels, and elevated blood pressure. These researchers concluded in their study what many people would see as the obvious: it is much easier to intervene at the stress stage than to intervene in the cancer and heart disease stage![5]

- According to a Mayo Clinic study of people with heart disease, psychological stress was the strongest predictor of future cardiac events.[6]

- In one ten-year study, people who were *not* able to manage their stress effectively had a 40 percent higher death rate than those who were "unstressed."[7]

- In a study of people with heart disease, researchers found a 74 percent reduction in cardiac events—including death, bypass operations, and heart attacks—in the study group that had stress-management training.[8]

FOUR BASIC TRUTHS ABOUT STRESS

At the outset of this book, let's establish a foundation of basic truths about stress. There are four concepts that I hope you will hold in your memory as you read about specific causes and treatments of stress.

Principle #1: Not all stress is bad.

Not all stressful moments are bad. In fact, the right amount of stress helps to spice up a person's life. Too little stress can make a person feel tired, listless, and less stimulated. Life would be boring without a little stress.

Some events in life are a mixed bag—a little stressful, but fulfilling and exciting as well. A wedding, buying a new home and moving into it, starting a new job, or facing an important must-win sporting event are all events that can be stressful, but they can also be personally rewarding or beneficial to a person's performance. Other events, such as facing an angry boss after blowing a "big contract," are just sheer stress!

Finding the right amount of stress can be similar to tuning the strings of a guitar—too tight and the strings snap, too loose and the tone is lousy.

Principle #2: Too much stress is bad.

Excessive stress is extremely damaging to the human body. Excessive stress can be either too much stress of the acute or short-term variety, or it can be stress for too long a time—the chronic or long-term variety. Excessive stress predisposes a person to develop:

- Cardiovascular disease and hypertension, elevated cholesterol levels, arrhythmias (abnormal heart rhythms), mitral valve prolapse, and palpitations, as well as heart attack and stroke.

- Skin eruptions such as seborrhea, eczema, hives, psoriasis, and even acne.

- GI disorders such as irritable bowel syndrome, gastroesophageal reflux disease, gastritis, ulcers, and inflammatory bowel disease (such as ulcerative colitis and Crohn's disease).

- Autoimmune diseases such as rheumatoid arthritis, lupus, and multiple sclerosis.

- Genitourinary problems including impotence, infertility, chronic prostatitis, recurrent urinary tract infections, recurrent yeast infections, imbalance of sex hormones, decreased sex drive, and frequent urination.

- Immune impairments that lead to chronic and recurrent ear infections, colds, sinus infections, sore throats, bouts with the flu, bronchitis, or pneumonia, as well as chronic and recurring infections of all types.

- Pain and inflammatory conditions such as tendonitis, migraine and tension headaches, carpal tunnel syndrome, TMJ problems, fibromyalgia, chronic back pain, and other chronic pain syndromes.

- Other ailments including chemical sensitivities, chronic allergies (both environmental and food), and chronic fatigue.

Chronic stress has been shown to slowly erode bone mass and may eventually lead to osteoporosis.

Long-term stress can affect a person's mental state and has been known to cause memory loss. Chronic stress exposes the brain cells to high levels of cortisol, which actually causes brain cells to shrink in size. Long-standing stress can cause progressive damage of these brain cells and may lead to Alzheimer's disease.

Stress has been associated with many emotional problems, including all forms of anxiety: generalized anxiety, phobias, obsessive-compulsive disorder, post-traumatic stress disorder, panic disorder, as well as plain ol' everyday worry. Depression, addictions, and overeating—as well as most emotional and mental diseases—are associated with long-term, excessive stress.

Long-term emotional stress often results from deep feelings of unforgiveness, unresolved anger, chronic anxiety, fear, grief, guilt, shame, depression, or any feelings that include a loss of control or feeling overwhelmed without hope. People with dead-end jobs, with no hope of promotion or transfer—or people who have a stormy marriage marked by contention, arguing, and fighting, with very little joy, peace, or love—are strong candidates for long-term stress. So are those who are addicted to drugs or alcohol, or those who have an ongoing financial or relationship struggle.

Excessive stress even affects a person's appearance. Many stressed individuals develop brown marks under their eyes (a condition known as periorbital pigmentation in the medical community and "stress stain" in more common language). Other people develop frown lines in the forehead and around the eyes and mouth. Still others develop bulging eyes, a tight jaw, and flared nostrils. Cosmetic surgeons are making millions off all this, of course, with treatments ranging from Botox injections to various methods of doing face-lifts to the application of facial fillers.

Principle #3: What you perceive to be stressful to you…is.

Your perceptions determine what you label as stressful or not stressful. There's no such thing as an event that is automatically stressful—unless you are the victim of a shark attack or grizzly bear attack. Stress is largely a matter of what you think about external stimuli. In other words, a very high percentage of stress is highly individualized. What you see as stressful may not be stressful to another person.

Do you become anxious when you are asked to address your superior or an important client during a business presentation?

Do you "stress out" at the thought of an upcoming performance interview with a supervisor you can't seem to please?

Do you feel stressed as you pull onto the freeway every morning?

Do you find yourself feeling stress at the thought of a "certain person" possibly being at the same upcoming party or gathering?

One person's stress may be another person's pleasure.

Perception is everything when it comes to stress—what one person perceives, interprets, or believes to be an extremely stressful situation…is. Another person may not consider that same situation to be stressful at all. He may even find it enjoyable or exciting.

Principle #4: You can choose to control much of the stress level in your life.

How does a person begin to do this? First, I recommend that you become informed about stress. Hosea 4:6 says, "My people are destroyed for lack of knowledge." This verse does not point to a shortage of love, faith, or hope. It points to a lack of knowledge! There are certain things we each must come to know about the causes of stress, and then take action on what we learn.

Second, you need to make a decision about what you are going to do in response to the information you gain. Just before he died, Moses reminded the Israelites of the need to choose carefully about what they would do when they entered the land of promise. He said:

> I call heaven and earth as witnesses today against you, that *I have set before you life and*

death, blessing and cursing; therefore choose life,
that both you and your descendants may live.
—DEUTERONOMY 30:19, EMPHASIS ADDED

Choosing life means to choose God's way over our way; it means to choose a relationship with Him and obedience to Him over our own self-centered desires.

Most factors related to stress are subject to your choice. You can choose to discover why you are stressed out, and you can choose not to be stressed out. Given a number of options about treatment, you can choose which options are of greatest benefit to you. Make this choice today: "I will come to grips with the stress level of my life!" You can start right now by answering the questions below.

HOW STRESSED ARE YOU—RIGHT NOW?

How can you tell if you are "stressed out?" Monitor your own body!

Without seeking to relax, quickly check these five parts of your body:

- Do you have a furrowed brow?
- Is your jaw clenched?
- Are your shoulders slouched?
- Are you toes curled under?
- Do you feel "tight" in your shoulder muscles, arms, legs, hands, or buttocks?

If so, your body is showing signs of stress!

3

Fight, Flee ... or Stew in Your Own Juices

God, our Creator, has built into each one of us a remarkable mechanism for staying alive. Even if we do not consciously activate this mechanism, the body responds intuitively and instinctively to danger, and our immediate response is to do one of two things:

1. Flee as quickly as possible from the source of danger
2. Stand and fight what is dangerous

This fight-or-flight mechanism was designed by God to work quickly. As soon as danger passed—because a person fled quickly enough or fought victoriously enough—the mechanism was designed to shut down and await the next incident of danger.

No longer is modern man facing dangerous predators or life-or-death struggles on a daily basis. Instead we are facing pressures at home, pressures at work, financial stressors, heavy traffic, and arguments with spouses, children, workers, or bosses. Rather than fighting or fleeing, which would eventually shut down the stress response, we are attempting to cope with the stress. As a result, we are literally stewing in our own stress juices.

These stresses are activating the stress response in our bodies just as they have been designed to do; however, many times the stress response does not turn off. It is similar to driving your car with the accelerator pressed to the floor. Eventually the result is biological disaster. The chronic drip, drip, drip of stress hormones continues daily, and this steady drip is fueled by stress.

SELYE'S THREE STAGES OF STRESS RESPONSE

Hans Selye is considered by many to be the "father of stress" since he was the first to document research related to the prolonged release of fight-or-flight hormones into the body.

An endocrinologist, Selye initially was attempting in his research to find the next new female hormone. He injected rats with an extract of ovarian tissue and then observed the effects of the hormone. Selye was a somewhat clumsy investigator, however, and he would frequently drop the rats after injecting them, chase them around his lab, and use a broom to get them to move from behind a desk or file cabinet. At the end of this experiment, he did autopsies on the rats and found that most had developed ulcers, shrunken thymus glands, and enlarged adrenal glands. He was surprised that the ovarian extract would produce these effects. He decided to perform another experiment with tighter controls.

The second time, instead of using an ovarian extract on all the rats, he injected half of them with saline, a form of salt water. Again, he was sloppy in his handling of the rats, dropping and chasing them as he had the first time. At the end of this experiment he again autopsied the rats and found the same findings—in both groups! He used the phrase general adaptation syndrome to describe how the rats had responded to chronic stress, and eventually he identified three stages of this syndrome: the alarm stage, the resistance stage, and the exhaustion stage. His findings have been replicated a number of times and still stand.

STAGE #1: THE ALARM REACTION

The first stage of stress, the alarm reaction, triggers a fight-or-flight response. When sudden stress is experienced—for example, if a person finds himself in a serious car accident or the victim of a violent crime—an emergency hormonal system in the body automatically kicks in. The alarm reaction occurs when a person *perceives* he is being attacked or is in a dangerous situation, not only when a person is actually in such a frightening circumstance.

The alarm reaction generally produces a short-term burst of adrenaline, which creates a temporary "high" and produces energy. These elevated levels of adrenaline can make a person feel great. People in highly stressed professions such as attorneys battling cases in courtrooms, emergency room physicians, and top business executives have reported that, through the years, they have become addicted to their own flow of adrenaline.[1] It also makes a person feel excited and allows a person to function well with less sleep. Eventually, however, a prolonged release of adrenaline into the human body can take a tremendous toll on a person's health.

Another name for this emergency system is SAM (for sympatho-adreno-medullary response system).[2] The two primary hormones during the alarm stage are epinephrine and norepinephrine, which have a dramatic effect on the sympathetic nervous system.

Epinephrine is released by the adrenal glands. It impacts sympathetic nerves located throughout the body's organs and tissues. The sympathetic nerves govern heart rate, blood pressure, and respiratory rate. Blood vessels constrict as blood is diverted away from the skin and digestive tract and is shunted to muscles and the brain. Sugar and fatty acids are dumped into the blood stream to supply fuel to the muscles and brain as well. Blood clots faster and the pupils dilate so the person can see better. The brain becomes very focused.

There was a time when this alarm response enabled my wife, son, and nephew to survive a vicious attack from a large pit bull dog. The incident happened when the three of them were on a boat on a small lake in a residential area. Just as they stepped out on shore, a pit bull saw them and began chasing my son, Kyle. Kyle ran and jumped off the pier into the lake. The dog jumped in after him and began swimming toward him. Kyle took off his sandal and began hitting the dog on top of the head. Finally the dog turned around and swam back to shore.

Foaming at the mouth, the dog then caught sight of my nephew and ran toward him, barking ferociously. My nephew once had a pit bull as a pet, so he attempted to befriend this angry dog. The dog, however, lunged at him, attempting to maul him. Each time the dog lunged, my nephew would punch it with his fist in the head with all his strength. My nephew was a strong eighteen-year-old young man at the time, but the dog would simply shake off the punch and attack again.

Across the way, my wife, Mary, began yelling, "Don't look in its eyes." Mary had seen a television program on the Discovery Channel that depicted brutal dog attacks. The program had given the warning that a person being attacked should never look into the attacking dog's eyes. My nephew, however, was scared to death and dared not take his eyes off the dog as it lunged toward him with teeth bared.

Finally the dog got hold of my nephew's leg and began tearing at his flesh. Mary screamed loudly, and the dog turned and began to race toward her. Mary put into practice what she had learned from the program. She turned her back to the dog. The dog tried to run around Mary to gain eye contact, and she began to spin like a top with her arms folded in. This frustrated the dog, and he eventually turned and ran back toward my nephew. In the nick of time, the police arrived and apprehended the dog.

I truly believe Kyle's life was spared because the alarm reaction in him caused him to run and jump in the water—it was extreme "flight" behavior. The alarm reaction saved my nephew's life, as well, since he punched the dog repeatedly with all his strength—it was an extreme "fight" behavior. Mary neither fled nor fought, but afterward, when both my son's and nephew's hormonal responses had returned to normal, Mary's hormonal response continued. Her heart raced, and she couldn't sleep that night as her mind replayed the attack over and over. Fortunately, we had booked a five-day cruise to the Caribbean, scheduled to leave just a few days later. Mary slept for almost two days once we were on board. Her body gradually unwound as she was able to relax.

STAGE #2: THE RESISTANCE STAGE

A person at this level is seeking to adapt to an ongoing negative situation. In this stage, the body no longer reacts with a fight-or-flight response, but rather a *coping* response. The body continues to produce a large amount of stress hormones, especially cortisol.

Cortisol is also the stress hormone secreted when a person just thinks or rehashes a stressful event in such a way that the endocrine system stays revved up.

Let me quickly run through a simple explanation of what happens in the brain and body: The brain perceives excessive stress, and the hypothalamus in the brain secretes a hormone called CRH. This, in turn, stimulates the pituitary gland to secrete another hormone, ACTH. ACTH then stimulates the adrenal glands to produce cortisol. Cortisol is a steroid hormone that stimulates the release of fats, glucose, and amino acids for energy.

Cortisol is also very important in helping to control excessive inflammation, maintain blood pressure, and maintain connective tissue. It helps improve a person's sense of well-being.

Under normal conditions, cortisol is secreted in a twenty-four-hour rhythm. The highest levels occur in the early morning, usually between six and eight o'clock in the morning, and decrease gradually during the day. The lowest levels are around midnight.

When the body is under prolonged stress, cortisol remains elevated. At times, cortisol levels can remain elevated throughout the day, and for many people, well into the night. This often leads to insomnia and sleep disturbances. The brain eventually loses its sensitivity to cortisol and is unable to regulate cortisol production. This causes the body to produce even more cortisol, and at the same time, to produce inadequate levels of another adrenal hormone called DHEA, which is the youth hormone. DHEA has an anabolic (tissue building) effect, in contrast to cortisol, which has a catabolic (tearing down) effect.

In the early 1900s, a British physician, Sir Harvey Cushing, described a syndrome characterized by the following symptoms:

- Truncal obesity (slender arms and legs with fat deposits in the abdominal area)

- Hypertension

- Weakness and fatigability

- Glucose in the urine (diabetes)

- Osteoporosis

- Amenorrhea (absence of menstrual bleeding)

- Hirsutism (excessive body hair in women)

- Purplish abdominal striae (stretch marks)

This became known as Cushing's syndrome. People who experienced these symptoms also experienced other symptoms such as an accumulation of fat on the back of their necks; thin, shiny skin; and telangiectasias (spiderlike blood vessels under the skin). They typically developed high blood pressure, diabetes, reproductive problems, and suppressed immune systems. Many of them had memory problems, sleeping problems, and were depressed, often to the point of committing suicide. When an autopsy was performed, a tumor found in the pituitary gland had produced large amounts of ACTH, which is the hormone that causes the adrenal glands to produce excessive amounts of cortisol.

I certainly realize that Cushing's syndrome is rare and is a severe form of cortisol excess. At the same time, I can't help but note that Americans today are suffering from many of the symptoms of Cushing's syndrome: obesity, hypertension, diabetes, syndrome X, hypercholesterolemia, depression, insomnia, osteoporosis, thin skin, fatigue, and weakness. Individuals with these diseases routinely have elevated levels of cortisol with salivary hormone testing.

Let's take a look at some specific consequences of elevated cortisol levels.

Obesity and cortisol

It is common for people under chronic stress to have elevated levels of cortisol and insulin. If insulin levels remain elevated, the body responds by storing fat, the elevated levels preventing the body from burning stored fat for energy. Most overweight individuals can't break out of this cycle since elevated cortisol stimulates a person's appetite, producing a near constant craving for sugars and carbohydrates during the day—foods that keep insulin levels elevated. In the end, these people keep their bodies programmed for fat storage.

High cortisol and high insulin levels combine to create the ideal formula for obesity, and especially to accumulate fat in the truncal area. Truncal obesity is also called apple-shaped obesity because excessive weight is carried in the middle of the body, the abdominal area. People with this condition often exercise for longer periods and at greater intensity to try to shed the extra pounds. Unfortunately, this usually only elevates cortisol levels further! When people with high cortisol levels diet, they usually end up breaking down muscle tissue into glucose. This can eventually lead to muscle weakness and muscle atrophy. The result is that they lose muscle and, in turn, decrease their metabolic rate, which leads to even greater weight gain. Meanwhile, any excess sugar intake is generally converted to fat—usually fat that is stored in the abdomen. It's a vicious cycle!

Truncal obesity greatly increases a person's risk for developing heart disease, hypertension, syndrome X, type 2 diabetes, elevated cholesterol and triglycerides, gallstones, and certain cancers. (Individuals with pear-shaped obesity—fat accumulations in the hips and thighs—are not at increased risk for these diseases.)

Syndrome X and type 2 diabetes

At normal levels, cortisol counterbalances the effects of insulin. However, elevated cortisol decreases the transportation of blood sugar (glucose) at the cellular level. In essence, elevated cortisol decreases cells' sensitivity to insulin, which leads to insulin resistance. The person who develops insulin resistance and continues to eat a diet high in sugar or processed carbohydrates will generally develop Syndrome X, "metabolic syndrome."

Syndrome X is at epidemic proportions in our nation today—research has shown that about one-third of the United States population has this syndrome. The syndrome has been linked to an increased risk of heart problems, diabetes, and Alzheimer's disease, as well as certain cancers.[3]

Metabolic syndrome is actually the name given to a cluster of metabolic disturbances that include elevated blood sugar, elevated blood pressure, elevated cholesterol, and increased body fat, especially in the truncal area.

Sex hormone difficulties

Cortisol is a major marker of a complex "control loop" that regulates the sex hormones. Elevated cortisol is associated with a drop in DHEA and testosterone, which can lead to a decreased sex drive and erectile dysfunction. In women, elevated cortisol is associated with lower levels of progesterone and testosterone. During periods of chronic stress, progesterone is actually converted to cortisol in the body, which can lead to a progesterone deficiency. This, in turn, can lead to menstrual problems and PMS, as well as significant menopausal symptoms. Levels of estrogen become imbalanced in the presence of high cortisol.

Memory loss

Physicians have known for decades that individuals with Cushing's syndrome develop memory problems, because in these people the hippocampus begins to atrophy or shrink. The hippocampus is the portion of the brain most involved in memory. The shrinking effect occurs because the neurons or brain cells in this part of the brain lose their ability to take up the glucose they need to remain functioning. Recent research has revealed that high cortisol levels are associated with atrophy or shrinkage of the hippocampus.[4] The memory loss that occurs may be related to Alzheimer's disease.

Depression

Chronic stress has commonly been associated with depression. Elevated cortisol levels cause an imbalance of neurotransmitters in the brain, notably serotonin and dopamine.

In normal patients, dexamethasone is a synthetic form of cortisone that exerts a "negative feedback signal" to turn off cortisol production. However, many depressed patients are resistant to dexamethasone, and they continue secreting cortisol despite receiving this potent cortisone medication. In one scientific study, as many as seven out of every ten patients with depression had enlarged adrenal glands, some with glands that were 1.7 times the size of a normal gland in a person who is not depressed.[5]

Bone loss

Excessive cortisol has been known for years to cause osteoporosis. Individuals with Cushing's disease and patients on long-term prednisone or other synthetic forms of cortisone are predisposed to osteoporosis.

Decreased immune function

Dr. Hans Selye showed that rats exposed to chronic stress developed shrunken thymus glands. Chronic stress in humans has also been associated with atrophy or shrinking of the thymus gland, as well as decreased function of the thymus gland.

Elevated cortisol levels are associated with as much as a 50 percent reduction of natural killer cells that destroy cancer cells, bacteria, and viruses. Elevated cortisol levels increase a person's susceptibility for developing recurrent infections. Students in one study were shown to be more prone to catch a cold, develop cold sores, or get infections when stressed during final-exam week.[6]

Epidemic in proportion!

Some of the conditions described above are rampant in our society. Approximately two-thirds of Americans are overweight.[7] One out of four adults has hypertension (high blood pressure),[8] and one out of two American adults has elevated cholesterol levels. One out of every two women over fifty years of age will develop an osteoporosis-related fracture,[9] and more than nineteen million Americans have depression. Fatigue is epidemic, and diabetes is increasing at an alarming rate.

STAGE #3: EXHAUSTION STAGE

The final stage of the stress process is the exhaustion stage. In this stage, the body actually begins to break down, and the risk of chronic disease increases dramatically. The exhaustion stage is technically referred to as adrenal exhaustion.[10]

The most severe form of adrenal fatigue is Addison's disease, which is quite rare. The sufferer needs to take medication in the form of corticosteroids for the remainder of his or her life. President John F. Kennedy had Addison's disease. Millions of Americans today are suffering with a milder degree of adrenal exhaustion because their stress response mechanism has been activated for so many years.

Adrenal exhaustion usually leads to being burned out mentally, physically, and emotionally. As adrenal function is impaired, every organ and system in the body is affected. Those who experience adrenal exhaustion often feel very tired. They usually suffer from hypoglycemia or low blood sugar and often need a snack every two to three hours to prevent a drop in blood sugar. They typically have memory loss, cloudy thinking, problems concentrating, and episodes of confusion. They may be prone to being depressed. They generally suffer from recurrent infections of all types, along with allergies (both environmental and food), chemical sensitivities, and immune system impairment.

People in the exhaustion stage are very prone to developing autoimmune diseases such as Hashimoto's thyroiditis, lupus, rheumatoid arthritis, psoriasis, or multiple sclerosis. They usually lose muscle mass and gain fat. They typically suffer from digestive problems. They generally produce inadequate amounts of hydrochloric acid and pancreatic enzymes, which leads to heartburn, bloating, and gas. They are prone to chronic fatigue, fibromyalgia, irregular menstrual periods, hormonal imbalance, severe PMS, loss of sex drive, irritable bowel syndrome, and psychiatric disorders. Individuals in the exhaustion stage are also more prone to develop Alzheimer's disease and cancer.

Sadly, many of those who truly are burned out turn to drugs, alcohol, or cigarettes as a way of compensating for their burnout. Some over-medicate themselves or self-medicate themselves into real physical problems. Many feel stuck in a rut. To further the problem, most physicians do not recognize adrenal exhaustion as a real concern and won't treat it. Patients are generally placed on antidepressants and are labeled by physicians as lazy patients or "drug seekers."

Eventually, a person in a state of adrenal exhaustion becomes subject to both debilitating and deadly diseases.

LIVING UPSIDE DOWN FROM GOD'S DESIGN

God designed the hormonal emergency alarm system to save our lives. But what happens if a person activates this system too many times for too many reasons? The alarm system is turned upside down into something that *destroys* life.

In some people, stress chemicals are triggered and released into the body hundreds of times a day. An argument with a child or spouse, gridlocked traffic, financial pressure, a stressful encounter at work, or any of hundreds of other situations can trigger the alarm stage. And then it begins...that steady drip, drip, drip of damaging hormones that wreak havoc on health.

Can we stop this process and turn things right side up again?

Yes! The first line of defense is to come to grips with our mental and emotional habits.

4

Mental and Emotional Habits Preprogram Us for Stress

We are all hardwired differently and have been programmed to a certain degree by our past experiences, genetics, and environment, as well as by our choices in life.

We each have a unique set of memories, based upon a unique combination of events, experiences, and relationships. We each perceive the world from our own unique vantage point.

We each have developed a unique set of emotional habits that are almost automatic. These habits set us up to respond to the world in unique ways.

If your parents were anxious people who worried excessively, you may have acquired that tendency as well. If you were raised in a hostile environment in which parents or caregivers were easily angered or frustrated, you may have learned some of these emotional habits and adopted them as your norm. Nobody actually teaches us how to respond to what we perceive to be negative situations in life. Rather, we model or copy the behavior of adults around us. We respond as we see them responding, and over time our response becomes an emotional habit.

By the time we are teenagers, most of our emotional habits are deeply ingrained in us. We simply react when we are exposed to a stressful situation. When we feel anger, worry, fear, or depression, we do what has become intuitive to us rather than stop to consider rationally our behavioral options.

What is the end result? We are preprogrammed for a stress reaction, just as a television remote-control device can be programmed to go to favorite channels or a radio in an automobile can be preset to favorite stations.

EMOTIONAL HABITS SOUND THE STRESS ALARM

Your body can't tell the difference between real-world causes of stress and mental or emotional causes of stress. The mind filters the perceptions of the outside world, and the way that filter works will either trigger a stress response or let the body continue on a status quo basis.

You may have been shown or read about the "spider response." Many people have a fear of spiders. The very sight of a spider of any size triggers all the normal alarm responses in the body. What we also know is that a piece of lint on the floor can trigger this response if a person thinks that piece of lint is a spider. Now, the piece of lint is not a spider. But because the mind perceives the lint as a spider, the body responds just as it would to a real spider.

EMOTIONAL MEMORY

It is also helpful to many people to know that we attach an emotion in our brains to every event or experience we have in life. We don't simply remember an event—we remember how we *felt* at the time of the event. We don't just remember where and when we first met our future spouse; we remember how we *felt* after first meeting our future spouse. We don't just remember going to the prom; we remember how we *felt* being with our date at the prom.

Our emotional memory is actually faster than our conscious memory at recalling an event. We remember the basic perceptions and the feelings we attached to them even before our mind can recall an idea or conclusion about that memory.

The amygdala is an area of the brain where emotional memories are stored. It is then able to compare emotional feelings with stored emotional memories. It then makes immediate decisions about the threat level of the incoming information. Once that instantaneous decision is made, the amygdala activates the autonomic nervous system, triggering both the physical stress response and an emotional reaction. All of this happens before the higher brain centers can even receive the information! In other words, we react both in our bodies and our emotions before we think.

What external circumstances can serve as a trigger or emotional signal? The circumstances are varied and nearly infinite. An old song on the radio...the aroma of a particular perfume or aftershave...seeing an old, familiar face in a crowd...picking up a long-forgotten object...or finding oneself in an old, familiar place are among the circumstances that become an emotional signal for most of us at some point in our life.

And what emotional memories are triggered? Perhaps the memory is a good one—a nostalgic one of a time with a parent or grandparent, a first date or first love. But there are other times when the emotional signal stimulates a memory that is not at all positive, such as a time of feeling rejected, abandoned, betrayed, hurt, depressed, anxious, or angry.

The resulting biological response and emotional reaction can be as powerful as the first time the emotional signal was received. The memory of an event can produce chemicals in the body and emotions in the soul that duplicate in intensity the person's initial reaction to being hurt, wounded, abused, or rejected.

Over time, the repetition of these perceptions imprints a pattern in a person's neural circuitry. Once these are imprinted, an emotional habit has been established.

Why is this important to understand? Because emotional habits are the basis for many of the most important decisions we make in life, especially decisions that seem "intuitive" to us. We may prejudge people or environments on the basis of these emotional habits, without ever getting to know a person or explore an environment.

EMOTIONAL RESPONSES TO VICARIOUS EVENTS

One of the interesting and most potentially damaging aspects of all this is the fact that a person doesn't need to personally experience with his or her five senses the event that triggers the emotional signal. The signal might be triggered vicariously by simply watching another person or even by watching a character on television!

Consider the impact of media violence as it relates to stress.

Have you ever been in an armed robbery? Have you ever been attacked viciously? Have you ever been carjacked?

The vast majority of people in our nation never experience any of these events, but you certainly wouldn't know it from the programs aired on prime-time television!

Very few of us are actually threatened in a way that is truly life-threatening, or even dangerous. Yet our bodies are called into action as if we are!

Why do media producers use such frightening experiences so frequently? They do so in hopes of triggering a little bit of the pleasure-causing adrenaline to rush into our bloodstreams. They are attempting to elicit a little excitement—and we fall for it because we perceive that we want a little excitement in our otherwise dull and boring lives.

The more desensitized we become to the violence, the more violent the images must be to trigger an adrenaline release into the bloodstream.

In terms of the violent content of television programming, prime-time television programs portray an average of three to five violent acts per hour. Children's Saturday-morning programming offers an average of twenty to twenty-five violent acts per hour. According to a 1996 report from the American Psychiatric Association, adolescents will have viewed sixteen thousand simulated murders and nearly two hundred thousand acts of violence by the time they are eighteen years old![1] Worse yet, the current portrayal of violence is highly graphic and realistic, offering anatomically detailed simulations of killing, maiming, and wounding. At the same time, violent acts portrayed in the media go unpunished a whopping 73 percent of the time![2] Countless "good guys" are portrayed as perpetrators of violent acts, which sends a message that violence is justified and a viable method for dealing with problems.[3]

Is it any wonder that date rape is at an all-time high?

Is it any wonder that one in four adult women reports having been sexually abused?

Is it any wonder that stress levels associated with being raped or abused are at an all-time high?

A person doesn't need to have ever been molested, raped, shot, stabbed, or otherwise abused or violated in order to feel as if he or she has been! As we become more excited during an action-packed or scary movie, there is a greater release of adrenaline, which is a stress hormone. Elevated levels of this hormone are able to lock in the brain whatever image is producing the emotional excitement. This in turn causes us to involuntarily remember frightening movies and traumatic experiences, as well as extremely pleasurable experiences. High adrenaline levels literally brand these experiences into our neural circuitry.

Now you can see the wisdom in putting no evil before your eyes, as the psalmist David wrote, "I will set nothing wicked before my eyes" (Ps. 101:3).

WHAT YOU PERCEIVE IS YOUR REALITY!

Are you aware that a person is more likely to die from a heart attack or stroke between nine and eleven o'clock on a Monday morning than at any other time of the week? Why? Most Americans *perceive* Monday morning as the most stressful time of the week![4]

Your perceptions are at the root of a very high percentage of the stress your body experiences!

The Mitchum Report on Stress in the '90s showed that work, money, and family issues are the most common constant sources of stress for most people in the United States. This report emphasized, however, that it is actually our perceptions of work, money, and family interactions that are at the root of most stress.

Your perceptions determine how you see the world.

The mind is similar to a computer—the brain is the hard drive, and the perceptions are the "software." It is the perceptions of people, demands, issues, and circumstances—not the actual people, demands, issues, or circumstances in and of themselves—that dictate how a person will react.

Perceptions can become distorted.

Perceptions determine whether something is positive or negative. The problem in most highly stressed individuals is this:

they are preprogrammed with distorted perceptions to the point that even trivial circumstances or demands can trigger a massive reaction. Their perceiving ability has become flawed or faulty.

This has been shown in a number of studies about abuse. It doesn't take anything major to trigger extreme anger in an abuser. Very often the person being abused cannot even point to something that was said or done. The problem is not in the external circumstance—the problem is in the internally distorted perceptions of the abuser.

Children and teenagers today are especially vulnerable to distortional perceptions. They see perceptions of life on television programs—from MTV, VH1, *The Jerry Springer Show*, and various interview programs as well as prime-time shows and videos—and they conclude, "This is the way life operates." They see tattoos, body piercing, drug use, alcohol consumption, cigarette smoking, and promiscuous sexual relationships as being normal human behavior because these behaviors are so prevalent in what they see and hear. They begin to act accordingly, and in so doing, they set themselves up for real-life experiences that further reinforce their emotional memories and emotional habits.

Behaviors such as the ones I noted above are nearly always associated with expressions of spiritual rebellion, social isolation, and various forms of cultural or racial prejudice. These states, in turn, tend to be marked by fairly intense emotions, usually anger, frustration, depression, and even suicidal despair.

Randy was an eighteen-year-old who came from a strong Christian family. In rebellion against the beliefs of his parents, he began experimenting with drugs and alcohol and eventually got involved in the Gothic movement. He dyed his hair jet black and wore all black clothing. He had multiple piercings on his face (eyebrow, nose, tongue, and lip). His physical appearance was quite shocking to me the first time I saw him—he looked like images I had seen in horror films about vampires! Randy slept all day, worked at night, and then partied after work with like-minded friends who were also using drugs and alcohol.

His life had spiraled out of control, and he had fallen deeper and deeper into depression. His mother finally persuaded him to come to me for an evaluation. I explained to the mother that her son had become self-programmed for depression by the music he listened to, the friends he hung out with, the drugs and alcohol he consumed, and the constant black color he wore. He couldn't stand to see the light of day—and thus, he had chosen a night job so he could sleep during daylight hours.

I strongly advised him to change his life if he wanted to change his emotional state of depression. I prescribed this to him: "Attend church, hang out with Christian teenagers, get a daytime job, stop listening to the music you are listening to, and stop using drugs and alcohol." He refused my prescription. He insisted, instead, that the only prescription he would follow was one for an antidepressant medication.

I saw Randy a month later, and his condition had not changed. I increased the dose of his medicine. His condition still did not improve. I tried other medications, all to no avail. Then he began having suicidal thoughts, and I immediately referred him to a psychiatrist for immediate hospitalization.

Some time later Randy's mother called to tell me that her worst nightmare had happened the previous day. Her son had overdosed on drugs while partying. His friends had abandoned him, leaving his lifeless body in a dark alley behind a club.

Randy had refused to reprogram his own life. His autopilot was set on depressing thoughts, drugs, and drunkenness. Eventually that programming led to his death.

Emotional habits trigger the release of stress hormones. When these hormones are chronically released into the body, they become "killer hormones."

Many people try to manage their stress without ever addressing the real root of the stress. They purchase relaxation tapes, take vacations, or practice stress-management skills. Some turn to alcohol or substance abuse—including overuse of prescription medications—to control their stress level. But often they do not change their mental or emotional habits. The perceptions that give rise to stress go unaddressed.

To address and treat stress definitively, we need to come to grips with our perceptions. We need to face up to our own distortional thought processes.

5

Addressing Distortional Thought Patterns

Anna was walking to her community college class one day and met Barry on the sidewalk. He was a good friend from high school, and she said, "Hello." Barry didn't even acknowledge her presence. At first she thought, *What a snob! Does he think he's better than me?* For a short time she was quite angry. Later, however, she thought that perhaps she had done something to upset him, and she felt guilty about that, even though she couldn't identify anything she had done. Lying in her bed that night, she began to worry that she would lose his friendship.

The next day, still upset, she intentionally ignored Barry even though she met him again as she was walking to class. Barry, however, walked right up to her and said, "Anna, why are you ignoring me?"

Anna then burst out that he had ignored her yesterday and that she had been upset by his behavior. Barry replied, "What are you talking about? I didn't even see you yesterday." Anna reminded him that she had spoken to him the day before. Barry said, "I must have been so focused on my big calculus exam that I zoned out and didn't even see you, even if you did say hello."

Anna had jumped to many different conclusions in the twenty-four hours between these two encounters and had felt angry, guilty, and anxious. None of the conclusions were rooted in the truth of her relationship with Barry. She had allowed herself to engage in a distortional thought process.

One of the primary causes of stress—if not the foremost cause of stress—is distortional or irrational thinking. I encounter distortional thinking every day in my practice. A distortional thought process can alter a person's mood and emotional outlook. It can cause a misperception or misinterpretation of events. People very often think their way into stress, worry, anxiety, fear, depression, anger, hostility, rage, guilt, and shame.

CHANGING OUR THOUGHTS THROUGH COGNITIVE THERAPY

The bad news is that every person is prone to distortional thinking on occasion.

The good news is that we can change distortional thought processes. We first must analyze our own thinking. We must become informed about our own mental and emotional habits. These principles are at the heart of what is known as cognitive therapy. This form of therapy is grounded in the belief that men and women are capable of replacing faulty thoughts with accurate ones.

Psychologist Albert Ellis developed Rational Emotive Therapy in the 1950s to help patients replace irrational beliefs and perceptions with rational, realistic statements. In 1961 he published *A Guide to Rational Living*. His work became a foundation stone for Dr. Aaron Beck, a psychiatrist.

In working with depressed patients, Dr. Beck found that they experienced streams of negative thoughts that seemed to pop up spontaneously. He termed these cognitions "automatic thoughts" and discovered that their content fell into three categories: negative ideas about themselves, the world, and the future. He began helping patients identify and evaluate these thoughts and found that by doing so, patients were able to think more realistically, which led them to feel better emotionally and behave more functionally.[1] This approach became known in psychology as cognitive therapy or cognitive-behavioral therapy (CBT).

In cognitive therapy, a patient learns to no longer accept automatic thoughts at face value. Rather, he is taught to dissect, examine, and question his thoughts, and especially to examine those thoughts, beliefs, assumptions, or projections that might be negative. Patients are taught to recognize and question old assumptions, such as "If something bad is going to happen, it will happen to me." Beck found that when a negative thought pattern is broken, painful expectations lose their self-fulfilling power.

Renowned psychiatrist Dr. David Burns popularized cognitive therapy in his best-selling book *Feeling Good: The New Mood Therapy*. Having conducted more than thirty thousand cognitive therapy sessions in his career, Dr. Burns believed rational thinking was crucial in helping people gain control over their negative thought patterns.

Burns taught that thoughts create moods. Cognition is the process of beliefs, perceptions, and mental attitudes that gives interpretation to events. These interpretations can create, in turn, emotions such as anger, hostility, depression, sadness, anxiety, fear, shame, or guilt. The problem is that many people who become caught up in these emotions often have a distorted view of the event and have allowed an irrational, twisted, or unrealistic thought pattern to determine how they feel.[2]

A cycle can develop. The more stress a person is under as a result of negative emotions, the more prone he or she is to misinterpreting events and to seeing things in a distorted, irrational way. The negative perceptions fuel negative emotions.

TEN TYPES OF DISTORTIONAL THINKING

Dr. Burns has identified ten types of distortional thought patterns, which are listed below.

1. All-or-nothing thinking

For this kind of person, there are no gray areas. Anything less than his standard of "perfect" is worthless.

Marty had this type of thinking. She was a high school senior assigned to write a term paper. She worked on the paper every night and weekend for two months, and when the paper was due, Marty didn't feel at all ready to turn it in. She feared receiving an

F for not turning in a paper, however, so she hesitantly handed in the work she had done. She made an A- on the paper, but because she demanded perfection of herself, she saw an A- as a totally unacceptable grade. It might as well have been an F to her.

A healthy thinker recognizes that even in the best of circumstances, nothing or no one is perfect.

2. Overgeneralizations

A person who overgeneralizes thinks that if one thing goes wrong, nothing will ever go right for him ever.

Ed was an experienced civil engineer who had been with his last employer for more than twenty years. After his last employer filed for bankruptcy, he knew he would have to find another job that could offer the same pay scale, but he wondered who would hire an older, experienced engineer when they could hire a college graduate for less. After three interviews, a phone call, and two rejection letters, Ed concluded that third company would reject him, so he gave up any hope of finding another job.

If Ed were a healthy thinker, he would recognize that simply because company #3 has not replied, it is not a sign that he did not get the job. Instead he should remain positive, follow up the interview with a phone call thanking them for the interview, and wait for their reply.

3. A negative mental filter

This kind of distortional thinking causes a person to hear a half hour of praise after a job evaluation but leave the meeting depressed because of one area "needing improvement."

Anne was going to her high school prom. Her mother bought her a new dress and shoes and took her to have her hair professionally styled on the day of the prom. At the prom everyone complimented her on how beautiful she looked and how pretty her dress and hair were. One classmate who was jealous of Anne pointed out a run in her stockings. It was a very tiny run that was barely noticeable. Anne, however, felt mortified, as if every person in the room were aware of this flaw.

When Anne returned home that night and her mother asked about the prom, Anne focused so much on her embarrassment and her classmate's negative comment that Anne completely forgot about all the compliments she had received.

Choosing to focus only on the negative causes unnecessary stress. On the other hand, choosing to always focus only on the positive and not dealing with the negative is equally harmful and unrealistic. A person has to find the balance between the positive and negative situations in life.

4. Disqualifying the positive

Even more distortional is when a person takes a positive experience and turns it into a negative one. These kind of thinkers feel they are not worthy of any praise under any circumstance.

Harry was a faithful, hard-working salesman who had made his sales quota each of the last five years. Harry was promoted to sales director over the entire company, which was a great surprise to Harry. With the promotion came nearly a doubling of his salary. Rather than showing excitement about the possibility for this advancement, Harry immediately began to tell his supervisor that he didn't deserve the position. He pointed out several of his weaknesses and said that he thought a fellow worker named Steve was better qualified. Even though his supervisor pointed out several of his strengths, Harry discounted each of them. In the end, Harry sabotaged his own promotion.

DEFINITIONS OF COGNITIVE DISTORTIONS

1. ALL-OR-NOTHING THINKING: You see things in black-and-white categories. If your performance falls short of perfect, you see yourself as a total failure.

2. OVERGENERALIZATION: You see a single negative event as a never-ending pattern of defeat.

3. MENTAL FILTER: You pick out a single negative detail and dwell on it exclusively so that your vision of all reality becomes darkened, like the drop of ink that colors the entire beaker of water.

4. DISQUALIFYING THE POSITIVE: You reject positive experiences by insisting they "don't count" for some reason or other. In this way you can maintain a negative belief that is contradicted by your everyday experiences.

5. JUMPING TO CONCLUSIONS: You make a negative interpretation even though there are no definite facts that convincingly support your conclusion.

   a. *Mind reading.* You arbitrarily conclude that someone is reacting negatively to you, and you don't bother to check this out.

   b. *The Fortune Teller Error.* You anticipate that things will turn out badly, and you feel convinced that your prediction is an already-established fact.

Enjoy receiving compliments and praise, and use them to validate your self-esteem. There is nothing prideful about graciously accepting praise or a compliment when rightfully given. Not only will this reduce stress, but it will also add richness to your life.

5. Jumping to conclusions

People who jump to conclusions predict the worst possible outcome or circumstance without having any, or all, the facts to support their conclusions.

One day Jeanette overhears her boss speaking with someone about a job description very similar to her own. Immediately Jeanette thought, *He's not happy with my work, and he's going to replace me with this person. What am I going to do if I get fired?* Her boss notifies her that he has something to tell her later in the day. All afternoon her stomach is in knots. Trying to concentrate on her work is impossible. It is almost time for Jeanette to go home, when a young woman walks in the door and her boss says, "Jeanette, I'd like for you to meet my niece. She was just hired as a receptionist at our other office. We are so pleased with your work that I want you to train her." Jeanette jumped to the

6. MAGNIFICATION (CATASTROPHIZING) OR MINIMIZATION: You exaggerate the importance of things (such as your goof-up or someone else's achievement), or you inappropriately shrink things until they appear tiny (your own desirable qualities or the other fellow's imperfections). This is also called the "binocular trick."

7. EMOTIONAL REASONING: You assume that your negative emotions necessarily reflect the way things really are: "I feel it, therefore it must be true."

8. SHOULD STATEMENTS: You try to motivate yourself with shoulds and shouldn'ts, as if you had to be whipped and punished before you could be expected to do anything. "Musts" and "oughts" are also offenders. The emotional consequence is guilt. When you direct should statements toward others, you feel anger, frustration, and resentment.

9. LABELING AND MISLABELING: This is an extreme form of overgeneralization. Instead of describing your error, you attach a negative label to yourself: "I'm a loser." when someone else's behavior rubs you the wrong way, you attach a negative label to him: "He's a...louse." Mislabeling involves describing an event with language that is highly colored and emotionally loaded.

10. PERSONALIZATION: You see yourself as the cause of some negative external event, which in fact you were not primarily responsible for.[3]

conclusion that she was losing her job to another person, which was not the case at all.

Instead of getting stressed out about the thought of losing her job, Jeanette should have waited until her boss spoke with her before drawing a conclusion about the situation.

6. Magnification or minimization

Dr. Burns refers to magnification also as *catastrophizing.* A person who "awful-izes" the possibility of a disaster tends to magnify, or blow out of proportion, the importance of circumstances or a situation. A simple mishap, however small, is regarded as a monumental disaster. Some people also call this "Murphy's Law" mentality: "If anything can go wrong, it will go wrong, and it will be worse because that's just my luck."

Beth realized her boss was overwhelmed and volunteered to help prepare a report for the stockholder's meeting. The day after the meeting, her boss came in very grumpy. He complained about a few things, and Beth became flustered. She thought, *What made me think I could prepare that report? Maybe there was a spelling error. I feel terrible!* She began visualizing her boss giving the report and becoming embarrassed because of her imaginary mistakes. Later that day her boss apologized for his behavior. He explained that he hadn't slept well the night before because he had a painful backache. He thanked Beth for being so understanding and for the fine job she did composing the report.

The person who magnifies perceived weaknesses also tends to minimize his personal success as inconsequential. In this example, Beth underestimated her ability to put together a well-written report.

The healthy thinker sees life as a sequence of events, all of which are factored into an overall track record. No single event is perceived as being overly important or of no consequence.

7. Emotional reasoning

This person allows the truth to be based upon his feelings. If he feels incompetent, then he thinks he must be doing a lousy job.

Terry had just graduated from college and had accepted a position for a large company selling life insurance. He was very excited about the possibility of making a lot of money. However, after the first week, he had been turned down by every prospect. He felt rejected, depressed, and worthless. He took it personally that people were rejecting him instead of realizing that they were rejecting the life insurance. He allowed his feelings and emotions to affect his job, and he eventually quit.

The healthy thinker separates his emotions from his overall self-worth.

8. "Should" statements—fixed-rule thinking

This person is a "should," "must," or "ought to" person. He confines people and events to his rules and fails to realize the fact that he can't force anyone to adhere to them. The more rigid the rules, the greater the person's disappointment. That disappointment usually plays out as worry, depression, frustration, irritation, or guilt.

Mr. Smith, CEO of XYZ Company, is attending an industry convention. He has Susan, his executive assistant, make hotel reservations months in advance at the host hotel. The day before he is scheduled to check in to the hotel, he has Susan call to confirm. She reports back that the hotel could not find his reservation, even though Susan has a confirmation number. Now there is no room available because they are booked solid due to the convention. Mr. Smith blows up at Susan, blaming her for the lost reservation. After all, "she should've made sure his reservation was secure."

The person with fixed-rule thinking tends to live in "should" statements. People should do certain things, society should act a particular way, or a situation should turn out in an expected fashion.

The healthy thinker knows that the only "should" statement a person should make is one in the form of a question: "How should I approach this situation now and in the future?"

9. Labeling and mislabeling

A person who attaches a negative label to himself or someone else tends to do so because of his own low self-esteem.

Many children, unfortunately, are called names such as *stupid, lazy,* or *no good.* Then those children call other people by these names or may call themselves by these names, at least in their own minds. If a person labels himself as stupid or lazy long enough, eventually he will live up to that label. It becomes a self-fulfilling prophecy.

Early in his childhood Johnny had been diagnosed with attention deficit hyperactivity disorder (ADHD). He frequently fought with other children and would end up in the principal's office. He had difficulty staying quiet in class and wouldn't do his homework. He ended up failing two grades and, as a result, was much bigger than the other kids in his class.

When Johnny became a teenager, he began using drugs and alcohol, and eventually he became a drug dealer. He covered his body with tattoos and had piercings in his ears, tongue, lip, eyebrow, and chin. He was big, strong, and scary-looking—highly intimidating to other teenagers. Those who had picked on him and called him names when he was younger were now frequently threatened with bodily harm if they didn't buy drugs from him. As a result, a number of his schoolmates were hooked on drugs and dependent on him to supply them. Johnny had no respect whatsoever for those to whom he sold drugs. His "names" for them were often spoken in derision and with expletives.

Johnny was a victim of labeling and name-calling, but he also became a person who labeled and called others names. The cycle of name-calling is often a downward one.

Remember that God has called you precious and beloved, and you are His child.

10. Personalization

This kind of thinking shifts the blame of an outcome on self. Unfortunately in our society, many children who come from dysfunctional homes become trapped in this kind of thinking: "Daddy left Mommy because I was bad."

After Amy's father died, her mother, Nancy, was left with the financial burden of a home and raising Amy alone. Amy's mother began drinking to numb her emotional pain and drown her problems. Amy blames herself for her mother's alcohol addiction and feels that if she were not in the house, then her mother would be free to sell the house and go on with her life. Rather than feel guilty, Amy needs to realize that her mother is an adult who needs help and needs to learn to cope with life's situations.

Free yourself of stress and guilt by realizing that you are not responsible for another person's actions or decisions. In the case of a child, the child needs to be reassured that he did nothing wrong and that his dad's decision to leave was not his fault.

For more information on distortional thinking, read my book *Deadly Emotions*.

OTHER DISTORTIONAL BELIEFS

Perhaps there are other distortional beliefs that do not take on the magnitude of the ten mentioned above. Here is a list of ten other common distortional beliefs.

1. "Life is fair, and everybody is entitled to a good life."

The truth is that life is *not* fair. What we are guaranteed at some time is an experience of pain, hurt, or inconvenience. Every life has a measure of problems and joys. Pain and pleasure come into our lives "randomly"—certainly as God allows, but not always in the proportion we perceive as fair. The Bible tells us that God "makes His sun rise on the evil and on the good, and sends rain on the just and on the unjust" (Matt. 5:45).

2. "People should behave properly."

This is an unenforceable rule. Not everybody has your definition of "properly." If you expect other people to always behave toward you in the way you consider "proper," you will live in a state of frustration, anger, and stress.

3. "I need to be liked and accepted by everyone."

Not everybody will like you. It is impossible to please all of the people in your life all of the time. Neither can you find agreement with every person. Whenever it is possible in those situations, agree to disagree. If you live with a deep desire to be accepted by every person you meet, you will become a very passive person and likely suffer from low self-esteem.

4. "The worst outcome will probably occur."

The worst outcome is rarely what comes to pass. Worrying about things beyond your control leads only to excessive stress.

5. "I am unable to change the way I am."

This belief is guaranteed to lead to stress! Not only can you change, but also in any number of ways you need to change in order not to be bound to your past. Some change is inevitable, such as physical changes as you grow older. Other changes are highly desirable, such as the forging of new friendships and learning new skills.

6. "Life is awful when things don't go my way."

I call this the "spoiled-child syndrome." Not everything is going to go your way. That doesn't make life awful. Rather, it means you have an opportunity to mature emotionally and to solve problems and overcome difficulties in order to become stronger and more confident as an individual.

7. "I must be perfect or almost perfect in everything I do."

No person—except Jesus Christ—has ever been perfect, is perfect, or ever will be perfect in this life—and you are *not* the Son of God. As we grow in our relationship with God, He calls us to experience greater levels of wholeness in this life. Unfortunately, some Bible translations use the word *perfect* instead of *wholeness*, which has led many people to believe that God calls us to perfection, and He gets very angry with us when we fall short of this mark. The truth is that God calls people to *wholeness*, and He will help any person attain greater wholeness if that person desires to do what is necessary for wholeness.

8. "The past has much to do with determining the future."

The past only has as much impact on your future as you allow it to have. Mistakes in the past can become learning experiences so that we do not repeat the past. Bad habits of the past do not need to continue. Human beings are capable of overcoming the pain and limiting experiences of the past, with God's help.

9. "My personal worth is dependent on how much I achieve or produce."

People who believe they have no value apart from their accomplishments are usually striving to find fame, fortune, or positions of power. That is a stressful life! Your worth as an individual is dependent upon how much God loves you and cares for you—and that amount is infinite.

10. "It is easier to avoid the difficulties and responsibilities in life than to face them."

A person who dodges life's difficulties and responsibilities sabotages his own success. Such a person usually feels more stress than the person who takes on life's challenges because the person who avoids difficulties suffers from an inferiority complex, feeling like everybody's doormat or feeling guilt and embarrassment.

ANSWERING THE QUESTION: WHO OWES WHOM?

Many of these distortional thoughts are rooted in a general overriding belief that life *owes* a person something. There is nothing written in the cosmos or the Word of God that declares this to be true. Life owes you *nothing*; you owe life something!

People who think life owes them something are always blaming others for their own failures, shortcomings, and even their own stress! How often do we hear statements like these: "My boss makes me nervous." "My husband frustrates me." "My children annoy me." "My neighbors stress me out." Many things don't happen to us intentionally; things happen as part of the overall "life experience."

Sadly, most stressed-out people don't realize that a very high percentage of their stress is the result of distortional thinking. This is especially true if they are blaming others for their stress. Such a person rarely looks in the mirror and says, "I'm causing these stressful feelings in my life."

THE ABCD—AND E—APPROACH TO THOUGHT ANALYSIS

Dr. Albert Ellis, a psychologist, came up with what he called the "ABC process" for identifying how thoughts impact our emotions.[4] When a thought occurs, he calls this the "antecedent," or activating *A* factor. The event is usually followed by an emotional "consequence," or *C*. The antecedent, or activating event, may be your spouse speaking to you. Feeling angry about what your spouse said to you might be a *C* response. In many cases, a distortional belief occurs between *A* and *C*—in other words, there is a *B* factor that occurs between what is experienced and what is felt. In our example above, the distortional thought might be one of these thoughts:

- *My spouse shouldn't be speaking to me in that tone of voice.*

- *My spouse is nagging me, and nagging is wrong.*

- *My spouse is angry, so I will respond in the same manner.*

Dr. Ellis encourages people to move beyond the ABC of this process to add a *D*, which is to "dispute" the distortional thought and to replace it with a rational thought.

We also need to add an E step to his process—"exchanging" the irrational thought pattern with a positive, rational thought pattern that leads to concrete specific action aimed at alleviating future "activating events." Allow me to give you an example.

A patient visiting a physician's office for the first time is an hour late for his annual physical examination. (This is the **activating** event.) The physician starts thinking, *Patients are always late and ruin my schedule and my day; this patient will probably always be late.* Now the physician's **beliefs** are distorted. The emotional **consequences** are frustration, anger, and anxiety. He can, however, **dispute** or challenge this distortional belief by telling himself that thinking patients are always late is an over-generalization and that he is "catastrophizing" by believing his entire day is ruined.

What would be a rational thought to replace the irrational responses?

Maybe this patient had trouble finding the office or a parking space, which is why he was late. There is very little emotion attached to such a rational thought and, therefore, little stress.

A person who gets wound up with irrational thoughts such as those identified in this example is likely to be a person who does this frequently during the day. By the end of the day, this type of person can be seriously frustrated, angry, and stressed out.

I identified for you the A, B, C, and D factors. Now for what I call the "E" factor; that is, "exchanging" the distortional thinking with rational thoughts and behavior. Using the example once again, the physician would be wise to ask these "rational" questions:

- Is there any **evidence** to support any of these irrational thoughts? No.

- Is there **evidence** to support the rational thought? Yes. A first-time patient may very well have difficulty finding the office.

- Is there an **alternate** activity that can be done rather than dwelling on the emotions associated with the tardy patient? Absolutely.

The physician would be wise to come up with a rational decision that produces rational behavior. For example, the physician could say, "I will do some charting and dictation in the time I allotted for this person's physical exam, move the other patients up on the schedule as I am able, and see if the annual exam patient arrives by the end of the day. If so, I will see him. If not, then I will enjoy going home at an earlier time." The physician might also be wise to implement a few new policies in his office. In the future, he could remind patients of their appointments with a phone call, or give them a written statement stating that if they do not keep an appointment, they will be charged a fee. New patients will be given clear directions about how to find the office. All of these are very rational approaches that might alleviate future frustration. Just the thought of them in the present tense is likely to alleviate current frustration.

Try this ABCD-E process using an example from your own life.

Thought-Emotional Analysis Worksheet

A = Activating experience
B = Distortional belief
C = Emotional consequence
D = Disputing/challenging the distortional belief
E = Exchanging distortional thinking with rational thoughts and behavior

Take a long look at your own life today. Slow down your life so that you can recall specific incidences or experiences. Look at specific relationships. Are you engaging in distortional thinking about these incidents, experiences, and relationships? If so, what might you start doing to take responsibility for your own faulty thinking?

If you are unable to do Dr. Ellis' ABCD process or to look with objectivity at various incidents or experiences in your life, you may be wise to consult a rational emotive therapist or a therapist skilled in cognitive therapy. Sometimes couples can help each other identify these patterns.

With practice, a person can become adept at identifying and disputing distortional thoughts, and in their place, begin to practice rational thinking. As a person changes his thinking, his mood changes, which often melts away stress.

OVERCOMING DISTORTIONAL THOUGHTS THROUGH "REFRAMING"

One of the best techniques I have found for changing distortional thinking is called "reframing." I have always enjoyed looking at illustrations that have a hidden message or image. I remember a patient giving me a cartoon picture of a beautiful princess. She asked me to find the other hidden image on the sheet of paper. At first I saw no hidden image, but when she finally suggested that I turn the piece of paper upside down, the image of a wrinkled old woman became obvious! The "hidden" image appeared when I shifted my perspective.

Reframing is similar to this technique. It calls upon a person to shift his focus or attention away from his present point of view in order to attempt to "see" another person or a situation from a new perspective. This is similar to putting a new picture frame on an old picture. Do you remember viewing pictures through a View-Master? (That is the toy where you slide in a photo disk, and every time you click the lever, it advances to the next frame.) In many ways, reframing is similar to taking new information into one's mental "View-Master" and advancing the "frame" of a new portion of the world at large.

Years ago my wife, Mary, began to develop anxiety about driving an automobile. She had heard a statistic that the more a person drives a car, the greater the chances of being involved in an accident. She got to the point where she dreaded driving because she feared the risk of an accident. One day as she was driving with my father, she expressed these fears. He helped her "reframe" her thinking by suggesting to her that the more she drove her car, the more she could develop her driving skills and decrease the likelihood of having an accident. When Mary reframed her thinking, the fear and dread of driving left.

When you alter the way you "see" the world, something not only happens to you emotionally and mentally, but also physically. Many stressful situations can cease to become stressful.

In 2004, Hurricane Charley blew through Orlando, Florida, which is where we live. By the time this hurricane reached our city, it had been downgraded from a category 4 to a category 2 hurricane. Nevertheless, it packed winds in excess of one hundred miles an hour. Most of Orlando lost electrical power, and many people lost portions of their roofs to the storm. The day after the hurricane was a sweltering August day, and without power and air conditioning, the heat seemed like adding insult to injury.

I was listening to a radio talk show that day. Caller after caller phoned in complaining about the heat, lack of power, roof damage, and food spoiling. Finally an African American woman phoned in and began shouting for joy. She said that she wanted to thank God, shout, and dance that no one in her family had been injured in the hurricane. She was so happy that her husband and children had escaped injury.

When asked about her house and if she had power, she said, "Oh, a tree fell on my house and there is no power, but we are safe and unharmed!"

This woman had reframed the situation and refocused her perspective on her blessings. She refused to dwell on the negative.

In many ways, Hurricane Charley brought out the best in people as they pitched in and helped their neighbors. It also brought out the worst in others who complained, were impatient, and became angry at having to wait in long lines and being without certain amenities, such as ice.

Thomas Edison worked long hours and failed literally hundreds of times in his efforts to create an effective filament for the carbon incandescent lamp. One story about his life claims that as each experiment failed, Edison simply tossed the experiment outside his second-story window. Eventually, the pile reached almost to the second floor of his house! So many failures would have discouraged most people. Edison, however, reframed his failures by saying, "I am not discouraged. Every wrong attempt discarded is another step forward." We too can choose to see our failures in this manner.

Years ago I seemed to always be standing in the shortest line at the grocery store, only to have it turn into the longest line. Someone ahead of me would have a credit card declined, the clerk would need a price check on an item, the cash register would run out of tape, or the manager would need to approve a check. I would become very frustrated. I decided to "reframe" these situations, and instead of seeing the delay in terms of frustration, I chose to see it as an opportunity for a relaxation break—a time to practice a couple of deep-breathing exercises along with some posture-related exercises. The delayed lines became not only beneficial to me, but also even pleasurable. James 1:2–4 says:

> My brethren, count it all joy when you fall into various trials, knowing that the testing of your faith produces patience. But let patience have its perfect work, that you may be perfect and complete, lacking nothing.

Failures can be reframed as learning experiences—a problem can be perceived as a "teacher." Certainly problems have a great potential to function as character builders.

REFRAMING CAN REVEAL "MEANING"

A few months ago a patient named Jenny came to me complaining that she had experienced very sore and tender thighs and calves for three days. She had just returned from a relaxing vacation with her husband and their three children. They had stayed in a friend's two-story townhome where, much of the time, they were on the beach. The leg pain began on their drive back home.

I asked if she had exercised any while she was away, and she replied that she did not have any time to exercise. I later discovered that Jenny lived in a single-story home, and during the vacation she had spent considerable time and effort running up and down the stairs of this townhome chasing her three-year-old child. Jenny was not used to climbing stairs, and the result was that her thighs and calves were sore. It was an easy diagnosis, and a week of taking natural anti-inflammatory products helped her considerably.

When Jenny first came into my office, she thought she was suffering from some strange malady. She had let her mind wander off to all sorts of possibilities, most of them related to terrible diseases. Once she knew the reason for her pain, she was able to reframe her thinking and laugh at her former fears and concerns.

This is often the case. When we find the meaning behind an experience or event, we often are able not only to resolve issues related to the memory of that event, but also to let go of all fears and residual pain from the event. Reframing can help us move out of the past and toward the future.

"FRAME" EACH DAY IN ADVANCE

I have found it especially helpful to "frame" my day each morning. I started doing this several years ago after I took a trip to Toronto, Canada. As I prepared to leave Toronto by plane, I had to fill out a card, required of all United States citizens, with my name, address, and the contact information of a spouse, relative, or close friend so the airline would have someone to contact should our plane crash. Although I knew that extra security measures had been instituted after the September 11, 2001, attacks on America, I was a bit startled at this policy. It made me think, *What if this flight is my time to die? How would I want to spend the next couple of hours?*

Most people I know are postponing the things they really enjoy and really want to do in life until some distant time when those dreams seem more doable or affordable. I have become a firm believer that we need to live each day as if it is our last one on earth. If we "frame" a day with that perspective, we often find that petty things no longer bother us; in fact, there are very few big problems that bother us! James lived with this frame around his life. He wrote, "You do not know what will happen tomorrow. For what is your life? It is even a vapor that appears for a little time and then vanishes away" (James 4:14). Life is precious and fragile. Frame your days with the people and activities that matter most to you.

Years ago a long-term patient came into my office one morning crying hysterically. Earlier that morning she and her husband had a terrible fight, and shortly after he left for work, she received news that he had died in an automobile accident. She deeply regretted the fight they had and wished she had the opportunity to tell her husband one more time that morning, "I love you. Good-bye." Frame a day with this goal in mind: "I will tell every person in my family today that I love him or her."

THOUGHT FIELD THERAPY

One viable solution to eliminating painful, stressful, or traumatic memories and negative thought patterns is through a psychological treatment called "Thought Field Therapy." Using the same network of energy pathways as acupuncturists, clinical psychologist Dr. Roger Callahan has discovered that these energy pathways can be accessed to heal emotional distress. This cutting-edge psychological treatment is used to treat anger, addictions, anxiety, compulsions, grief, guilt, phobias, trauma, and stress. Dr. Callahan states that 70 to 80 percent of individuals can expect to have their negative emotions completely resolved.

By simply tapping with your fingers on specific acupuncture points, you will be able to eliminate imbalances in the body's energy system and eventually eliminate negative emotions in only a few minutes. However, you need to tap specific points in a particular sequence—similar to opening a safe. When the correct points are tapped in the proper sequence, the negative emotion is released. In the context of psychology, the term release usually means a sudden, intense expression of the emotion.

Proper treatment usually results in the immediate, complete disappearance of the emotion, and the typical patient will often say, "I can't think of it anymore." But this is an incorrect assumption. Actually, since the emotion is gone, when they think of the problem, they no longer can find the disturbing emotion associated with the problem.[5]

REFRAMING IS "TRANSFORMING"

The Bible tells us that we are not to live with distortional thought processes. Rather, we are to have a "transformed" mind. Paul wrote to the Romans, "Do not be conformed to this world, but be *transformed* by the renewing of your mind, that you may prove what is that good and acceptable and perfect will of God" (Rom. 12:2, emphasis added).

How do we develop a "transformed" or "renewed" mind? We steep our thinking in God's Word. We find out how God sees reality. We find out what God calls true. We find out what God commands. And then...

We choose to see the world through God's eyes.

We choose to label right and wrong according to God's standards.

We choose to love and to forgive as God loves and forgives us.

If you haven't made these choices, or more specifically, if you have not made them today, I strongly encourage you to do so!

6

Reduce Your Frustration Factors

We live in a fast-paced society in which nobody seems to have enough time. I call most of my fellow citizens the "too-much bunch."

- They have too much to do.

- They are too hurried.

- They have taken on too much in the way of commitment or responsibility.

- They have too much debt.

- They have too much work to do in any allotted time frame.

- They have too much in the way of clutter and possessions.

- They have too many frustrations and, as a result, may take way too many tranquilizers and stomach medications!

The majority of Americans report that they are frustrated on a daily basis, and many report that they remain frustrated throughout any given work day. According to Webster's dictionary, the word *frustrate* means "to induce feelings of discouragement" or "to defeat another's plan or achievement of goals." In other words, frustration occurs when we are in a situation that keeps us from experiencing genuine joy and pleasure. We usually become frustrated when we have unmet expectations.

Jesus said, "In the world ye shall have tribulation: but be of good cheer; I have overcome the world" (John 16:33, KJV). This word *tribulation* in the Greek language means "afflicted, anguished, burdened, persecuted, troubled." It can also be translated "pressure." That is the way we feel when we are frustrated!

A great deal of frustration does not arise from real situations that thwart us or keep us from finding the joy we desire. Rather, it arises from distortional expectations. In other words, we develop a "distorted view" of what life should be like or should produce.

- We expect our children to be perfect...and they are not.

- We expect other people to do the right thing...according to our definition of "right"...and they do not.

- We strive to protect our children from harm, giving them love and guidance...and they rebel and seek out the very things from which we attempted to protect them.

- We expect our career to be fulfilling and rewarding...and it is not.

- We expect our new business venture to soar...and it falls flat.

- We expect our beloved to be the perfect spouse...and are surprised to find there is no such thing as a perfect person.

To our distorted expectations we often add a layer of the competitive spirit—"keeping up with the Joneses." We continually compare our level of achievement to that of other people and nearly always find ourselves coming up short in one or more categories of comparison.

The good news is that most of the external triggers that cause us to become frustrated can be managed, and most of our internal perceptions that are distorted can be reprogrammed in our own minds and hearts.

Bill was a patient of mine who was extremely frustrated. He had hypertension, and during his exam in my office he was constantly interrupted by his pager or cell phone, each time with an "important" message or call he had to take or return. After each call he appeared even more frustrated.

During one of the calls I decided to check his blood pressure. It was much higher than when I had taken his blood pressure at a resting state between calls! His resting blood pressure was 122/80, but his on-call blood pressure was 160/100. In addition to frustration, both anger and impatience—which are often manifestations of frustration—are known risk factors for hypertension.[1]

STRESS ACTIVATES THE STRESS ALARM

Bill was constantly in a hurry and was nearly always "running late." He complained of being in debt "up to his eyeballs." At the same time, he always seemed to be bragging about a new car he had just purchased. He talked often about needing to work longer hours and make more sales to keep his head above water.

Bill was stuck in a rut of frustration and couldn't get out. In addition to his hypertension, he had high cholesterol and was obese.

Frustration stimulates the stress response. Blood vessels constrict, and blood pressure rises; when this happens with great consistency, hypertension may develop. Frustration triggers the sympathetic nervous system into "overdrive."

It also tends to trigger our "psychological response" into overdrive.

What do I mean by this? When we become frustrated, rather than back off, clarify our values and priorities, and make choices that simplify our lives, we tend to fall into a frustration trap. We think the solution to our frustration will be to get even busier—and as a result, we work even longer hours. Or we think the solution is to buy more possessions to ease our frustration—and as a result, we tend to get deeper into debt. The longer hours and bigger debt do not solve the problem of frustration, of course. They usually simply increase our frustration!

In his book *Toxic Success*, Dr. Paul Pearsall tells a story about a thirty-two-year-old woman who was suffering through her last days with breast cancer. She was unable to lift her head, and she was shaking so badly that the rubbing sound of the sheet made it difficult to hear her weak and failing voice. She whispered, "If I could come back to life, I would pay attention to just being alive. I would pay attention to the chance to be with my husband and our kids. It seems like I spent too much of my life giving my time for money. Now, I would give all my money for just a little more time to be with my family."[2]

This woman had distortional thinking. She had thought her job and money would bring her happiness. She thought wrong.

Frustration tends to build the more we go over and over old situations that we cannot reverse and for which there is no immediate solution. Frustration also tends to build the more we try to figure things out when answers are unclear or cannot be found. Ultimately, if we want to free ourselves from frustration we need to come to two main conclusions:

- I cannot change the past. I can only forgive and ask God both to heal the pain I feel about the past and to help me move forward in my life.

- Some things I cannot figure out in advance. I simply cannot anticipate all that may happen or may not happen. I must take life as it comes, one day at a time, trusting that God is in control and He will help me with everything that comes my way.

We are wise to anticipate that life will have moments of pain, confusion, and fear. Weight lifters go into a training session *knowing* that if their workout is effective, they *will* have pain. In being able to anticipate the pain, they have no emotional response to the pain. Their response is purely physical. We can learn much from them.

DON'T LET A RESPONSE OF FRUSTRATION BECOME A HABIT

For many people, feeling frustrated is a habit. Frustration has become an emotional response that is programmed into their neural circuitry. Much of what we know about frustration is learned from our environment—from our parents, older siblings, relatives, teachers, coaches, or other authoritative figures. We also have been programmed by all sorts of media to expect frustration in relationships. In the end, however, the degree to which we become frustrated is related to our own mental and emotional habits. Over the years, we have "practiced" responding and reacting to certain situations. These responses and reactions have become habitual, and they are stored in the amygdala of the brain, which is the emotional memory storehouse of the brain.

Not only do we program ourselves through the years with emotional habits that lead to frustration, but we also program ourselves with "expressions" of frustration. Frustration very often leads to anger—usually explosive anger and rage. At times the anger becomes a seething resentment or bitterness.

When we explode in anger, we stimulate the sympatho-adreno-medullary (SAM) system. In other words, we stimulate the stress response that produces elevated adrenaline. When we seethe with anger, we generally stimulate the HPAC stress response, which is the hypothalamic-pituitary-adreno-cortical response that produces increased cortisol levels. Both of these anger responses over time lead to cardiovascular disease.

Venting anger may feel good to the person expressing it in the moment, because he or she usually gets an adrenaline rush. But this venting comes at a cost to health in the long run. In addition, the person who vents tends to leave behind him a wake of "broken" things—sometimes breakable items that have been smashed in a rage, and even worse, sometimes broken bones or shattered emotions in a loved one who witnesses the rage or is the recipient of violent behavior.

A female patient went to her physician's office one morning with an ice pack on her nose. As she removed the pack from her face, he could instantly see that her nose was broken. When he asked her what happened, she told him that she had just experienced road rage. As she was parking her car in a parking lot, another driver who wanted the same parking place had become outraged at losing it to her. When she got out of the car, the other driver approached her, ranting and raving, and because she refused to move her car, he punched her in the nose. He was so blinded by his anger that he didn't notice she had called the police. When they arrived, he was arrested on the scene. She later learned that this wasn't the first time this man had lost his temper. He ended up spending two years in jail. His expectations were that he deserved the parking place he had spotted, and when he did not get to it first, his frustration boiled over into anger and physical assault.

I remember a former patient who went through a very bitter and painful divorce. She was a successful businesswoman who worked hard to build her business. What she did not know was that while she was working, her husband was cheating on her with a younger woman. In the end, he received a substantial settlement, which made her seethe with bitterness and frustration. Prior to her divorce, her blood pressure was normal. During and after the divorce, she began to register high blood pressure readings. I placed her on medicine for hypertension. However, her blood pressure continued to rise, so eventually she needed three different blood pressure medications in order to control her blood pressure. A few months later, she suffered a mild stroke, which was a major wake-up call for her. She decided to forgive and no longer give so much of her mind to rehashing the old hurts of her divorce. It was not easy to forgive and to turn her mind away from the injustice she felt had been committed, but she took control of her own mind and emotions and forced herself to let go of all negative perceptions she held toward her former husband. The more she forgave, the more her blood pressure dropped, and in the end, she was able to wean off all her blood pressure medications!

THREE THOUGHT PROCESSES THAT PRODUCE FRUSTRATION

There are three main distortional thought processes that lead to frustration.

1. Preconceived "should-do" behavioral rules

As I stated in chapter five, this is what I call the "fixed-rule" thinking. Many people become frustrated because they believe things "should" be done a certain way—their way.

As an example, a person may have a preconceived idea that other people should be kind, respectful, and polite. When people who are unkind, rude, impatient, or offensive mistreat him, he discovers he has no recourse. He cannot make other people treat him well. He has no authority to insist that other people act in the way they should act, which results in feelings of frustration and, at times, anger or hurt.

There is only one rule that we should have, and that is the one Jesus gave us in John 13:34. He said, "A new commandment I give unto you, That ye love one another; as I have loved you, that ye also love one another" (KJV). This rule is not about how other people should treat you, but rather about how you should treat other people.

God requires that we love even those who do not live up to our expectations. In writing to the Corinthians, the apostle Paul said this about love:

> Love suffers long and is kind; love does not envy;
> love does not parade itself, is not puffed up;
> does not behave rudely, does not seek its own,
> is not provoked, thinks no evil; does not rejoice
> in iniquity, but rejoices in the truth; bears all
> things, believes all things, hopes all things,
> endures all things. Love never fails.
> —1 CORINTHIANS 13:4–8

What does this mean to the person who struggles with frustration? It means that *we* need to practice love any time a person does not live up to what we believe a person should do. We are required to be the ones who display:

- Patience
- Genuine appreciation for the accomplishments of others
- Humility
- Forgiveness
- Kindness
- Good manners
- Generosity of spirit—giving to others more than seeking to receive
- Refusal to be provoked into anger
- Perseverance in difficult times
- Belief and hope for the best
- Putting up with difficult people

And we are to do it all "without failing" or giving up! "But," you may be saying, "that puts all the burden on me no matter how obnoxious, proud, rude, unkind, or despicable another person might be!" Right. The truth is, you cannot force anybody to live up to your standards or expectations about character. You can only enforce those standards on yourself.

I live in a neighborhood where security guards patrol the neighborhood in patrol cars with flashing yellow lights on top. If a driver speeds through our neighborhood, a security guard can pull him over and give him a warning ticket. The guard, however, does not have the authority to issue tickets with mandatory fines as the police department does. The speed limit in the neighborhood is twenty-five miles per hour, and many residents quickly caught on that the security guards were unable to impose these fines. Therefore, people began to speed—up to sixty miles per hour—through some sections of the neighborhood; they simply ignored the flashing yellow lights of the security patrol. Finally, the neighborhood association had to call in police officers to patrol the neighborhood and issue tickets to speeders. As officers of the law, the police were able to enforce the law, whereas the security guards could only call attention to the problem.

Ultimately, when other people break the laws of God found in the Bible, only God can enforce those laws. You, however, do have the ability to enforce the laws of His Word in your own heart and mind.

If a fellow employee is overly critical or obnoxious to you, you may not be able to do anything about what is said. But you do have the ability to determine how you will relate to that person and act in that situation.

If a driver on the freeway cuts you off in an incident of road rage, you may not be able to do anything about what has been done. But you do have the ability to determine how you will drive.

If a cashier is rude to you, you may not be able to do anything to change that person's tone of voice, but you do have the ability to determine how you will respond.

My wife, Mary, and I were in England a few years ago to attend a seminar where I was scheduled to speak. We were waiting for a train to take us from London to another city. The train was scheduled to leave at five o'clock that evening. As we arrived at the station just a few minutes before five o'clock, we were feeling pressure to get our tickets as quickly as possible. When we were next in line to move toward the ticket window, two women suddenly walked to the front of the line and went to the ticket window. I said, "You can't do that," and one of the women turned around and said, "Oh, yes, we can." At that moment, I realized I had absolutely no authority to tell her to go to the back of the line and wait her turn.

I had a choice. I could become frustrated and angry, or I could switch my mind off the "frustration" channel and on to the "love" channel. Mary and I began to talk about the wonderful conference we were attending and to focus on details about various presentations we had heard or were scheduled to hear. Fortunately for us, the train was running a little late, and we were able to get our tickets and board the train without any difficulty.

- Would frustration and anger have made the line move according to our "rules"? No.

- Would frustration and anger have had any impact whatsoever on the train's arrival and departure time? No.

♦ Would frustration and anger have spoiled part of our trip? Yes.

And these emotions would have released stress hormones we did not need!

2. Jumping to conclusions

A second common distortional thought process linked to frustration is one that I covered in chapter five: "jumping to conclusions." This means that you believe that you know at all times with 100 percent accuracy what other people are thinking about you or what they are planning or intending to do.

3. Rehashing the problem

Frustration often arises because a person continues to rehash a problem or hurtful situation. Most overstressed individuals are "rehashers." They constantly contemplate, relive, and meditate on the hurtful and painful experiences of their past. An upsetting event may have occurred fifteen years ago, but a rehasher can recall that experience as if it happened yesterday. The incident has been brooded over, pondered, and deliberated to the extent that the person almost seems incapable of going for very long without reliving the event and talking about it. The experience is "relived" as an old record might be replayed again and again...the issues go round and round...and the scratchiness on the old record just increases with each playing.

As soon as a person begins to rehearse the incident in his mind, the stress response goes into high gear. Biologically, the brain does not make a distinction between short-term and long-term memories when it comes to a biochemical stress response.

After more than ten years of marriage, John left Jane while they were visiting friends in another state. They didn't have an argument, not even a minor disagreement. He simply got in his car and drove back home to his home state. When he finally returned home to Jane, he brought with him divorce papers. He packed up his things and left permanently.

Jane was devastated and tried to contact her husband repeatedly, but without success. She didn't have any explanation for his sudden and irreversible behavior. Eventually, she even hired a private investigator to find him and discover why the sudden change of heart, only to learn there was no reason for leaving.

I finally politely said to her, "Jane, you need to stop rehashing this. Let it go!" But every few months Jane would show up with a medical ailment and rehash the entire story one more time.

I finally recommended that she make an "appreciation list." I told her to list everything that was good about her life. I shared with her what the apostle Paul wrote to the Thessalonians: "Rejoice always, pray without ceasing, in everything give thanks; for this is the will of God in Christ Jesus for you" (1 Thess. 5:16–18).

I also shared with her that in my medical practice I have noted through the years that those who develop an attitude of gratitude, praise, and trust in God have far fewer feelings of frustration, anger, and resentment.

I also advised her to keep her mind busy by watching funny movies, reading the Bible, reading good wholesome books, and memorizing and meditating on Scripture. I instructed her to stop telling her divorce story to anyone who would listen. I told her that she needed to stop trying to figure out why her husband left her.

Something deep inside Jane told her that what I was saying to her was right. At first it was difficult for her to do the things I prescribed for her to do, but she eventually did them all. She is happier than ever these days, and she rarely speaks about her former husband.

When she stopped rehashing the problem, she moved into a new level of truth on which to base her life.

The apostle Paul wrote these words of wisdom to the early Christians who lived in Philippi:

> Whatever things are true...noble...just... pure...lovely...of good report, if there is any virtue and if there is anything praiseworthy— meditate on these things.
>
> —PHILIPPIANS 4:8

Paul told the Philippians that if they would do these things, the "God of peace" would be with them. What is the opposite of frustration? *Peace.*

How do you get peace? Change the way you think! Move from distortional perceptions, jumping to conclusions, and rehashing of problems to thinking about the good things of God! Focus on what is true, noble, just, pure, lovely, of good report, virtuous, and praiseworthy!

There may be lots of things you need to "turn off" in order to turn on these good and pure thoughts. You may need to turn off television, stop watching some kinds of movies, and put down some trashy novels. You may need to stop going to certain Internet sites. You may need to turn off some radio stations or change your music.

There may be some new habits you need to adopt—habits such as reading and memorizing the Bible, listening to wholesome Bible teaching and preaching, listening to good Christian praise music and hymns, and attending church regularly.

Most of all, you need to take control of your own thinking and choose to think the way God desires for you to think—with thoughts and attitudes rooted in love!

TAKING CONTROL OF FRUSTRATION—EXTERNAL FACTORS

You may need to take control over some external factors. If there are two cries voiced by overstressed Americans, they seem to be these:

- "I'm so busy!"
- "I'm so tired!"

Both cries stem from taking on too much to do in too little time.

Anytime I see a patient whose health is deteriorating because life is spinning too fast, I explain to him that life is not a sprint, but a marathon. He or she needs to slow down and enjoy the slow jog through life. Those who race through their days at a breakneck speed are "striving"—they are in hot pursuit of things temporal that they believe they personally must own, accomplish, or make happen.

In most cases, those who are too busy or too tired have a deep intuitive feeling that the one thing they truly need more of is "people time." They need to spend more time with a spouse or with their children. They may need to spend more time with elderly parents, grandchildren, or friends. To get more people time, a person simply needs to turn off some things—for example, the television, the computer, or the phone—and turn on activities that involve conversation, doing tasks together, or engaging in recreational pursuits with other people.

The third great cry I hear from overstressed people is this: "I have too much to do."

Usually this can be translated, "I've taken on too many commitments" or "I'm working too many hours."

What underlies these external factors? Usually a deep desire for more material possessions or a desire for more recognition, fame, or approval. Millions of Americans are living with an excess of possessions and inadequate space. Perhaps they are attempting to "buy" friendships or feelings of self-worth by taking on too many responsibilities (including participation in a variety of committees, clubs, and societies or care of another person for whom one is not truly responsible).

I have several patients who are "malling" themselves to death—they are addicted to the high they get while shopping and spending, oftentimes, money they truly do not have. The average American now carries the burden of $8,000 in credit card debt,[3] which means our nation as a whole has more than $600 billion in credit card debt.[4] Sears now makes more money on credit than it does on the sale of merchandise! And this from a company founded by a man who would only pay cash![5]

What happens when a very high percentage of our nation is too busy, too tired, and has too much to do for reasons that are often rooted in materialism and striving for self-worth? At least three consequences are directly linked.

1. Relationships suffer.

First, relationships suffer. The divorce rate in our nation has more than doubled since 1950, with approximately one out of every two marriages failing. The majority of new marriages won't last longer than seven years.[6] The one thing that people really need—deeper and more satisfying relationships—is the first thing sacrificed by being too busy, tired, or having too much to do.

2. An obsession with escapism develops.

Second, people become obsessed with new ways to try escaping from the pressures they feel. They seek out more "entertainment" in the form of books, television programs, videos, video games, and computer games. The average television viewer now watches between twenty and thirty-six hours a week of television.[7] These people seek out more "toys" to own, more vacation spots to visit, and more activities or hobbies to help them "unwind." As part of an attempt to escape the pressure, more and more people are eating out or turning to fast-food meals. And what do these various forms of escape produce? In the vast majority of cases, they produce an overwhelming amount of information (far more than a person can take in and use)...an overwhelming amount of sexual images (that tend to fuel lust and, eventually, behavior that destroys relationships)...an overwhelming amount of expense...and an overwhelmingly unhealthy dietary plan!

3. A distorted view of what is valuable develops.

Third, people who are too tired, too busy, or have too much to do tend to lose sight of what is important because they become preoccupied with what is urgent. They respond to the need of the moment rather than plan and pursue a life that is grounded in what they truly consider to be vital and valuable.

Consider what happens in the workplace. The "big goals" of doing a job often get bogged down in a sea of pager and cell phone rings, e-mails, voice mails, faxes, and instant messages. The average office worker now receives just over one hundred messages from e-mails, memos, and voice mails a day![8]

DON'T WAIT FOR A NEAR-DEATH EXPERIENCE!

It sometimes takes a near-death experience before a person will clarify his values and return to a life structured around self-generated priorities rather than external demands.

A patient named Bill suffered a massive heart attack in his mid-forties and was not expected to live. His family gathered around his bedside and reminisced with him about the joyful times in their lives. This man had been a highly driven executive who suffered extreme frustration. He sacrificed his family life to climb the corporate ladder. He was closing deals while his children had ball games. He felt driven to succeed.

Bill developed severe hypertension and sky-high cholesterol. He was overweight and had diabetes. His problems compounded at home, to a great extent, because of his absence as a father. His teenage children began experimenting with drugs and eventually became addicted. His son was arrested for drug possession and later for selling Ecstasy and served time in prison. His daughter became an alcoholic and had several abortions. She became so depressed that she tried to commit suicide on a number of occasions. His other son became a homosexual and contracted AIDS. His wife, depressed and overwhelmed, used food for her comfort. She was thin when she married Bill, but her emotional eating made her morbidly obese.

Bill's world was falling apart, literally. His body was broken. The people he loved the most were broken. It was at the time his son was sent to prison that he had his massive heart attack.

Bill defeated all odds and lived through this heart attack, and he made a decision to change his life dramatically. He no longer fought traffic to try to outmaneuver others to reach his destination three minutes earlier. He slowed down, noticed flowers he had never seen in his neighborhood, and took walks in the fresh air. He made a decision that he was truly going to enjoy every day of the rest of his life. He began to write regularly to his son in prison. He reconnected with his daughter and other son and began to attend church with his family every week. He and his wife began to work out at a gym, and they made a mutual decision they were going to stop striving and return to the priorities and goals they had when they first married: a loving, healthy, giving, God-centered marriage.

Did Bill and his wife find instant success in their turnaround efforts? No. But a great deal of pressure lifted from Bill the minute he decided to make these changes.

Are Bill and his wife still in pursuit of the goals and priorities they deeply desire? Yes. Both of them are at greater peace—with far less frustration clouding their days—and they are rebuilding broken relationships with "new bricks" of love, patience, and renewed understanding.

Viktor Frankl, a Jewish psychiatrist, was imprisoned by the Nazis during World War II. His parents, his brother, and his wife died in the camps or were sent to the ovens. He lived from day to day wondering if he would be next. Then one day, naked and alone in a small room, he began to become aware of the one freedom his Nazi captors could not take away. Frankl realized that, no matter what the Nazis did to him, they could not rob him of his right to decide within himself how it would all affect him. He had the power to choose his response.[9] He survived the camp and went on to become Europe's leading psychiatrist, with twenty-seven books published and translated into nineteen languages. His most notable work is titled *Man's Search for Meaning*. In it he wrote, "Everything can be taken from a man but one thing; the last of human freedoms—to choose one's attitudes in any given set of circumstances, to choose one's own way."[10] He developed his psychiatric theory into "logotherapy"—which is founded on his belief that man can choose his responses to life.

In many cases, this is a vital message for those who are frustrated. So often, people who have programmed their lives to respond with frustration, anger, and resentment seem to think that their lives are "out of control." This is another way of saying they don't believe they can exert control over their own external or internal factors. In truth, they can!

If you are living with tremendous frustration, anger, or bitterness today, you can change the way you respond to life. You can change the way you think, feel, and act.

And you can start making these changes right now!

Part of learning to deal with stress and frustration is learning to deal with offense, which we will cover in the next chapter.

7

Dealing With the Inevitable Offenses

Through the years I have had a number of patients who came to me after they had experienced a major "wake-up call" in their health. In some cases, they were diagnosed with an illness and told they had only three to six months to live. I have discovered in dealing with these patients that many of them began to spiral down into ill health at the time they began to harbor an offense. They had been emotionally wounded in some way and had refused to forgive.

An offense is similar to a grudge. It is any circumstance or complaint that is perceived as unjust or hurtful. An offense usually produces what I call a "grievance story." A grievance story is when something happens in our life that we did not want to happen, and we deal with the problem by thinking about it too much and talking about it too much.

A number of commentators have noted that Americans today are an angry and hostile people. Most anger is rooted in this issue of offense. The vast majority of people in our nation have a grievance story, and generally speaking, they are quick to tell it to you!

Here is a striking statistic: 20 percent of Americans have a hostility level that is high enough to be dangerous to their health.[1] This figure can be translated into approximately sixty million Americans! Hostility, of course, is a major risk factor for hypertension. One in four adult Americans has hypertension.[2]

Hostility and anger are also risk factors for heart disease. In one twenty-five-year study involving 255 medical students from the University of North Carolina, researchers found that subjects who were found to have the most hostility on the Standard Personality Test had a nearly five times greater risk of developing heart disease as their less hostile classmates. They were also more likely to die by age fifty—seven times more likely.[3]

HOW MUCH VIOLENCE DO YOU TAKE INTO YOUR MIND?

Anger and hostility are reinforced in us as a nation through constant bombardment of violent images and violent language. When was the last time you watched several hours of prime-time network television programming that did *not* have at least one act of murder, suicide, violence, use of drugs, illicit sex, or overt rebellion against parental authority or society's laws? I doubt if it is possible! Much of the music our teens listen to promotes violence, killing, suicide, immorality, and drug use. The "gangster rap" music and heavy-metal rock music are particularly violent.

Most of us would be repulsed by the lyrics of gangster rap—that is, of course, if we were able to understand the lyrics. Whether we understand the lyrics or not, our children and teenagers do! What is happening when these lyrics are played repeatedly and rehearsed frequently in the minds of young men and women? Nothing good!

Some parents are unknowingly purchasing video games for their children that teach children to kill, maim, and decapitate people. Among these games are "Resident Evil," "Doom," "Tomb Raider," "Killer 7," and "Dead Rush." We need to wake up and become alarmed!

A number of child psychologists and psychiatrists are recommending that their patients turn off television, stop going to the movies, and even stop watching the news. You may be thinking, *The news?* Often the media give graphic details about gruesome murders, kidnappings, drive-by shootings, and terrorist acts. The majority of movies that appear in today's multiplex cinemas have violence in them—even in the so-called "action movies" rated PG.

The problem with violence is that people become desensitized to it. They sear their own consciences and find they are able to watch more and more brutality and senseless killing with fewer and fewer emotional responses. While people may say they are against violence, by their actions in watching violence—and buying high-priced movie tickets to do so—they contribute to its increase. It takes more and more violence to stimulate feelings of "excitement," because the mind is growing more and more numb to the horror of violence.

This is not a new phenomenon linked only to the media. The Bible gives us a very detailed account of a person being "desensitized" to sin and violence. In Genesis 13 we read that Abraham and his nephew Lot had so many flocks and herds that the land was not able to support all the animals. So, Abraham separated himself from Lot and gave Lot his choice of lands. Lot chose a beautiful place along the Jordan River that was described as being "like the garden of the Lord." He made his dwelling in the city of Sodom on that plain. When four kings invaded Sodom and the nearby cities, Lot was captured and taken far to the north. Abraham, along with 318 of his servants, rescued Lot and brought him and all his goods back to Sodom. In Genesis 18, we read that the Lord regarded the sins of Sodom and Gomorrah as "very grave." Abraham negotiated with God to spare the cities for his nephew's sake, and the Lord finally agreed that if ten righteous people could be found in these cities, He would not destroy them.

Shortly afterward, two angels went to Sodom and visited Lot without his being aware they were angels. Lot invited the two men into his house to spend the night, but even before these men could lie down to go to sleep, the men of Sodom—young and old from every quarter of the city—surrounded Lot's house. The men of Sodom demanded that Lot's visitors be given to them so they might have sexual intercourse with them. The city was so perverse that strangers who came into town were considered "fair game" for violent sexual assault.

Can you imagine living in such a city? Lot had lived with Abraham, a great man of faith who was a "friend of God." He knew right from wrong. He had chosen Sodom as his home because of the beauty of the area. He had learned to tolerate the wickedness of the city. He had programmed his own thinking to tolerate the perversion all around him—such perversion that not even ten righteous people could be found in the entire city!

Lot went out to try to plead with the crowd to leave his guests alone. He even offered his two virgin daughters to them in place of the strangers. The crowd, however, pressed against Lot and nearly broke the door down. Finally the angels inside the house reached out, pulled Lot to safety, and shut the door. The men outside were struck with blindness by the angels, and the next morning, the angels led Lot and his family out of the city. Lot's sons-in-law stayed behind—they may very well have been homosexuals since Lot's daughters are described as still being virgins. As Lot's family left Sodom with the angels, the angels warned them not to look behind or linger on the plain lest they be destroyed by the fire and brimstone that was going to rain on Sodom and Gomorrah. Lot's wife looked back, however, and instantly became a pillar of salt.

What a tragic and horrible end to what had been a promising "career" and successful home life for Lot! He simply had grown accustomed to the sins of Sodom and had externally programmed himself to accommodate a high degree of violence and perversion in the immediate world around him.

Do we do the same? Those who desensitize themselves to sin and violence ultimately may "preprogram" themselves to deal with an offense in a violent manner.

Jesus spoke of Lot in describing His Second Coming. He said:

> Likewise as it was also in the days of Lot: They ate, they drank, they bought, they sold, they planted, they built; but on the day that Lot went out of Sodom it rained fire and brimstone from heaven and destroyed them all. Even so will it be in the day when the Son of Man is revealed.
> —LUKE 17:28–30

We do not want to become desensitized to sin and violence; however, on the other hand, we do not want to take a personal offense toward the sinner who commits the sin and violence.

HOW EASILY ARE YOU OFFENDED?

Countless millions of people have been internally preprogrammed to be easily offended. Most learned this from their parents. They then reinforced an "offense habit" as they encountered various circumstances in their own lives. Jesus said that "it is impossible but that offences will come: but woe unto him, through whom they come!" (Luke 17:1, KJV). In other words, offenses are inevitable. We cannot avoid situations that hurt us physically or wound us emotionally. But, Jesus said, woe to the person who *causes* such offenses.

Most of us would say "That's right!" in response to Jesus' words. God should punish the person who causes an offense against us.

But what if the offense is one that we have imagined or perceived in error? Not all "offenses" are truly offenses! Many offenses are the product of our own distortional thinking—we imagine offenses, we perceive offenses, we see accidental acts as being intentional acts. And when we harbor offense—in other words, when we refuse to let go of an offense that is either real or perceived—we are choosing to remain offended. In these cases we are offending ourselves!

Jesus' word to us is plain, "Woe to you!"

It is impossible to avoid all painful situations, but when you turn those painful moments into offenses and grievance stories, you are causing your own body and soul great harm.

Joe was a patient of mine who sold life insurance for a living. After he had been selling insurance for five years, Joe was surprised when a fellow worker who had been selling insurance for only two years was promoted to the position of manager in their insurance office. Joe was very upset at this and immediately went home to rant and rave to his wife, telling her how unfair this promotion was. He concluded that his boss "hated" him and, therefore, was out to destroy him. Joe became offended and turned his offense into a grievance story. He didn't care who heard his story, including customers. As a result, he began to sabotage his own sales. His customers reasoned that if Joe was not satisfied with the company, they probably shouldn't be satisfied with it either. People began to cancel the policies Joe had sold them.

Joe eventually was placed on probation and was told that if his production did not improve, he would be terminated. Joe took further offense! At hearing his boss's reprimand, Joe exploded with anger and told his boss to his face how unfair he had been.

The boss explained to Joe that he was gifted in sales, not in management, and that his colleague was not particularly gifted in sales but was very gifted in management. He explained that he did not hate Joe but rather had always enjoyed his company. He told him that he valued his work and respected his abilities.

Joe had sabotaged his own career by perceiving an offense when none had been intended. It took him months to recoup his losses.

I once had a patient who had a very cantankerous mother-in-law. This man decided to have a surprise birthday party for his wife. He asked his secretary to send out invitations to all of her friends and family members. In doing so, the secretary inadvertently forgot to send an invitation to his wife's mother! The mother-in-law perceived that this was a deliberate act meant to hurt her. She retaliated by having a rusted-out junk car behind her house towed to her son-in-law's house as an act of spite.

When the car arrived, neither the man nor his wife was at home. Their ten-year-old daughter, however, was at home. She decided to play in the car while waiting for her mom to return home from an errand. When my patient and his wife finally came home and saw the car, they began to examine it and found two rattlesnakes in the vehicle! This cantankerous mother-in-law could have killed her own granddaughter because she had concluded—on the basis of distortional thinking—that she had suffered an offense when no offense had been intended!

AVOID DEVELOPING A HABIT OF "TAKING OFFENSE"

Becoming a person who is easily offended is a habit. It is not unlike the habit exhibited by Pavlov's dog. Years ago Russian scientist Ivan Pavlov performed experiments in which he would ring a bell prior to feeding his dogs. The dogs initially salivated only when food was put before them, but over time, they associated the sound of the bell with the presence of food and began salivating every time the bell rang. This response became known in psychology as a "conditioned response."

Many people have allowed themselves to develop a "conditioned response" of being offended. They see an offense in virtually everything that happens to them. Even if a person gives them a compliment, they misinterpret what is said to the point that it becomes an offense to them.

My wife, Mary, and I were shopping at a home improvement store one day when Mary saw a woman pull out a paint can and then set it down in the aisle. She then walked several feet away from the can, turned, and walked toward the can, purposefully tripping over it. Sitting in the aisle where she had fallen, she complained of pain in her twisted ankle. She called for the manager of the store and said she was going to sue the store for leaving a paint can in the middle of the aisle. Mary had witnessed the entire incident, and she called the store manager aside and told him what she had seen. She left her name and phone number with him.

Sure enough, a few weeks later, the customer tried to sue the store, and the store manager called my wife. Mary signed an affidavit about what really had happened. We both were appalled that somebody would willfully try to "create" an offense with the intent of gaining money, but we know from our personal experience that it does happen.

A patient named Rebecca came to me when she was thirty-five-years old. She had long-term asthma. Periodically she had such severe asthmatic attacks that she would end up in a hospital emergency room. Rebecca was also very easily offended, and I noticed that at times when she was severely stressed over an offense, she nearly always had an asthma attack. I asked her to tell me her earliest memory related to asthma, and she recounted for me a story that happened when she was just a toddler. She remembered being in a mist tent in the hospital, and another girl was in the same room under a mist tent. The other little girl received lots of toys as presents from her parents—including a beautiful Barbie doll. Rebecca's parents, however, did not bring her any toys, only books to read. Rebecca had become "offended" at her parents for providing only "ugly old books." This offense was still so real in Rebecca's mind—having rehearsed and retold her grievance story for so many years—that in just telling this story to me, she brought on an asthmatic attack!

I told Rebecca that she was stuck in the past and that if she truly wanted to help her own asthmatic condition, she needed to quit repeating her grievance story and forgive this offense, which was primarily a perceived offense and nothing her parents ever intended to do to hurt her. Rebecca agreed, and when she quit telling her grievance story, her asthma attacks decreased dramatically.

The Bible gives us several stories of people who became offended. One of these people was Saul, the first king of Israel. On one occasion, as David returned from winning a battle, women came out from the cities to line the road, where they sang his praises and danced in joy. Specifically, they sang, "Saul has slain his thousands, and David his ten thousands." Saul responded by saying, "They have ascribed to David ten thousands, and to me they have ascribed only thousands. Now what more can he have but the kingdom?" Saul became both angry and jealous, and he sought to kill David from that moment onward. (See 1 Samuel 18:6–9.)

In contrast, the New Testament tells us of another Saul, this one better known as the apostle Paul. Paul had every reason to be offended by what people had done to him, often misconstruing what he said and misinterpreting his actions. He wrote to the Corinthians that he had been whipped by the Jews five times, each time receiving thirty-nine lashes (which was the maximum allowed). He wrote that he had been stoned once, had been beaten with rods three times, and had been shipwrecked three times; and on and on he recounted the terrible experiences he had been through. (See 2 Corinthians 11:23–29.) Then Paul says of his suffering that he had come to see it as all being for the purposes of God! He told the Corinthians how the Lord had spoken to him, saying, "My grace is sufficient for you, for My strength is made perfect in weakness" (2 Cor. 12:9). Paul did not feel offense at those who had injured him, but rather, he had great joy that when he was in a weakened state—no matter the cause—Christ was strong!

Paul said to the Roman governor Felix, "I myself always strive to have a conscience without offense toward God and man" (Acts 24:16). Paul was choosing to live free of offense.

DEALING WITH AN ACCIDENTAL OFFENSE

Some offenses are purely accidental. The "accident" seems to be something we are failing to recognize in our society today. The caseload in our tort system and the resulting costs are staggering. Attorneys seem only too quick to conclude that everything must be intentional and "blame-able." We spend more than $233 billion, which is equivalent to a 5 percent tax on all wages, on lawsuits in our nation, the majority of which would be classified as "frivolous" by previous generations and certainly by many people in other nations.[4]

Perceived offenses can also be dangerous. I have heard of a story where a man faced years of legal trouble simply because he did not know how to handle his perception of an offense. The man, a very large one, was seated on an airplane, drinking a cup of coffee. A young army recruit carrying a duffel bag passed by the man and accidentally bumped this man's shoulder, making the man spill the coffee onto his lap. The recruit, unaware of what happened, kept walking to the back of the airplane, looking for his seat. The man, believing the recruit's nudge was intentional, became infuriated and, with fire in his eyes, began yelling at the recruit and charged him from behind. The man shoved the recruit, forcing him to fall forward onto an elderly lady. Both the elderly lady and the recruit fell, and she suffered a hip fracture resulting from the fall. Her fracture was so severe she almost died as a result of complications from her injury. Clearly this man could have avoided the legal issues had he controlled his perception of offense.

Accidents happen. We need to acknowledge that reality, and when we find ourselves on the wrong end of an accident, we need to refrain from turning an accident into an offense.

DEALING WITH AN INTENTIONAL OFFENSE

An intentional offense is when someone maliciously hurts you, slanders you, or gossips about you *willfully*. The person's *intent* is to cause emotional or physical injury. Very often the offenses are verbal. James 1:19–20 admonishes us, "My beloved brethren, let every man be swift to hear, slow to speak, slow to wrath; for the wrath of man does not produce the righteousness of God."

Don't allow an offense against you to trigger anger or retaliation.

The truth is, in nearly all cases, that willful acts of offense come back to harm the offender, not the person who is intentionally wronged.

John was an up-and-coming junior executive in a huge corporation. He was on track to break all records in climbing the corporate ladder. Everyone seemed to like John, and he had a spirit of excellence in everything he did.

Paul was also a junior executive and very jealous of John. He started a rumor that John, who was married, was having an affair with a fellow employee, and the news spread throughout the company. When John heard the rumor, he was offended—and rightfully so. He traced the rumor back to its source and confronted Paul about what he had said. Paul quickly lied and said that someone else had told him John was having an affair.

Paul's boss, however, had heard the same rumor and also traced it back to Paul. In the end, Paul was terminated as a result. The stone that Paul had tried to cast at John had come back to strike him.

Proverbs 6:16–19 tells us:

> These six things the LORD hates,
> Yes, seven are an abomination to Him:
> A proud look,
> A lying tongue,
> Hands that shed innocent blood,
> A heart that devises wicked plans,
> Feet that are swift in running to evil,
> A false witness who speaks lies,
> And one who sows discord among brethren.

Intentional offenses very often bear several of these characteristics. Intentional offenses nearly always have an element of "lie" or "falseness" about them. They are the device of a heart that intends evil against innocent parties. They sow discord. Offenders are often very proud people who seek their own way and seek to be "number one." A great deal of offense can be generated by idle gossip. Jesus warned specifically about this, saying, "For every idle word men may speak, they will give account of it in the day of judgment. For by your words you will be justified, and by your words you will be condemned" (Matt. 12:36–37).

DON'T SIGN FOR A BOX OF RATTLESNAKES

You can choose to reject an offense. If something hurtful happens to you, you can choose to respond in a way that reverses the hurt rather than retains and "nurses" the hurt. You can refuse to carry an offense in your heart, or you can turn it into a grievance story.

Consider for a moment what would happen if the UPS man arrived at your front door with a large box and asked you to sign for it. When you ask what is in the box, he looks at his clipboard and says, "The form says this box is full of rattlesnakes." At that point, you shake the box and hear the snakes rattling away inside it; if you are remotely sane, you hand the box back to the UPS man and say, "There's no way I'm signing for this. Return it to the sender!"

Jesus has already said "Woe!" to the person who causes offense. God will take care of those who willfully offend you. Trust Him to do it. For your part, refuse to sign up for the offense—refuse to think about it or talk about it.

When we receive an offense, we may as well be signing for a box of rattlesnakes when it comes to our health. Feelings of offense trigger the stress response in our body, and the longer we hold on to an offense, the more we experience the negative long-term effects of an activated stress response.

The more we allow offenses to occupy our minds, the more we begin to develop a grievance story. And the more we rehearse and retell that grievance story, the more we keep alive the stress response that is activated in us by an offense. Truly we do ourselves harm in the long run!

HEEDING GOD'S COMMAND TO FORGIVE OTHERS FIRST

What are we to do when we feel offended? The Bible has a prescription that can be expressed in just one word: *forgive!*

We are commanded to forgive in the Bible. Jesus said:

> If you forgive men their trespasses, your heavenly Father will also forgive you. But if you do not forgive men their trespasses, neither will your Father forgive your trespasses.
>
> —MATTHEW 6:14

> Judge not, and you shall not be judged. Condemn not, and you shall not be condemned. Forgive, and you will be forgiven.
>
> —LUKE 6:37

The teaching of God's Word is clear. If we refuse to forgive others, God cannot forgive us. Christians need to understand that if they continue to harbor resentment and bitterness—refusing to forgive—they face serious judgment from God. I have heard my friend Joyce Meyer say that bitterness and unforgiveness are like drinking poison and wishing the *other* person would die.

To forgive does not mean that a person is saying, "This didn't matter," or "This wasn't a huge wrong committed against me," but rather, it is saying, "I choose no longer to hold on to this feeling of unforgiveness toward the person who hurt me." Forgiveness isn't letting a person off the hook so that no justice is required. Rather, it is trusting God to deal with the offending person, the horrible memories, and the hurtful situation.

Forgiving in its simplest form is "letting go" of old hurts and releasing people into God's hands for Him to deal with those people as He desires.

Always remember that much of the bitterness and resentment people have is based upon a perceived or accidental offense, or upon just "plain ol'" distortional thinking. Perceived and accidental offenses take on the nature of a lie. The person believes something that wasn't real or certainly wasn't intended. In forgiving, the person is "letting go" of the past—and it's an especially good thing if the person lets go of a lie of the past.

The apostle Paul taught, "You must make allowance for each other's faults and forgive the person who offends you. Remember, the Lord forgave you, so you must forgive others" (Col. 3:13, NLT).

We must learn to forgive immediately for the sake of our emotional, physical, mental, and spiritual health. Jesus said, "If you bring your gift to the altar, and there remember that your brother has something against you, leave your gift there before the altar, and go your way. First be reconciled to your brother, and then come and offer your gift" (Matt. 5:23–24). Forgive immediately whether or not the person asks for forgiveness.

Many people are married to a spouse who is violent, an alcoholic, or a drug addict. If someone repeatedly injures you, you are still commanded to forgive them instantly, but you are not expected to trust them immediately—and you are not required to remain in close proximity so they can continue to abuse you. I recommend you contact a domestic violence hotline. Here is the number for the National Domestic Violence Hotline: (800) 799-SAFE (7233).

Trust takes time to rebuild and requires a track record of mutually beneficial behavior. A person needs to gain or regain your trust over a period of time. Forgiveness is a quick action; establishing trust is a slow process.

I know of a woman who was sexually abused by her father during her teenage years. As a teenager, she would push her dresser against her bedroom door in an attempt to keep her father out of her room at night. When this didn't work, she began to sleep with a butcher knife under her pillow. She actually began to look forward to the potential opportunity to stab her father through the heart. Then she was born again by accepting Jesus as her Savior.

Even after her conversion experience, she had extreme hatred and unforgiveness toward her father. She was nearly in shock when she heard a preacher say that if she didn't forgive, God couldn't forgive her. She immediately began to "negotiate" with God on this point. She didn't want to forgive her father. As she prayed, however, she heard a still, small voice speaking in her mind, "If I could make an exception right now for anyone, I would for you, but if I do, I am not the One the Word says I am. I cannot change. You must change."

She began to see a vision of the baggage of pain, hurt, and resentment she was carrying. In her vision, her wounds appeared as old, torn, ragged, beat-up luggage. The load of all this luggage was heavy, and it was keeping her back from walking quickly and boldly into great blessings. Then she heard the still, small voice speak to her: "I have a claim check for this baggage. I died for this, and it is rightfully Mine." She began to weep, and as she did so, she found she was able to release her hurts to Jesus and, at the same time, totally release her father. As she forgave, all the hatred and bitterness left her heart.

The question is never whether someone deserves to be forgiven. Nobody ever truly "deserves" forgiveness. But we are not forgiving a person who has hurt us for their sake. We are doing it because it is a commandment of God, and ultimately, forgiving them is for our sake. God does not want us to be shackled by unforgiveness, resentment, and bitterness. He doesn't want us to poison our own health. He wants to free us from the energy-draining, disease-inducing, deadly emotions of resentment, bitterness, and unforgiveness.

It is also critically important that you forgive yourself. You may have done things in your life that you regret. I have encountered a number of patients who can't seem to forgive themselves for an affair, an abortion, or an addiction. Some can't seem to forgive themselves for a failure, a lie, or something they stole from friends or family. Unforgiveness against one's own self is just as damaging as unforgiveness of another person.

The Bible tells us that if we confess our sins, God is faithful and just to forgive us our sins and to cleanse us from all unrighteousness. (See 1 John 1:9.) We simply need to go to God with a humble heart, admit our sin to Him, ask for His forgiveness, and then by an act of our faith and will, receive His forgiveness.

A patient named Joanne had an abortion when she was eighteen years old. Then when she was twenty-five years old, she married, but she was never able to have a child. I first met her when she was fifty years old and menopausal. She was also suffering from fibromyalgia and chronic fatigue. Emotionally, she was depressed and hated herself. She constantly made degrading remarks about herself. At the root of her self-loathing was unforgiveness for what she had done in having the abortion.

I taught Joanne about self-forgiveness, especially emphasizing the point that we have no right before God to continue to hold on to our own sins once God has forgiven us for them. To do so is to say that God is not able to forgive us or that God shouldn't forgive us. It is an act of rebellion against God, putting ourselves into a greater position of authority when it comes to our sin. Joanne had never thought she needed to forgive herself. This was "new" information to her.

When she finally came to the point of confessing her sin to God and receiving His forgiveness to the point that she forgave herself, her energy returned rapidly and her fibromyalgia cleared up.

"I FORGIVE YOU, BUT..."

Some people claim that they are only able to forgive *partially*. There is one aspect of the sin they just cannot forgive. Others don't make this claim, but by what they say, it's easy to conclude that they have forgiven only partially. They tend to say, "I forgave so and so, *but...*" Any time there is a qualifier placed on forgiveness, the forgiveness is only partial. Other people claim to have forgiven, but the mention of a particular person's name or an event in the past causes a grating in his soul that is somewhat like fingernails scratching on a chalkboard. That "shudder" at a memory is often a very clear signal of partial forgiveness.

I liken partial forgiveness to a person having been stuck with a thorn. The bulk of the thorn is removed, but the tip of the thorn has broken off and remains deep under the skin. There is a "festering" that remains. Until the tip of that thorn is removed, the skin cannot completely heal.

How can a person move to a state of total forgiveness? I believe there are several things that help tremendously.

1. Acknowledge

First, acknowledge that you have only forgiven partially, and ask God for help in forgiving completely. Admit to the Lord the struggle you have in forgiveness, and ask Him to show you how you can release the person fully into His care.

2. Meditate on Scripture

Second, meditate on passages of the Bible that address the issue of forgiveness. Become very clear in your thinking about God's commandments related to forgiveness.

3. Speak forgiveness

Third, any time the name of a person or the memory of an event comes to mind or is spoken, choose immediately to say in your mind, "I forgive that person. He or she is in God's hands." Make this a conscious act.

4. Praise and worship God

Fourth, spend more time in praise and worship before the Lord. I have found the Hillsong worship CDs to be very helpful to my patients in helping them come before the Lord with an open heart—a heart willing to praise and a heart willing to be healed.

Forgiveness is ultimately a choice that a person makes. It is an act of the will. It is an act of faith. When we do our part in seeking to forgive, God does His part in enabling us to forgive. In return, He forgives us and restores our joy and peace. In most cases, He takes our joy and peace to new levels!

8
_____

Wiping Out Worry

I once heard someone say, "I don't worry anymore. I've been a pallbearer for too many of my friends that did." Every day I encounter patients in my office who tell me they are worried about a wide variety of things:

- "I'm afraid I'm going to lose my job."

- "I'm worried that I might have cancer."

- "I'm worried that I might develop heart disease or Alzheimer's disease."

- "I'm worried about my children."

- "I'm worried that I might lose my hair."

- "I'm worried that my wife might have an affair."

- "I'm worried that I won't be able to pay all my bills."

The list of things people worry about seems endless at times! We seem to be a nation of worriers.

I'm not talking now about the anxiety disorders that have been diagnosed in approximately nineteen million Americans. These anxiety disorders include generalized anxiety disorder, post-traumatic stress disorder, obsessive-compulsive disorder, panic disorder, and phobias of many types. Rather, I'm talking about the tens of millions who suffer from mild anxiety that has not yet reached the level of a disorder. They have developed a habit of worrying.

Being a "worry wart" does not mean that a person is mentally ill. It just means that worry has become a mental habit. The habit can lead to a neurotransmitter imbalance in the brain, so in one sense, worry may lead to mental illness. In most cases, people who worry do not need medication. They simply need to change their mental habits!

In *The Purpose-Driven Life,* Rick Warren writes, "When you think about a problem over and over in your mind, that is called worry."[1]

The trouble is that chronic worry stimulates a chronic stress response.

WORRY AND ANXIETY ARE UNHEALTHY

Anxiety is commonly referred to as the "common cold of mental illness." Worry and anxiety are virtually interchangeable terms. In fact, one dictionary defines *worry* as "to feel anxious." That same dictionary defines anxiety as "a concern that causes worry."

Both worry and anxiety are internal, unpleasant clusters of "nervous" or agitated thoughts and feelings that something unpleasant may happen or may already have happened. Worry and anxiety tend to be related to things we think about, imagine, or perceive. Worry and anxiety can be short term or long term—they can become almost a state of mind. Some people worry about everything!

The terms "anxiety attack" and "panic attack" have now been given to an intense bout of worry or anxiety in which the heart rate increases and a person may hyperventilate, sweat or tremble, feel weak, or have stomach or intestinal discomfort.

DISTORTIONAL THOUGHT PATTERNS THAT LEAD TO CHRONIC WORRY

Chronic worriers nearly always have distortional thoughts. The two main distortional thought patterns linked to worry are catastrophizing, which we covered in previous chapters, and the "what if...?" thought pattern.

"What if...?"

The most common distortional thought pattern linked to worry is a repetition of "What if...?" questions. People ask, "What if I get fired?" "What if I don't finish my project before the deadline?" "What if I have a heart attack?" "What if my son becomes an alcoholic?" "What if the food burns and catches the house on fire?" "What if my daughter is in a car wreck and is paralyzed as a result?" The "what if-ers" usually analyze a potentially dangerous situation without ever drawing any conclusions or mapping out any solutions...and they nearly always carry the "what if..." scenario to its worst possible conclusion.

Mark Twain once quipped, "I have been through some terrible things in my life, some of which actually happened."[2]

Maureen was a chronic worrier. She was a hypochondriac, and I saw her in my office almost monthly back in the 1980s. She had hypertension, but the real reason she came so often to my office was to ask "what if...?" questions in hopes of alleviating some of her worry. She knew enough about anatomy and medical conditions to be suspicious of a wide variety of symptoms! She'd ask:

- "What if that sharp pain in my arm is a symptom of a heart attack?"

- "What if that pain in my abdomen is caused by an abdominal aneurysm?"

- "What if that flutter in my chest is a dangerous arrhythmia?"

As a result of Maureen's chronic worry, she had been to see three different cardiologists who had put her through three different nuclear stress tests, three echocardiograms, and two heart catheterizations, as well as numerous other cardiac tests...and

Maureen was only thirty-five years old! There was very little likelihood of her having a heart attack or angina. The main reason she had all these tests was because she pressed for them, convinced that she "needed to be sure," and the physicians she saw feared that if there was something truly wrong with her and they did not do the tests, they might be sued.

When her cardiologists and I finally convinced her that she had a healthy heart and cardiovascular system, she switched diseases on us. Her questions became, "What if that occasional abdominal discomfort is a cancerous tumor?" "What if that occasional headache is a sign of a brain tumor?"

Maureen was beginning to make the rounds of specialists who would order various CT scans and MRIs to rule out cancer in various parts of her body when I finally convinced her that the specialist she really needed to see was a psychiatrist. Maureen agreed to go primarily because her "what if…" preoccupation had already cost her a marriage, custody of her children, her job, and bankruptcy.

The psychiatrist placed her on medication and referred her to a cognitive behavioral therapist. Over time the therapist helped Maureen reprogram her thinking, but perhaps the simplest and yet most beneficial thing the therapist did was to insist that Maureen wear a thick rubber band around her wrist. She was instructed that each time she found herself thinking or saying, "What if…?" she was to pull the rubber band and let it snap back to her wrist, which brought a little sensation of pain. Over time, she reprogrammed herself to get rid of "what if…?" thinking. She went on to remarry her husband and to be a wonderful wife and mother.

The person in the Bible most commonly associated with "what if…?" thinking is Job. Job was considered the most righteous of all the people on the earth in his day. He was an exceedingly wealthy man with a very large household that included seven sons and three daughters. Each son had his own home, and each son invited his brothers and sisters to feast with him on appointed days throughout the year.

As these feasts ended, Job offered burnt sacrifices on behalf of his children, saying, "It may be that my sons have sinned and cursed God in their hearts." Job had a great concern that his children be in right standing with the Lord.

One day a messenger came to Job to inform him that a nomadic tribe had raided Job's flocks and had taken all his oxen and donkeys. The raiders had also killed all of the servants attending these animals, except this messenger. Just as he finished speaking, another servant arrived and said that a fire had burned up all of Job's sheep and the servants attending them. A third messenger showed up just as the second one was finishing his report. He reported that three bands of Chaldeans had come to steal Job's camels and had killed all the servants attending the camels, except the messenger.

One more messenger came, and this one had the worst news of all. He reported that while all of his children were eating and drinking in the oldest brother's home, a great wind had caused the house to collapse on top of them. They were all dead, including their servants. Only the messenger had survived.

In a single day of "reporting," Job learned that he had lost all of his possessions and children. Even so, he fell on his face and worshiped God. He did not sin or blame God for what had happened.

After this, Job was struck in his own body. He suffered painful boils from the soles of his feet to the crown of his head. He began to scrape the boils with a piece of broken pottery to try to gain some relief. His wife encouraged Job to curse God and die, but Job refused. Three of Job's so-called "friends" came to convince him that he had done something terrible to deserve all of his misfortune. Job refused to concede that he had sinned. He finally said, "The thing I greatly feared has come upon me, and what I dreaded has happened to me" (Job 3:25).

The great implication is that Job had thought repeatedly in his life:

- "What if my children sin and I'm not able to offer a sacrifice for them?"

- "What if I lose all my possessions and wealth?"

- "What if I lose my health?"

Aren't these the three most common worries people have today? People are worried about their children or relationships with people they love. They are worried about their finances and material possessions. They are worried about their health.

EVEN A FAITH-FILLED PERSON CAN CATASTROPHIZE

In many ways Abraham, the man the Bible calls the "father" of all who have faith, was a catastrophizer. When famine swept the land in which he was dwelling, he went to Egypt with his wife Sarai, a very beautiful woman. Abraham told Sarai that when the Egyptians saw her they would think she was his wife and would kill him so they might have her. Abraham immediately projected the worst possible outcome!

Abraham asked Sarai to say that she was his sister instead. When Abraham and Sarai arrived in Egypt, this is exactly what happened. Sarai was taken to Pharaoh's harem, and in turn, Pharaoh gave Abraham a great quantity of livestock, sheep, oxen, male donkeys, male and female servants, female donkeys, and camels. But the Lord sent great plagues on Pharaoh and his house because of Sarai, and eventually Pharaoh called Abraham in and asked him why he hadn't told the truth about Sarai. He returned Sarai to Abraham and sent him out of Egypt. (See Genesis 12:10–20.)

This happened a second time. Abraham found himself in the land ruled by Abimelech the king of Gerar. Abraham again introduced Sarah as his sister. (By this time God had changed her name from Sarai to Sarah.) The king took Sarah to be one of his wives, but before he could have sexual relations with her, God warned him in a dream that she was actually Abraham's wife and that he needed to restore her to Abraham. Abimelech did so immediately! Again, Abraham had "catastrophized" an outcome that wasn't anything close to what God had designed for his life.

Joel Osteen, pastor of one of the largest churches in the United States, tells a story about himself in which he had anticipated a worst-case scenario. He had driven home and pressed the garage door opener, but the door didn't open. He parked the car and went to the front door, but found it locked. He didn't have a key, so he began knocking on the door. At first he didn't hear anything, but he knew his wife was home. Then he heard some racket in the house and a knocking noise. He began to knock harder on the front door. Then his imagination kicked in. He began to envision a large muscular guy attacking his wife. He felt he just had to save her!

He ran to the back of the house to see if another door or window was open. Finally, he picked up a large log and was about to use it to break down a door when his wife opened the door, smiled, and said, "Joel, what are you doing with that log?" Joel replied that he was about ready to knock down the door to save her. She laughingly said, "What are you going to save me from?"

She had simply been hanging pictures upstairs when he knocked on the door.[3]

Too many people, it seems, focus on what Jesus told His disciples: "In the world you will have tribulation." They know that tribulation means anguish, burdened, troubled, and persecuted. They raise every minor hassle and inconvenience to that level. They forget that Jesus followed this statement immediately by saying, "But be of good cheer. I have overcome the world" (John 16:33).

CARE VERSUS OVERCARE

"But," you may be saying, "I'm not worrying; I'm just concerned. Isn't it right to 'care'?" Yes, it's right to care, but not to overcare. Doc Childre, founder of the Institute of HeartMath, coined the term *overcare* to describe an emotional state. He says overcare is "simply too much care and concern that leads to worry."[4]

Overcare is one of the main reasons why clergy members experience such a high burnout rate.

> Focus on the Family's H. B. London has called the pastor an "endangered species." Denominational executive Dr. David Rambo reported that 90 percent of pastors say they are inadequately trained to cope with ministry demands, 80 percent say their ministries have had a negative effect on their families, and 70 percent have a lower self-image than when they started in the ministry.[5]

I personally believe that pastors experience a high burnout rate in part because they do not fully count the cost of ministry prior to entering this profession. Many seem to have an idealistic belief that all they need to do is prepare a sermon for Sunday morning. They don't realize that they will be called upon to be a church administrator during the week, even as they visit the sick and conduct funerals and weddings. Many are on call every night. Excessive care can turn into overcare—taking on too much responsibility for too many people.

The person who is called upon to do too much for too many is a person who soon finds that he or she cannot succeed in helping everybody all the time, and perhaps not even succeed in helping some people some of the time. There's a growing sense of inability, inadequacy, insufficiency...in a word, failure.

When overcare exhausts a person's emotional reserves, there doesn't seem to be enough "energy" left to deal with the rest of life's practical issues. People with joy and a relaxed attitude can become irritating—rather than be a joy, they become an added burden. The result is that life seems futile, with no hope for any real change. Overcare can lead to "cease to care."

I had a patient who worried constantly about her chronically ill son. Her son lived with her, but he was not too ill to care for himself or to work. He had a night-shift job at a factory. She worried about him until she knew that he was home safely each night, and on some nights, she would wait up until he arrived at three o'clock in the morning. Other nights, she would awaken four or five times to check to see if her son was home and safe. She had crossed the line into "overcare." The result was that she became sleep-deprived, and over time, she developed chronic fatigue.

She began listening to Christian teachings on television and on audiotape. The taped messages kept her mind off her worries. She also began to memorize Scripture and frequently quoted Psalm 23 to herself. She made a diligent effort to change the channel of her mind from "worry" to "Word of God." Over time, she overcame worry and overcare. Not only is she happier and better rested, but also her son is happier. That is often the case. Those who are the recipients of overcare generally don't want to be!

Overcare can kill.

A young girl I know received a beautiful flowering plant for her twelfth birthday. She was so excited! She had never taken care of a plant all her own, but she was determined to keep it alive and beautiful. She knew that where she lived in Florida, people often watered their lawns daily, so she began to water her plant daily. After two weeks, she noticed a couple of leaves turning yellow. She decided she wasn't watering the plant often enough, so she began to water twice a day and to add fertilizer to the water. Within a week, all the leaves had turned yellow. and the next week, all the leaves fell off. She killed her plant with overcare.

Some of us are doing the same thing with our health. We are applying so much worry to our lives in the name of care and concern that we are setting ourselves up for disastrous results that could become deadly results. For more information on overcare, read my book *Deadly Emotions*.

CHOOSING FAITH AND PEACE

Worry and fear are the opposite of faith and peace. We are told in the Bible to cast *all* our care upon the Lord. (See 1 Peter 5:7.) God did not say "some of your cares"—He said "all."

Jesus had this to say about worry:

> Therefore do not worry, saying, "What shall we eat?" or "What shall we drink?" or "What shall we wear?" For after all these things the Gentiles seek. For your heavenly Father knows that you need all these things. But seek first the kingdom of God and His righteousness, and all these things shall be added to you. Therefore do not worry about tomorrow, for tomorrow will worry about its own things. Sufficient for the day is its own trouble.
>
> —Matthew 6:31–34

Faith is simply trusting God to do what He has promised to do in the Bible. It means trusting Him to forgive you because He said He would forgive you if you confessed your sins to Him and asked Him to forgive you. (See 1 John 1:9) It means trusting Him to care for you because He says He cares for you. (See 1 Peter 5:7.) It means trusting Him to love you because He says He loves you. (See 1 John 4:19.)

How do we acquire faith? The Bible tells us that we each have already been given a measure of faith (Rom. 12:3). The challenge before us is to grow in our faith. We do this by hearing the Word of God (Rom. 10:17). This does not simply mean we listen to sermons and tapes of good Bible preaching and teaching. It means that we study and meditate on God's Word. As part of studying and meditating, we are wise to read God's Word aloud and to memorize Scripture so we can meditate on God's Word any place and any time.

When we read the Bible aloud to ourselves, we are "hearing" the Word of God.

When we repeat God's Word aloud to ourselves in the process of memorizing it, we are "hearing" the Word of God.

When we recite God's Word from memory to ourselves, we are "hearing" the Word of God. The two ears closest to your mouth when you speak are likely to be your ears! The Bible tells us, "You will keep him in perfect peace, whose mind is stayed on You" (Isa. 26:3).

9
_____

The Power of Attitude to Create or Relieve Stress

Can a person's attitudes cause a stress response? Yes. Certain negative attitudes trigger a long-term stress response. Can a person's attitudes relieve stress? Yes! Attitudes are very powerful.

What exactly is an attitude? It is a manner of acting, feeling, or thinking that reveals a person's disposition or opinion. I personally like the definition of attitude given by one of America's finest Bible teachers and preachers, John Hagee. He sums up attitude with four statements:

> *Your attitude is an inward feeling expressed by outward behavior.* Your attitude is seen by all without you saying a word.
>
> *Your attitude is the "advance man" of your true self.* The roots of your attitude are hidden, but its fruit is always visible.
>
> *Your attitude is your best friend or your worst enemy.* It draws people to you or repels people from you.
>
> *Your attitude determines the quality of your relationships with your husband, your wife, your*

children, your employer, your friends, and God Almighty.[1]

Thoughts and feelings shape attitude, so it is important first and foremost for a person to identify his own thoughts and feelings.

What are the attitudes that can trigger the stress response in a person's body? They tend to be criticism, pessimism, impatience, and attitudes that might be described as "pushy," "grumpy," and "contentious." Rudeness and self-centeredness are definitely attitudes that impact the body negatively.

These attitudes, of course, give rise to behaviors that most people hate in others but often do not see in themselves: whining, murmuring, grumbling, backbiting, and arguing.

The apostle Paul had a tremendous concern about the impact of negative attitudes. He warned the believers in Corinth about the bad attitudes that were permeating their church. He said, "I am afraid that when I come I may not find you as I want you to be....I fear that there may be quarreling, jealousy, outbursts of anger, factions, slander, gossip, arrogance, and disorder" (2 Cor. 12:20, NIV).

In writing to the Galatians, he identified a number of attitudes among the "works of the flesh," including hatred, jealousies, selfish ambitions, dissensions, heresies, and envy. (See Galatians 5:19–20.) These were just as potent and just as sinful as behaviors such as sorcery, idolatry, murder, adultery and fornication, and "outbursts of wrath." The apostle Paul went so far as to say that those who engaged in these attitudes and behaviors "will not inherit the kingdom of God" (v. 21).

As Moses led the Israelites in the wilderness, the people at one point became very discouraged and began complaining. The Bible tells us, "The people spoke against God and against Moses: 'Why have you brought us up out of Egypt to die in the wilderness? For there is no food and no water, and our soul loathes this worthless bread'" (Num. 21:5). The people had such a complaining attitude that the Lord sent fiery serpents among them, and many died because of the serpents' bites.

Paul wrote to the Philippians:

> Do all things without grumbling and faultfinding and complaining [against God] and questioning and doubting [among yourselves], that you may show yourselves to be blameless and guileless, innocent and uncontaminated, children of God without blemish (faultless, unrebukable) in the midst of a crooked and wicked generation [spiritually perverted and perverse], among whom you are seen as bright lights (stars or beacons shining out clearly) in the [dark] world, holding out [to it] and offering [to all men] the Word of Life.
> —PHILIPPIANS 2:14–16, AMP

Jude 14–16 speaks of a prophecy from Enoch, who said that the Lord would one day come with ten thousand of his saints to execute judgment on all. He would come to convict the ungodly sinners, among whom were "grumblers, complainers" and those who walked according to their own lusts, with mouths of "great swelling words, flattering people to gain advantage."

A complaining, disgruntled, manipulative, and lustful attitude puts us on God's judgment list. All of these attitudes are markers of a distortional thought process. People who complain rarely see the goodness or the greatness of God. They are totally focused on self, upon what they want, when they want it, and how they want it. That focus on self, which might be summed up as an attitude of pride, lies at the root of virtually all sin. It is a preoccupation with me, myself, and I.

We've all heard the phrase, "Get better, not bitter." The only difference between the words better and bitter is the letter "i." In our emotions, a positive attitude that is forward looking is nearly always an attitude that includes God and others. A negative attitude that is marked by bitterness is nearly always an attitude that is totally self-centered, with the "big I" of self as the focal point.

What are some of the attitudes that turn off the stress response? These are among them:

- Contentment
- Appreciation
- Forgiveness

- Joy
- Love
- Compassion

If you have become preprogrammed to complain or to be critical, pessimistic, grumpy, or impatient, make a decision that you will not continue to hold or display these attitudes. Recognize that the attitude you have is a choice you can make. Begin to practice new attitudes that bring healing not only to your emotions, but also to your body.

BEGIN TODAY TO PRACTICE CONTENTMENT

How can you practice being content? First, recognize that contentment has nothing to do with our circumstances. The apostle Paul wrote to the Philippians these words from a Roman prison:

> I have learned in whatever state I am, to be content: I know how to be abased, and I know how to abound. Everywhere and in all things I have learned both to be full and to be hungry, both to abound and to suffer need. I can do all things through Christ who strengthens me.
> —Philippians 4:11–13

Take note of three things in this passage.

1. Paul said that he had *learned* to be content. It wasn't an automatic instinct or a personality trait. Contentment was something he trained his mind to experience.

2. Paul said that contentment had nothing to do with circumstances or provision. Paul had lived "low" and "high." He had been "full" and "hungry." He had experienced sufficiency and need. Contentment is not an external state; it is an internal one.

3. Paul relied upon Christ to give him strength.

Your relationship with Jesus Christ is the source of all the contentment you can ever need or desire.

Sadly, most people—including many in the church—don't really believe this. They still believe contentment can come with a hefty bank account, a balanced stock portfolio, a paid-for mortgage, or a sufficient pile of possessions. We Americans seem to have an insatiable desire for the newest, most, and best. We need the latest-model cell phone, the fanciest car, and the biggest television screen in order to feel a deep satisfaction and self-worth. Contentment cannot be purchased at any price. It only comes in knowing Christ Jesus.

One of my patients is a five-year-old boy named Tommy. He came to me with recurrent sore throats and ear infections. I discovered that his mother worked all day and his nanny allowed him to eat anything he wanted. Well, what Tommy wanted were Popsicles, Oreo cookies, and Reese's peanut butter cups during the day, and for dinner, a pizza. He absolutely refused to eat vegetables and picked at his food to the point that his parents routinely gave in to his demands for the foods he wanted. I sat down with Tommy's parents and his nanny and said, "The time has come to tell Tommy enough is enough." I told them to remove all junk food from their cupboards and to toss out the Popsicles, cookies, and candy. I told them Tommy could have pizza only one night a week. I recommended they give him vegetables and fruit on a daily basis and that they keep healthy, wholesome snacks around the house. I gave them a well-balanced meal plan for the entire family to follow.

Tommy's sore throats and ear infections cleared up and did not return. He has become content with eating pizza once a week and eating fruit in place of sugary snacks. But if given his choice, Tommy would still be eating the very foods that suppressed his immune system to the point where he was an easy target for any virus that floated by.

Adults, like Tommy, often do not know when enough is enough. They strive to obtain more and more, do more and more, and climb higher and higher. They trigger a stress response in their own bodies from a rampant attitude of striving.

Give up stress-causing striving!

Perhaps more than any other single attitude, an attitude of striving to get more…get ahead…do more…accomplish more…have more…own more…receive more…is the attitude that triggers a stress reaction. Striving is such a dangerous attitude because there is never a stop point for it! The person who has a striving attitude always wants more. The "something more" may manifest itself as greed or gluttony. It may manifest itself as a prideful grasping or as a manipulative ploy to get others to yield to them the right of way, recognition, or material substance. The person with a striving attitude never "is" enough and, therefore, never has enough.

The striving person says, "I must do it. I must make things happen."

The person who truly is trusting Jesus Christ to be the Lord of his or her life is a person who says, "I cannot make anything of real worth happen. I trust You, Lord, to give me what I need, when I need it, and in the ways I need it most. I trust You to bring me peace and satisfaction."

When I sense that a patient has a striving attitude, I often prescribe for them a simple exercise of taking inventory of their homes. They often are appalled at this idea because they know their homes, closets, and attics are bulging at the seams with too much "stuff." They don't know all that they have; in fact, they often readily admit that they have storage units to store their "extra stuff," and they have no idea what all is presently in the storage unit.

Have you taken an inventory of your home lately? As you write down the items you own, make two columns next to the items on the sheet of paper. Label one "Need" and the other "Want." Put an X in the appropriate column.

I have learned through the years that many people don't know the difference between a need and a want. A need is what is actually required to sustain your life. What you want are things you believe will improve the quality of your life. Our needs are very few. Our wants, however, are many.

In the vast majority of cases, it is our wants that control our life and add stress to it. Conversely, a great deal of stress could be eliminated from many lives if people would only choose to be content with what they have rather than seek to possess more and more.

Take a moment to consider how many things you have that were once new and exciting to you, but now are boring or out-dated. Those things are nearly always in the "want" category. Once we get something we want, we rarely find it satisfying. We begin to hunt for something else that is new and exciting.

A woman told me that she had taken her nine-year-old car into the dealership for a minor repair. She said to the service representative in the repair shop, "I suppose I should be thinking about a new car, but hey, this one runs pretty well and it's paid for." She said to me, "I was surprised when the service rep, who worked for the dealership, replied, 'If it isn't broken, don't fix it.' There was a little irony in that since he had just arranged to have my slightly broken engine fixed, but overall, I was impressed with his attitude. He wasn't at all trying to sell me a new car. I decided this [car] will do for another fifty thousand miles!" This woman has the correct perspective about needs versus wants.

If you have a house, do you really need a new one? Why?

If you have a car, do you really need a new one? Why?

If you have ten pairs of shoes, do you really need more?

If you have a dozen work shirts, do you really need more?

(You may think ten pairs of shoes and a dozen work shirts represent large quantities, but trust me, there are people who consider themselves impoverished if they have so few of these items!)

There is something wonderfully therapeutic about having a garage sale or packing up boxes of excess possessions and giving them to a charitable cause.

One of my patients was stricken with lung cancer at the age of fifty. He had been a successful businessman, but he was in debt. He had a second mortgage on his home, two new cars with large car payments, and his credit cards were maxed out. He was a collector of antiques and several specialty items. His home was packed with "stuff," plus, he had two extra storage units. He had smoked two packs of cigarettes a day for more than thirty years, and his bad habit finally caught up with him.

He was so weak from chemotherapy that he needed to stop working, but the bills kept pouring in. He decided to sell his home, one of his cars, and move to a smaller condo in order to pay his bills. But he had no way to move all his stuff into a smaller living space. He said to his wife with a great deal of regret, "I spent all these years collecting these things, and now I have no room to enjoy them." He regretted ever purchasing them.

This man's illness forced him to come to grips with the priorities of his life. He realized that his wife and family were all he truly needed, except for more "time." It was a wonderful insight, but it came very late in his life.

Jesus said very plainly, "Do not lay up for yourselves treasures on earth, where moth and rust destroy and where thieves break in and steal; but lay up for yourselves treasures in heaven, where neither moth nor rust destroys and where thieves do not break in and steal. For where your treasure is, there your heart will be also" (Matt. 6:19–21). One commentator has noted about this last sentence that it could also have been translated, "What you value determines what you do." Your attitude is directly involved in attaching "value" to items. Take a close look at what you value. How much do you want your "wants"? Is there anything—any object or possession—with which you are very reluctant to part? Would you sacrifice your health to keep the "stuff" you have acquired?

Memorize this prayer.

I recommend to nearly all of my patients that they memorize a very simple prayer that is known universally as the "Serenity Prayer." I have found it to be a powerful tool in helping a person turn from a negative attitude to developing a more positive attitude.

> God, grant me the serenity
> To accept the things I cannot change;
> Courage to change the things I can;
> And wisdom to know the difference.

Begin to thank and praise Him.

I wholeheartedly believe that appreciation—or gratitude—is one of the most powerful stress busters available to every person. It doesn't require a prescription, and it's free. Furthermore, it works mightily if a person will practice it! Those who are thankful and have a strong attitude of gratitude have far less stress in their lives than those who are striving, jealous, or greedy, or who feel desperate for more recognition, more self-worth, or more value. The outward expression of gratitude is the voicing of thanks and praise.

Psalm 100:4–5 says, "Enter into His gates with thanksgiving, and into His courts with praise. Be thankful to Him, and bless His name. For the Lord is good; His mercy is everlasting, and His truth endures to all generations." The very portal through which we enter God's presence is thanksgiving and praise. We thank and praise God for His great goodness, His acts of mercy toward us, and the truth that He never changes in His nature or His love. All things that are beneficial and eternal come from Him, and all praise is due His name!

When the apostle Paul and Silas, his companion in ministry, found themselves in prison, they certainly must have been uncomfortable. They had been beaten with rods and had many stripes laid on them. In prison, they were put in the innermost chamber and fastened by their feet in stocks. If two people ever had a license to whine and complain, it would have been Paul and Silas.

Paul and Silas did not whine, however. At midnight, Paul and Silas were praying and singing hymns to God, and the other prisoners were listening to them, no doubt encouraged by them. (See Acts 16:20–25.) As they were singing praises to God, God caused a great earthquake that freed them from their bonds.

Did Paul and Silas suddenly jump up and run away? No! They stayed where they were, and when the keeper of the prison came, fully expecting the prisoners to have escaped, he was stunned to find Paul and Silas and all the other prisoners still in the prison. He was so moved by this that he cried out, "Sirs, what must I do to be saved?" Paul and Silas led this man and his entire family to Christ that night. They baptized all of them, and the prison keeper and his family, in turn, washed their wounds. They ate and rejoiced until dawn.

Hebrews 13:15 admonishes us, "Let us continually offer the sacrifice of praise to God, that is, the fruit of our lips, giving thanks to His name." Praise is a sacrifice. We may not always feel like praising God or think we have the time to praise God, but we must praise God anyway. That is one of our primary purposes for being on this earth. Jesus said that if people don't praise God, even the very rocks will cry out in praise. (See Luke 19:40.) We were created to have thankful hearts and praise on our lips. When we do otherwise, we are failing to live up to our full human potential.

Praise is the one sacrifice about which the Lord has always been and always will be pleased. Praise is offered in heaven continually! The sacrifices of the Old Testament were blood sacrifices made in order to maintain a right standing with God. When Jesus came and died on the cross, He became the last blood sacrifice. His shed blood atones for sin. Instead of offering a blood sacrifice, we are to offer the "sacrifice of praise to God" and to do so continually. These days many Christians don't even offer a prayer of thanksgiving or praise when they sit down to a meal. They certainly haven't developed an abiding attitude of thanksgiving and praise so they can offer this sacrifice to God continually. We need to begin to thank and praise God with intention—moving by "baby steps" in the right direction until praise and thanksgiving seem to flow from us at all times and in all situations.

God does not ask us to praise and thank Him for all situations and circumstances, but rather, to praise and thank Him in the midst of all situations and circumstances. No matter what happens to us, it is temporary. God is eternal and unchanging. He alone is worthy of our praise.

APPRECIATION IMPACTS HEALTH IN MEASURABLE WAYS

One of the ways that physicians can measure the function of the autonomic nervous system is by what we term "heart rate variability." A person's heart rate variability is the measure of the beat-to-beat changes in the heart rate as the heart speeds up and slows down in different patterns. Heartbeat changes are especially influenced by a person's emotions and attitudes. Thoughts, perceptions, and reactions can greatly affect heart rhythms, and heart rate variability is a good measure of the impact that various emotions have on the body.

Appreciation, joy, and love create a coherent spectrum on the heart rate variability EKG tracing. These emotions and attitudes enable a person to enter into a healthy state called "entrainment." When a person has entered into entrainment, the sympathetic nervous system and the parasympathetic nervous system are fully synchronized or balanced. This allows a person to enjoy just the right amount of stimulation and the right amount of relaxation. If a person consciously chooses to focus on things that evoke a sense of appreciation or gratitude, the nervous system comes back into balance, and all systems of the body—the brain included—function in greater harmony.[2]

What about frustration, anger, anxiety, bitterness, resentment, and other toxic emotions? They create an incoherent spectrum on heart rate variability. The sympathetic and parasympathetic nervous systems get out of balance and are not fully synchronized.

The Institute of HeartMath has also found that compassion and kindness add energy to a physical body. According to the Institute, these core heart feelings increase synchronization and coherence in the heart rhythm patterns, and these in turn decrease stress.[3]

God knew this all along, of course. It has just taken several thousand years for medical science to develop the technologies to show the truth of this in more graphic terms.

The good news about appreciation is that it is much easier for the average person to feel appreciated than it is to feel either love or compassion. I believe that is why Psalm 100:4 says we enter into His gates with thanksgiving and into His courts with praise. A person can move quickly from frustration, depression, worry, irritability, anger, or resentment to appreciation. Even if a person doesn't feel very thankful, he can begin to voice thanksgiving and praise, and the feelings will follow. As the feelings begin to well up, the stress response in the body declines.

Isaiah 61:3 says that the Messiah will give a "garment of praise for the spirit of heaviness." Certainly it is a garment of praise that Jesus makes available to every believer by the power of His Holy Spirit flowing in him or her.

Psychologist Abraham Maslow had an interesting insight into appreciation. He said, "All you have to do is to go to a hospital and hear all the simple blessings that people never before realized were blessings—being able to urinate, to sleep on your side, be able to swallow, or scratch an itch."[4] Could exercises in deprivation educate us faster about all of our blessings?

In my work in the hospital, I met one of the most appreciative patients I have ever encountered. He was also one of the sickest patients. He was at death's door. This man was dying of metastatic colon cancer, but he was so appreciative and thankful for the most basic of functions and services. He was grateful that he could go in a wheelchair and sit in the beautiful garden that was in the hospital courtyard. He was thankful that he could breathe with the nasal cannula of oxygen in his nose. He was thankful that he could keep food down and not vomit. He was thankful that his family came to see him regularly. Even though he was filled with cancer on the inside, and he was bald, emaciated, toothless, bent over, and his body covered with bruises, he was thankful to the end. He was a tremendous inspiration to me.

Dr. Bill Bright, one of the greatest Christian leaders of this generation, was a patient of mine. He was a man of great faith, and I visited him regularly after he was bedridden. Every time I saw him, he smiled and voiced words of sincere appreciation.

His wife told me that once when she was talking to him, she said, "Bill, I'm so sorry you have to suffer."

Dr. Bright looked at her, surprised, and said, "Suffer? I'm not suffering. I am in a beautiful home, lying on a comfortable bed, and surrounded by people who love me, care for me, and are willing to do anything to help me. Jesus is the One who suffered. He died alone. They beat Him unmercifully. They put a crown of thorns on His head, made Him carry the cross, and nailed Him to the cross. This isn't suffering. Jesus is the One who suffered."

Dr. Bright's attitude of gratitude, even as he was dying, was a tremendous inspiration to my wife, Mary, and me. He showed us what it means to be a person of true appreciation. He taught me a great deal about how to live as he lay dying.

AN ATTITUDE OF GRATITUDE

A young man who was the star running back of his high school football team had a bright future full of promise. In a small town where everybody knows everybody else, his coaches, family, and even the townsfolk knew he was going places. Some of the best colleges in the country were scouting him, offering full scholarships; surely he would end up playing in the NFL.

Then one day he started complaining of pain in his right knee. The pain persisted, and finally his coach said, "Son, you have to go to doctor. You have to get that knee checked out." The young man reluctantly did as he was instructed. While he was at the physician's office, the physician took an x-ray of the knee and saw something in the x-ray. Rather than alarm the boy and his family needlessly, the physician sent the young man with his x-ray to an orthopedic specialist for a definitive diagnosis.

The orthopedic surgeon put the x-rays up, and said, "Yep. There is something definitely wrong right above that knee." More x-rays were ordered, and ultimately a CT scan was also done.

After studying all the test results, the physician called the young man and his parents into his office to give them the bad news.

"The orthopedic surgeon said this is a case of osteosarcoma. Osteosarcoma is worse than any cancer. It is literally eating into your bone, and if we don't remove your leg, it will spread over your entire body and eventually kill you."

As the young man sat and listened to the doctor give the prognosis, tears began to well up in his eyes. When he first started having knee pain, he simply pushed the pain aside, thinking it was nothing that some time in the whirlpool or some physical therapy couldn't fix. Now all of his hopes and dreams of being the first one in his family to attend college seemed to be slipping away. So were his dreams of becoming a football star in college and eventually the NFL. This was not what he had expected to hear.

On the day of the surgery, lying in his hospital bed, he stared at his legs. He began to move his leg, bend his knee, and wiggle his toes, thinking, *This is the last time I will ever be able to do any of this.*

After the surgery, he awoke in his hospital room and absent-mindedly began wiggling his toes. He opened his eyes, alarmed by what he had done. He thought to himself, *Wow! They told me that it might feel like my leg was still there, but in fact it wouldn't be.* Yet he still couldn't believe what he was feeling.

His eyes widened as he scanned his lower body and saw that his right leg was still there! He asked the physician what happened. The physician reassured the young man that he did indeed go to surgery; however, what they thought was osteosarcoma was simply a bone cyst.

"You're going to be able to walk, run, and play football again," the physician told him.

The young man was so filled with emotion that tears streamed down his face. He knew that he had been given a second chance and was grateful for something that many took for granted—their legs and their ability to walk, run, and play. Every day from that day forward he thanked God for giving him back the promise of a life he had so desperately wanted.

He realized that perhaps this was a lesson he needed to learn. You never appreciate the things you have until something threatens to take them away. The young man now awoke with a whole new mind-set. Each morning he started the day with the same prayer. He thanked God for his arms and legs, his sight, and his ability to walk and run.

Never take anything for granted, for you never know when something so precious can be taken away. Life is a gift, and it is up to you to cherish every moment. First Thessalonians 5:18 says, "In everything give thanks; for this is the will of God in Christ Jesus for you." This is God's will for you. Whatever your situation, give thanks in the process.

TAKE THE GRATITUDE SURVEY

Michael McCullough and Robert Emmons are leading investigators into the effects and nature of gratitude. They developed the very simple gratitude survey below and used it to poll a large sample of people.[5]

Using the scale below as a guide, write a number beside each statement to indicate how much you agree with the statement.

1 = strongly disagree
2 = disagree
3 = slightly disagree
4 = neutral
5 = slightly agree
6 = agree
7 = strongly agree

_____   I have so much in life to be thankful for.

_____ If I had to list everything that I felt grateful for, it would be a very long list.

_____ When I look at the world, I see much to be grateful for.

_____ I am grateful to a wide variety of people.

_____ As I get older, I find myself more able to appreciate the people, events, and situations that have been part of my life history.

_____ Very little time goes by between opportunities to say thank you to someone about something.

Add up your scores. If you scored 35 or below, you are in the bottom one-fourth of people who took the survey. If you scored 36 to 38, you are in the bottom one-half of people who took the survey. If you scored 39 or 40, you are in the top one-fourth of people taking the survey. If you scored 42, you are in the top one-eighth of those surveyed.

As a side note of interest, generally speaking, women who took this survey scored slightly higher than men, and older people scored higher than younger people.

MAKE AN EVEN LONGER APPRECIATION LIST

I believe one of the most powerful things you can do in relieving stress is to begin to make a gratitude list or an appreciation list. Let me add a few suggestions about that list here:

- Put on it things great and small for which you are genuinely thankful.

- Update the list periodically.

- Review and recite the list aloud frequently.

As you make your appreciation list, include various parts of your body and bodily functions: your eyes and your eyesight, your ears and your hearing, your tongue and your ability to taste, your skin and your sense of touch, your nose and your ability to smell. Include the ability to walk, to be pain free in the use of your fingers, arms, legs, back, and neck. Be grateful for your health! Be grateful for a body that functions and can be strengthened and renewed.

I still remember a story I read several decades ago in one of Dale Carnegie's books. It was the story of a man who complained about having no shoes until he met a man who had no feet.

Be grateful that you can take a hot shower every day. Be grateful for owning a refrigerator, a stove and oven, a dishwasher, a car, a home, a bed, air conditioning, sufficient food, clothing, a sofa, toilet paper, and ice.

A pastor's wife from Zimbabwe once told me that when she first came to the United States, she went into a supermarket and was simply overwhelmed at the abundance and variety of food she found there. She couldn't get over the bread racks that were filled with dozens of types of bread. She said that in her nation people sometimes stood for three hours in line just to purchase one loaf of bread, which was all that was permitted a family. This woman overheard a customer in the supermarket complaining because her particular brand of bread was sold out. The pastor's wife left the store sobbing.

We Americans tend to take so much for granted.

Regardless of circumstances, don't stop adding to, reviewing, or reciting your appreciation list. Keep the praise and thanksgiving flowing to God, especially when you are facing a difficult situation.

One gentleman suffered from hypertension and anxiety. He began to learn appreciation, and as he did, his performance at work improved dramatically. Co-workers and supervisors both recognized this improvement. But then came a time of severe company cutbacks, and since he did not have much seniority, he was terminated in spite of his excellent job performance. He continued to thank God, regardless of this setback.

One of this man's fellow employees landed a higher-paying job at another company that was a competitor of their first company. He praised this gentleman so highly to his new boss that the company called the man for an interview and hired him on the spot. When we have an attitude of gratitude, God is able to move us freely into precisely the position He desires for us to be in. There isn't anything holding us back—no "reputation" that we have to overcome or alter.

As you make your appreciation list, avoid any tendency to compare what you have, are, or have experienced with the possessions, personality, gifts, or history of any other person. Thank God for what you have. Avoid any consideration of what you may not have or what others have. God gives to each of us what He knows we need and can handle. He always gives to us what is beneficial to us now and for all eternity.

The more we learn and experience in life, the greater our list of appreciation should grow.

AVOID THOSE WHO ARE SCORNFUL

As one final word related to attitude, I strongly encourage you to avoid those who are scornful. Stay away from those who are constantly critical, cynical, or sarcastic.

Psalm 1:1 tells us, "Blessed is the man who walks not in the counsel of the ungodly, nor stands in the path of sinners, nor sits in the seat of the scornful."

The word *scorn* literally means "an expression of mocking, contempt, or derision," or to scoff. To "sit in a seat" refers to adopting an attitude as a mind-set and means to take a position of being critical and judgmental.

Many people today seem to think it is "sophisticated" or a desirable trait to be sarcastic or cynical—to be just a little critical of things that do not come up to certain standards of style or perfection. God calls such an attitude scorn, and He hates it. God does not bless the scornful.

Choose instead to associate with those who are positive, upbeat, encouraging, and edifying. If you want to be less stressed, avoid associating or becoming yoked in any way with highly critical people. The people with whom you are in frequent contact will influence you. Attitude is contagious!

To deal with the stress, respond with an attitude that displays contentment, appreciation, forgiveness, joy, love, and compassion. When these characteristics are manifested in your attitude about life's situations, you empower yourself in overcoming stress. An attitude of gratitude is the easiest attitude to access in order to relieve stress.

10

Learn to Be Assertive

Assertiveness training has been around for years. This training helps people communicate clearly, confidently, and boldly. It gives people an opportunity to practice expressions of their thoughts, feelings, desires, and needs.

Assertiveness is not aggression. Assertiveness is simply a confidence in voicing who one is—what one thinks and feels, hopes and dreams, desires and doesn't desire—without fear of ridicule, reprimand, or punishment.

I believe God intended for the family to be the place where children learn assertiveness skills. A child who grows up in an environment filled with love, encouragement, and the freedom of expression grows confident that his ideas are valuable. He grows up learning that he has the right—and privilege—to set his own emotional boundaries and to determine when he wants to offer an idea and when he wants to be silent.

Assertive children have a healthy and strong sense of personal identity. The home environment, of course, is not one in which a child gets to do solely what the child wants to do. Homes that help children grow up with good assertiveness-training skills are homes that are also filled with discipline and guidance. Unfortunately, many people are not raised in loving, encouraging homes. They grow up doubting themselves and continually look to others for guidance and validation about what is appropriate and inappropriate in the setting of boundaries and the offering of ideas. These people often become either very passive—thinking their ideas and feelings are of no importance—or they become aggressive, demanding that they be heard and recognized as valuable.

If you are a passive person, I encourage you to spend a little time exploring why that is the case. In many cases, passive people are far more prone to stress than aggressive people. Assertive people—with a strong self-concept and well-defined personal boundaries—are less prone to stress than either passive or aggressive people.

DO YOU HAVE A PASSIVE PERSONALITY?

People tend to develop passive personalities for one of two reasons: they have been forced into submission as children, often in abusive ways, or they have been ignored as children. Those who are forced into submission through heavy-handed discipline or physical abuse are likely to have fears and residual anger, frustration, resentment, and bitterness over the way they were raised. They do not buck authority, but rather cower in the face of it. That does not mean, however, that they are not seething inside or in turmoil emotionally.

Those who are ignored as children tend to grow up feeling as if their ideas are of little consequence and that their presence is largely unwanted or not valued. So why offer an idea? Why voice an opinion? These individuals are often starved for affection and attention, but they don't know how to reach out and request what they want. They also feel rebuffed if others set emotional boundaries, and they feel shut out.

In general, passive individuals are unable to express their thoughts and feelings adequately, because they simply do not know how to stand up for themselves. They seek out others who will do battle on their behalf. Often they share their anger or hostility with a person and then expect that person to vindicate their cause. Passivity can lead to manipulative behaviors, which can destroy a relationship.

One reason that people seem to remain in nonassertive, passive behavior is a fear of rejection. Passive people often have good hearts and good motives, but they live behind a wall of fear that they are not acceptable or worthy. They may not want to reveal their thoughts and feelings out of fear that others will criticize or ridicule them.

If you recognize yourself as a passive personality type, know this: God wants to set you free. He wants you to learn how to express yourself and to come to the place where you can boldly declare who He made you to be and to pursue with confidence what He desires for you to do.

DO YOU HAVE AN AGGRESSIVE PERSONALITY?

Some people who grow up under an iron-fisted child-rearing approach become the very opposite of passive—they become openly and sometimes violently aggressive. They refuse to be bullied further, often reject authority, and, in turn, may become bullies themselves.

Some aggressive people were children who had a very different upbringing—their parents gave them too little discipline, allowing them to express defiant and rebellious behavior without any boundaries or restraints placed upon them. These aggressive children grow up to become pushy, intimidating, domineering adults.

Aggressive behavior is often confrontational behavior. Aggressive people may get in your face and point their finger at you, or they may resort to open and sometimes loud belittling and deliberately hurtful comments. They are good at shouting and throwing things.

Aggressive people seem especially prone to displaying their aggression on the highway. An aggressive driver will look you directly in the face as if to "stare you down." Aggressive people often glare, cross their arms, point, or clench their fists. In the corporate business environment, aggressive personalities are those who enjoy hostile takeovers and win-big situations in which other people must grovel as they lose; they also see all actions by other people as threats to their own survival or promotion. They are especially adept at walking over people to get to what they want or where they want to be.

Ambition is not aggression. To be ambitious is to set a high goal and actively and diligently pursue it. To be aggressive is to set a goal and pursue it as if you are the only person who can win the prize, and, therefore, all others around you must lose to some degree.

If you recognize yourself as having an aggressive personality type, the good news is that God wants to set you free! He wants you to learn how to be assertive without being aggressive. He wants you to develop a compassionate, generous, and loving heart—and if you are willing to do this, He will help you.

A BETTER WAY

No person is stuck forever with a passive or an aggressive personality style. Every person can learn to be assertive even if he or she was not raised in a healthy home environment. Here are a few suggestions.

Begin communicating your thoughts, feelings, wants, and needs more confidently.

Even if you don't feel confident on the inside, speak more confidently. The more you do this, the more confident you will feel on the inside.

Respect other people and their rights.

How can you develop a genuinely respectful attitude? One way is to purposefully yield to people on occasion. Give up the lane on the freeway or the parking space in the busy parking lot. Yield to another person in line. Another way is to be intentional about giving sincere compliments, even to strangers.

Do not let other people walk all over you.

Tell people what you expect and what you like. In so doing, you are also expressing—at least to some degree—what you do not expect and like. Communicate what you expect and like in terms of "appreciation" and "suggestion." For example, a person who says, "I really appreciate it when you pick up your dirty clothes and put them in the hamper each night" is a person who is setting a standard for what is desired. Without directly saying so, the person is also conveying the message, "I don't appreciate having to pick up your dirty clothes." The person who says, "May I make a suggestion that you wash the glassware before you wash the pots and pans?" is a person who is setting a standard that they expect a person to wash the dishes in the way that is most efficient and hygienic.

If others are rude, tell them that you find their behavior to be unkind.

If others are highly critical, tell them that you are sorry they are having a bad day, but you would really appreciate if they kept some of their criticism to themselves because it is not very helpful or encouraging to you.

Statements such as these can be made in a calm and kind voice. In fact, they are much more powerful and effective if they are made in a quiet, even-tempered, kind voice.

Do not respond to others apologetically.

Some people have a tendency to say repeatedly, "I know that you don't care what I think..." or, "I realize my ideas may not be worth much..." or, "I understand that I'm just a housewife and don't know about these things...." Such self-belittling remarks don't win anybody's respect, including your own self-respect.

Avoid putting others down.

If you don't have something positive or encouraging to say to another person, keep quiet. Praise does far more to change a person's behavior than criticism. Especially with our children, every constructive criticism should be balanced with two or more positive expressions of praise. A person who says, "I am so proud of you that you aren't like a lot of guys who wouldn't dream of helping with the housework; I think it's an amazing mark of maturity that you are willing to help out," is a person who gets a lot more housework and help from her husband. She likely gets more help than the wife who continually puts down her husband as lazy, inept, and chauvinistic.

Learn to say "no."

Know your own limits. Know when you have enough on your plate. You don't need to be unkind. You can say no in a gentle and respectful way. By not being able to say no, someone else's stress becomes your stress.

Saying no is a way of setting limits that impact your time, energy, resources, and emotions. The truth is that there will always be somebody who wants to borrow your car, wear your clothes, borrow or take your money, borrow your lawnmower, or who wants you to do something that is rightfully their chore or responsibility. When you "do" for another person what that person can do for himself, you take on a degree of responsibility for that person's life. Stick to being responsible for your own life and the resources of time, energy, talent, and creativity that God has given to you.

This isn't being selfish. It is being a good steward of your own resources—physically as well as emotionally and materially.

There are a number of kind ways of saying no. One of them is to add the phrase "right now" to your no. For example:

- "I don't think that is a good idea right now."

- "I'm not available to do that right now."

- "I can't take on that responsibility or task right now."

- "I'm not able to work that into my schedule right now."

At other times you may need to tell a person why you will never be able to participate in a certain venture or relationship:

- "I have a different set of priorities."

- "I am pursuing a goal that keeps me from participating in that."

- "I don't drink."

- "I don't think that's a wise course of action for me."

At times, you are wise to give a specific reason for your no. At times, you need only say, "No, thank you." At times it helps to tell the person that you are not rejecting him as a person; you are just saying no to a specific request.

There was a man who frequently asked to borrow tools or equipment from his neighbor. The man always seemed to return the lawnmower without fuel, or sometimes the equipment he had borrowed came back damaged or broken. He left his neighbor with a problem, and the burden and expense of repair was always the neighbor's responsibility. The last straw came when he borrowed an expensive power tool and brought it back broken. He didn't tell his neighbor that it was damaged.

The next time the man came over to borrow something, the neighbor told him that he was disappointed that he routinely mistreated his equipment and that he couldn't loan the neighbor his tools or machinery any longer. The man exploded in anger, calling the neighbor selfish for refusing to loan him the equipment when he was in need. In a kind and gentle voice, the neighbor simply restated the facts and told the man that he had to go.

This man was known for using this angry tone of voice to intimidate other neighbors into doing things for him. But the neighbor refused to let the man's anger intimidate him.

Later this man returned, apologized, and said he understood where his neighbor was coming from. The neighbor accepted the man's apology, but still didn't loan him equipment in the future.

Did this man feel any "stress" in using equipment, breaking it, and returning it broken? No.

Did the neighbor feel stress in finding that his equipment had been mistreated or broken? Yes.

In saying no, the neighbor may have experienced a brief outburst of anger from the man in the short run, but in the long run, he put himself in a position to experience a great deal less stress.

I have talked to a number of people who, momentarily, may have felt stress in telling a person they couldn't be on a committee or participate in a task force project. But in the long run, they have experienced relief and much less stress at not having to work with certain people or spend their time on certain tasks.

I have talked to a number of people who, momentarily, may have felt stress in telling a boss that they simply couldn't do more—that they were maxed out and were doing all they could do in a quality way. These people often feared they would be overlooked at promotion time or would be ostracized in the workplace for being an unwilling team player. They nearly always discovered, however, that in the long run, they had much less stress by not taking on more and more work. They found that their joyful attitude and the high quality of the work that they did do made them valuable employees to their immediate supervisors and their supervisors' managers.

One of the most important skills a person can adopt to prevent the buildup of stress in their lives is to learn to say no. Dr. J. Grant Howard has written: "Some people can't say no. They enroll in too many courses, hold down too many jobs, volunteer for too many tasks, make too many appointments, serve on too many committees, have too many friends. They are trying to be all things to all people all at once all by themselves."[1]

Learning to say no may be one of the most difficult things you ever learn to do, but it is also one of the most important things you can learn to do to control and insulate yourself from stress.

Tell them your doctor said so.

The passive person often ends up stewing in anger and frustration because he is unable to say no. I often find that my patients with chronic fatigue and fibromyalgia are passive people who have been unable to say no to people who have pressured them into doing more and more. I tell these patients to use me as an excuse. I say, "Tell them that your doctor refuses to allow you to do this." Or, "Tell them Dr. Colbert told you that you needed to resign from this position if you are going to remain his patient."

THE BASIS FOR YOUR "ASSERTIVENESS"

The underlying foundation for all assertiveness for the Christian needs to be a very strong understanding of God's plan and purpose. God's Word tells us that God has a plan for each and every life. He has built into each person a specific set of talents, dreams, desires, personality, faith, propensities, and "sense of fulfillment." When we have a very clear understanding about why we are alive on this planet today—and when we know the character and relationship with God that God desires for us to have—we find it much easier to be assertive. We know we don't have time or energy to waste—rather, we want to be focused and "on target" in everything we do so we can max out our witness for Christ and fulfill our reason for being.

Gain a vision for your life.

Many people are stressed because they have never had a vision for their life. They may have chosen the wrong job or the wrong career, or they are unwilling to obtain the education to enable them to achieve their vision. As a result, they never experience the passion, satisfaction, and joy of having a job that gives them a sense of fulfillment.

I strongly encourage you to spend some time imagining, fantasizing, or dreaming about the kind of life you really want to live. Imagine this life in a way that has no limitation on what you might do, become, or accomplish. Imagine that you have all of the friends, skills, resources, experience, time, and money you need to develop and fully implement the life you imagine.

What you imagine has unlimited potential.

Ask yourself:

- "What kind of family life would I like to have now? Ten years from now? In old age?"

- "What kind of spiritual maturity do I desire to have developed?"

- "What kind of health do I want to enjoy?"

- "What do I want a 'typical day' to be like now? Ten years from now? In old age?"

Now ask the critical questions: "How does this life line up with what I am living right now?" If there is very little similarity between the life you would like to live in the future and the life you are living now, what changes do you need to make? If there are only a few things different in the life you would like to live and the way you are living now, what changes or "fine-tuning adjustments" do you need to make?

Proverbs 29:18 says, "Where there is no vision, the people perish" (KJV). People sometimes think this vision is something that God initiates and plants into a person's "mind's eye." In the vast majority of cases, the "vision" we have is one that we see as a product of our own will. It is a vision rooted in our deep desires, dreams, and hopes. Does this make our vision any less godly? I don't believe so.

God is the One who plants within us from birth certain desires, propensities, dreams, goals, and hopes that are in keeping with our talents.

I have a friend who uses this metaphor to describe the way this works. She says, "God gives us the ability and the talent to be a 'hammer.' He has made us to be a hammer. That's our purpose in life. We have the responsibility to become the best hammer we can be—to develop all of the skills and to acquire all of the information necessary to be an outstanding hammer. But then, we must have a vision about what we will hammer. How and what will we build...when...where...and for whom? Those questions and answers are related to our vision. God has given us all of the raw elements for a vision, but it is up to us to identify our vision and to get it clearly in our mind's eye. We must be able to 'see' ourselves hammering successfully as we are building something noble and good!"

If we don't have a vision for our lives and "see" how we can be of maximum use in this life to the greatest number of people according to God's plans and purposes, we will languish. We will do very little. We will be lazy and self-absorbed. We will feel very little motivation and have very little reason to get up in the mornings. We will "perish" when it comes to fulfillment, satisfaction, and deep joy.

But if we do have a vision for our lives and can see ways in which to serve others in the Lord's name and for His purposes, we flourish! We accomplish more. We have a great reason to get up and get busy every day. We are motivated to do as much as we can do. We experience great fulfillment, satisfaction, and deep joy. We feel fully alive, and we thrive!

Most people dream or have a vision of a life that is marked by contentment, prosperity, joy, health, and peace. Yet most people don't live that life. We need to begin to line up our vision with our daily practice of life. Only then can the vision fully come to pass.

Martin Luther King Jr. once gave voice to a vision he had for his future and the future of his friends and loved ones. He said, "I have a dream that one day this nation will rise up and live out the true meaning of its creed: 'We hold these truths to be self-evident: that all men are created equal.'"[2] Think where we might be today if Martin Luther King Jr. had not dreamed of equality...if he had not had a vision...if he had not given voice to that vision...if he had not acted on it.

"See" a clear vision for your life.

Make the changes necessary to implement that vision fully.

Begin to act on those changes today!

Old habits and old attitudes will change as you begin to do what is necessary to make a glorious vision for your future come to pass.

Clarify your values and priorities.

Take some time to reflect upon and to clarify your values. Through the years I have talked to a number of people who were on their deathbeds. I have learned that people who are dying focus themselves on the love of family and making peace with God. They are very concerned with having "peace of mind." They often clarify values they previously ignored.

Don't wait until that day! Now is the time to clarify your values and identify your priorities in life. You might begin this process by answering this question: If you died and came back to life, what things would you do differently?

Jesus told a parable about a rich man and a poor man named Lazarus. Lazarus, a beggar, was full of sores. He lay at the rich man's gate and lived off the crumbs that fell off the rich man's table. Dogs came to lick Lazarus' sores.

Eventually Lazarus and the rich man died. Lazarus went to paradise, but the rich man went to Hades (hell). The rich man cried to Abraham, asking him to send Lazarus to dip the tip of his finger in water and cool his tongue because he was so tormented. Abraham, of course, couldn't respond to the rich man's request.

Then the rich man begged Abraham to at least send Lazarus to his father's house so that he could warn his five brothers about the place of torment. Abraham replied that if they didn't hear the message of Moses and the prophets, they wouldn't hear the message of a person who rose from the dead. (See Luke 16:19–31.)

What about you? Are there things that you are going to wish you had done or heeded? What are your answers to these questions:

- Imagine that you have only six months to live, but the disease you have causes no pain and will not cause a change in your present lifestyle. What would you still like to accomplish or experience? What would you want to do or obtain in the last six months of your life?

- What do you consider to be the top priorities of your life? Have you acted on your priorities today? This past week? This past month?

A PRIORITY CLUSTER

Nobody has just one priority in life—we all have a variety of priorities that impact all aspects of our lives. Our health, families, spiritual growth, a job or career, happiness, recreation and leisure time, finances, peace of mind, learning, friendships and fellowship, our homes, financial security, creativity, travel, companionship and communication—all of these can be part of our priority "cluster." I encourage you to identify your cluster of priorities by making a list of at least ten things you consider to be of utmost importance in your life.

SET GOALS FOR YOUR LIFE

Make a list of things you would like to do, accomplish, experience, earn, win, visit, or own in your life. These are "goal statements." A good way to phrase these is to start with a sentence that begins, "Before I die or fully retire, I would like to...." Goals pertain to every area of life. You may have a goal related to travel, work, ministry, family, spiritual growth, and so forth. In any area of your life, however, have only one main goal.

I encourage you to make a list of at least ten goals, and then number them according to importance in your life.

Vilfredo Pareto, an Italian economist, discovered that 20

percent of what a person does yields 80 percent of the results in that person's life. This is called the "80-20 principle." For example, about 20 percent of how a person spends his time yields about 80 percent of that person's income. About 20 percent of a person's mail is important, and about 80 percent is junk mail. About 20 percent of what we own is what we truly need to have a comfortable life, and about 80 percent is excess.[3]

I have found in my subscriptions to medical journals that about 20 percent of the information in these journals is very applicable and useful to me as a physician, and about 80 percent is of little value to me in my medical practice.

This principle likely holds true for our goals. About 20 percent of our goals are likely to be the real "motivators" in our lives. The others are likely to be things we would really like to do "if things work out" or "if we can." Ask yourself, "How much time do I really spend in pursuit of my top three goals in life? Do I schedule time each week for activities that are directly related to those goals?"

Be very specific and concrete.

Be very specific in setting goals for your life. Be practical and concrete—you should almost be able to close your eyes and "see" your goal—feel it, taste it, experience it, hear it. The majority of people never do this, and as a result, their life passes them by. They usually find they have regrets as they near the end of their life.

Ask questions about your goals.

Submit your goals to your own careful self-analysis. Below are some questions that you need to ask about your goals.

1. Is my goal achievable?

If your goal is to become an astronaut, but you never graduated from high school or college and don't intend to, then that is an unrealistic goal.

Achievable goals are ones for which you can do these things:

Make an action plan. For example, if your goal is to achieve better health, you should be able to map out a plan for accomplishing that goal. You very likely know what you need to do.

Most people who set this as a goal know they need to exercise more, make wiser food choices, and lose any excess weight they are carrying. They know they need to cut out junk food and sugars, get adequate sleep, drink sufficient water, and so forth.

Make a series of very specific "sub-goals" that serve as steps, or markers, that you are achieving a goal. For example, if your goal is to have better health, you should also be able to set very specific sub-goals. "What weight do I want to reach? What percentage of body fat do I want to have? I will exercise three days a week. I will lower my blood pressure and cholesterol level.

2. *Is my goal worth the time and energy it will take to accomplish the goal?*

Some people give voice to wonderful and lofty daydreams, but they have zero real desire to put in the time and energy it takes to achieve a goal. They have a serious lack of determination and perseverance to go along with their desire.

My desire to become a medical doctor took shape in my life when I was a teenager. I counted the cost. I knew that I was going to need to take out loans in excess of fifty thousand dollars in the 1970s and early 1980s to finish my college education and go to medical school. I knew that I was facing years of arduous study. I knew there were lots of nights and weekends in which I would need to study hard instead of play and relax with friends. I knew that I would be spending a lot more time in a library than at parties. I also knew the step-by-step process that was going to be required: I needed to get a bachelor of science degree, score well on the entrance exams required by medical schools, attend and do well in medical school, decide on a specialty, and, in my case, complete a family-practice residency.

I didn't just have a big vision, complete with details and a timetable; I had a big determination that I was going to turn this vision into a reality. I was willing to pay the price to see my vision come to pass.

Do you have that determination related to your vision?

Are you willing to make the sacrifices necessary to accomplish your vision?

3. Are the goals in various areas of my life balanced?

If most of your goals relate to your career or to finances, where does your family or your spiritual life fit in? If most of your goals are related to your hobbies and recreation, where does work fit in?

God's desire for us is that we live balanced, whole lives that reflect a harmony of spirit, mind, body, and emotions.

Short-term and long-term goals

In many ways the subset goals of an action plan become our short-term goals. People who have only long-term goals often feel frustrated because they don't know how to get from Point A today to Point B ten years from now. They are likely to be people who think they will truly start to "live" once they retire—it's at that point that they see themselves doing what they really want to do in their lives! Don't let that happen. Set short-term goals and midterm goals. They will give you enjoyment in life now and also be an indicator to you that you are on the right track toward your long-term goals. If your short-term goals are unsatisfying to you, perhaps your long-term goal is wrong for you.

Examples of short-term goals are: go out to dinner with friends once a week, spend quality time with family members every day, eat at least one meal daily as a family, or exercise three or four days a week.

Examples of midterm goals are: take a vacation once or twice a year, go away for a weekend vacation every eight weeks, pay off a car, reach a goal weight, read through the Bible, finish specific home improvements, or have a yearly family reunion.

Examples of long-term goals are: become debt free, become a vice president or own your own company, travel overseas, write a book, or own a vacation home.

Pray about your goals.

Your goals should become central to your personal prayer list. In other words, your goals should dominate the list of things that you pray for yourself. Voicing your goals to the Lord as a prayer is a way of activating your faith toward the accomplishment of those goals. Jesus said, "If you can believe, all things are possible to him who believes" (Mark 9:23). Begin to believe that

God will either help you fully accomplish the things you desire as your goals, or that He will convict you deep in your spirit that you have not truly voiced the goals that are most beneficial for you now and in eternity.

And then, be open to how God deals with you. If your goal is in line with God's plans and purposes for your life, you will have a joy in your heart when you think of your goals, and you will be eager to see them come to pass. If your goal is not in line with God's plans and purposes for you, you will have increasing doubt and a decreasing desire for these goals the more you pray about them.

If a goal is not something you truly believe God will help you receive and fulfill, then you need to reevaluate the goal or reevaluate your own faith. Jesus said, "Whatever things you ask when you pray, believe that you receive them, and you will have them" (Mark 11:24).

Share your goals with only a few.

Be wise in discussing your goals with other people. Certainly you will want to discuss certain goals with your spouse, family members, and close friends, because those goals may involve them or impact the amount of time you spend with them—either less time or more time. Some friends and acquaintances, however, may be jealous if you undertake a new challenge. Others may feel as if they are going to lose you as you pursue a new goal. Talk about your goal in positive terms, and be sure to include those you love the most in your plans and dreams.

Seek advice from trusted family members and friends, especially those who may have set a similar goal. Ask for suggestions about strategies or creative approaches to the accomplishment of your goal. Weigh the advice you are given for the applicability of the advice to your family life and particular goals.

Setting goals will enable you to eventually achieve your vision, which, in turn, relieves your stress. In chapter two I discussed that not all stress is bad and that you can choose to control the stress level of your life. Goal setting allows you to choose to control the stress level of your life. It also helps you clarify your values, which directs you toward your goal. Too many of my elderly patients regret never setting goals or making their life count for something. They reflect back over their life and wish they had set goals and stretched themselves.

Periodically reassess your goals.

Periodically reassess your goals to see if they are what you still desire. When I was a teenager, two of my goals were to own a gym and to drive a Corvette. I no longer have any interest in either of these goals, and I have absolutely no regrets about not doing either of these things.

A vision may change slightly as one pursues it. My vision certainly took a few turns I had not anticipated as the vision unfolded over the years. When I found myself as a family practice physician with a variety of debilitating ailments—chronic sinusitis, anxiety, fatigue, irritable bowel syndrome, and psoriasis—I knew that for me to pursue the vision I had for my own health, I was going to need to make some changes. I needed to change my diet, sleep more, decrease my stress level, drink more water, decrease my obligations, create more "margin" in my life, balance exercise with rest, and take supplements. I found that I had a need for more information than I had gained in medical school. I began to study nutrition, detoxification, and natural hormone replacement therapy. The more I studied and began to implement this information into my medical practice, the more I became interested in issues related to the emotional component of diseases, ways to balance neurotransmitters naturally, and "forgiveness therapy."

My vision broadened and changed, but my overall vision of being a person who might help others become well did not. The same is true for a genuine vision in your life. The "big picture" is not likely to change if it truly is God's plan and purpose for your life. The scope and details of that vision may change as you pursue the development of your talents and have experiences in your life.

Set deadlines and get busy.

For each of your goals and sub-goals, set deadlines. And then get busy.

Procrastination is one of the greatest enemies to achieving goals. Procrastination is usually based on distortional beliefs that a person has about himself. A person who grows up being told that he will never amount to anything, is a loser, or will never make it is very likely a person who will put off trying something because he has a hidden fear that what he was told as a child may actually be true. The only way to prove those old statements are lies is to actually make the effort and do your best to try to achieve a goal. People may not achieve a goal as quickly as desired, or they may not achieve a goal in as grand a manner as they had hoped, but those who try to achieve goals nearly always achieve far more than a person who fails to try. We have all heard the old saying, "Shoot for the moon, and if you miss, you'll still land among the stars!" That statement is true in the pursuit of goals. Aim high. You will accomplish far more than if you aim low.

In making an action plan, ask yourself questions such as these:

- "What do I need to start doing that I'm not doing?"

- "What do I need to stop doing that I'm presently doing?"

- "Do I need to read books or take courses to get the information I need?"

- "How am I going to keep myself motivated as I pursue my goal?"

You probably are going to need to make some time adjustments. Decide which activities you need to eliminate from your life. If you are spending a great deal of time watching TV or surfing the Internet, give yourself a time limit on these activities. Don't do them until *after* you have read the books or journals or listened to the tapes necessary to gain the knowledge or motivation that you need. You may be wise to decide which one program on television you enjoy the most and then limit your television watching to that one program.

Decide that every day you are going to do something that will either move you closer to your main goal or keep you motivated to pursue your goal.

FOLLOW THROUGH ON YOUR PLANS!

It isn't enough just to make these lists and goals described above. We need to do two things with them. First, we need to look for a balance and crossover principles among the three lists. Do we have priorities, values, and goals related to spiritual growth, ministry, or church activities near the top of our list? How do these priorities, values, and goals interrelate? Do we have priorities, values, and goals related to quality time spent with family members and friends? How do these priorities, values, and goals interrelate?

Second, we need to take a look at our calendars and checkbooks and see if the way we schedule our time and spend our money is actually in agreement with what we say are our priorities, values, and goals. Does our day planner reveal that we place high priority on family? Does our checkbook reveal that we place high priority on spiritual matters and evangelism?

Lists such as these can be wonderful motivators for change in a person's life. They can call a person to face the reality that what that person says he values is not necessarily what that person does in his daily life. Lists can challenge a person to bring priorities, values, and goals into greater alignment or synchronization. Keep your lists handy so you can review them periodically. They will help motivate you to stay focused and be more assertive.

Jim is a friend of mine who is an attorney. His main priorities are a close-knit family, good health, travel, and companionship with family and friends. For much of his life, Jim has enjoyed a high degree of financial security. He owns a large home and has a fulfilling job. His home life and work life have been in good balance with his spiritual life. Jim, however, was in fairly poor health, and while he had a desire to travel, he never seemed to have time to travel. After Jim made a list of his priorities, he decided that the time had come to do what he said he believed to be a priority: improve his health and travel. He began to change his diet, exercise regularly, and lose weight. He scheduled time to travel with his wife and son. He also made a choice to spend more time with his family and friends, which was also something he had as a priority. By identifying and clarifying his priorities, he felt compelled to "live them out."

The same thing tends to happen when we identify our values and goals. If we say we value "a big laugh every day" but we never laugh, then there is something wrong with that picture! If we say we value praising God but we never praise God, perhaps it's time we start.

Being assertive, learning to say no at the appropriate time, gaining a vision, clarifying your values, and setting goals will help reduce the stress factor in your life. And when you assert boundaries, know that the power of your words can add to—or subtract from—the stress in your life.

11

The Impact of Your Words on Your Own Stress Level

Through the years I have been amazed at how many of my patients come into the office with a complaining, whining, critical attitude—and speech. Certainly as a physician I expect people to come to me telling me that they feel sick, miserable, or are in pain—after all, a significant percentage of the people in my practice have depression, fibromyalgia, chronic fatigue, cancer, heart disease, or an autoimmune disease. What I have *not* expected is for people to be generally critical of the world as a whole.

When I prescribe "the speaking of stress-relieving words" to my patients—that is, the speaking of positive, life-affirming words and phrases—their conditions often improve dramatically.

We each need to be aware that the words we speak have a tremendous ability to cause or relieve stress—not only in other people, but also in ourselves. When we speak carelessly or critically, we can cause tremendous stress, even if those words are ones we carelessly and critically speak to ourselves verbally or mentally.

How do you characterize your own speech? Do you regularly choose positive, encouraging, comforting, kind, gentle, caring, and life-affirming words in your conversations with others or in the way you speak to your own self?

Or do you choose critical, complaining, rude, inconsiderate, hurtful, angry, negative, argumentative, or threatening words?

The choices you make regarding the words you speak are very important.

What you say and the tone of your voice are two choices that are solely yours to make.

King Solomon, considered to be the wisest man on earth in his time, said, "Death and life are in the power of the tongue, and those who love it will eat its fruit" (Prov. 18:21). Nothing that we say goes unnoticed by God or by our own subconscious mind. Everything we say contributes either to the promotion of life or death.

YOU ARE THE NUMBER-ONE "HEARER" OF WHAT YOU SAY

Many people have an understanding that what they say impacts others. Few seem to have an understanding that they themselves are the number-one audience of what they say! The impact of words on others is also an impact of words on *self*.

Edna was a patient who suffered from depression, fibromyalgia, and chronic fatigue. My staff dreaded her appointments. She invariably came into the office complaining and looking for things to criticize. She would become very upset if she was put on hold during a call to the office. She got upset if she had to wait for any amount of time in the office. Granted, Edna was in pain, but even people in pain have an ability to choose how they will respond to life and the words they will speak.

Edna complained about my nurses hurting her when they took her blood pressure or drew blood. She even complained about having to hold a thermometer in her mouth because it irritated her lips! My nurses are very caring and gentle, and they would never intentionally hurt any person. It was no surprise to me that they dreaded seeing her.

I too felt exhausted after spending only twenty to thirty minutes with her in medical consultation. She not only talked about her aches and pains, but she also complained about her husband or family members. Every phrase that came out of her mouth was a complaint or criticism, usually expressed in a whining tone of voice. I always left my appointments with her feeling drained of energy as well as enthusiasm, and I finally asked my staff to schedule her as the last patient of the day only so I wouldn't carry any negativity or exhaustion on to another patient.

I wasn't the first physician in Edna's life, of course. By the time I met her, she had been to fifteen different physicians, and she was only forty-five years old. She also had been married three times! Edna had attempted to sue some of her previous physicians for malpractice and was unsuccessful. It was something of a miracle that she stayed with me for a few years since none of the treatments I prescribed seemed to help her.

Then I became aware of the extreme importance of the words we speak. I prescribed for her: "Look for the good instead of focusing on the bad." I told her very plainly that she needed to start looking for and finding the good in everything she encountered, and that she needed to refuse to complain, criticize, or be negative. I pointed out that she had developed not only negative mental and emotional habits, but also negative speech habits. I described to her what I had witnessed in a gym where I work out.

I would see scrawny teenagers come to the gym to start lifting weights. Some of them didn't weigh more than 120 pounds, and their arms were so skinny I could encircle their flexed biceps with my thumb and index finger of one hand. After coming to the gym three to four times a week for an hour or two each visit—lifting weights and doing curls under supervision of a personal trainer—these young men would emerge six months to a year later with bulging biceps! The change didn't occur overnight, but change did happen.

I explained to Edna that she had developed bulging biceps of criticism and negativity. Her "muscles" of praise, appreciation, and encouragement were so small they were almost imperceptible. I asked her to make a diligent effort to turn that situation around and to shrink her critical and negative outlook and speech, and at the same time, seek to exercise praise and positive attitudes and speech. She was reluctant at first even to hear what I was trying to say to her, but finally I asked her if she would just try to do this for twenty-four hours.

How did she respond? With a negative comment. "There is no way I could go for twenty-four hours without complaining and criticizing." I suggested she just try to do this for an hour. She was silent—I could tell she was having trouble with even that small amount of "exercise" related to this new mental and speech habit. Finally, she agreed.

I insisted she stay in the office for that hour. She told me later that sitting in my office for an hour without saying anything negative was one of the most difficult things she had ever done in her life. I said at the end of the hour, "If you can do this for one hour, you can do it for twenty-four hours." I called her husband and explained to him what I had prescribed, and he agreed that he would work with Edna and the family to make this something of a "game." I got them to all agree that they would encourage, praise, and compliment one another, without criticism or complaint.

The next day Edna called to report that she had gone twenty-four hours without complaining or criticizing. She seemed excited at her accomplishment. I asked her to continue this process with her entire family involved until her appointment the following month.

The next month when Edna walked into my office I could hardly believe the change in her appearance. She came into the office with a smile on her face. She had energy. She said her depression had lifted and her pain from the fibromyalgia had decreased significantly. Each month thereafter her condition improved. Not only was Edna getting well physically, but also her marriage was healing, and her family and friends actually seemed to enjoy being with her more. Genuine love and appreciation were being expressed by Edna and to Edna.

My staff and nurses began to look forward to Edna's appointments because she came into the office with encouraging, appreciative words. She eventually came to the point where she did not need to come for monthly appointments—we were sorry not to see her but very pleased to know she was doing so well!

FOUR CATEGORIES OF STRESS-INDUCING WORDS

There are four main categories of words and phrases that cause stress:

- Cruel, hateful, and hurtful
- Critical, faultfinding, and judgmental
- Rude and inconsiderate
- Whining and complaining

Nearly all judgmental, angry, threatening, manipulative, and blaming words and phrases, and the attitudes that prompt them, can be placed in one of these four categories depending upon the unique and specific circumstance or situation. The same goes for lies, filthy speech (swearing and cursing), gossip, and argumentative, teasing, and bragging words and phrases.

Cruel, hateful, and hurtful words

What we sow verbally is what we often reap in our bodies and in our relationships. The Bible tells us, "Do not be deceived, God is not mocked; for whatever a man sows, that he will also reap" (Gal. 6:7). Not only do we tend to get back cruel, hateful, and hurtful responses from those to whom we speak cruel, hateful, and hurtful words, but we also get back into our own minds and bodies a negative consequence. Proverbs 26:27 tells us, "Whoever digs a pit will fall into it, and he who rolls a stone will have it roll back on him."

The apostle Paul wrote on several occasions about the impact of our words. He said to the Ephesians:

> Let no corrupt word proceed out of your mouth, but what is good for necessary edification, that it may impart grace to the hearers.
> —EPHESIANS 4:29

He also admonished the early believers:

> Let all bitterness, wrath, anger, clamor, and *evil speaking* be put away from you, with all malice.
> —EPHESIANS 4:31, EMPHASIS ADDED

Most of us grew up hearing and saying to other children, "Sticks and stones may break my bones, but words will never hurt me." That simply isn't true. Words we speak in a matter of seconds can cause emotional pain for years.

Most of us as children found ourselves saying to others who made critical or false remarks, "Take that back!" Once spoken, however, hurtful words can never truly be "taken back."

I once heard a pastor tell a story about a man he called Tim. Tim lived in a small town and was very jealous of Andrew, another man in that town. Tim began to spread vicious rumors about Andrew, and the lies and gossip caused Andrew's wife to leave him. Tim was ashamed when he heard this, and he went to his priest to confess his sin and to get advice about what to do. The priest instructed him to take a goose down pillow, open it up, and put a handful of feathers in front of the door of every person to whom he had spread his lying gossip. Tim did this, and the next day he returned to the priest for further advice. The priest instructed him to return to these doorsteps and gather up the feathers. When Tim attempted to do this, of course, he quickly discovered that the feathers had been blown away, and he had no feathers to bring back.

The wise priest said, "These feathers are like your words. Once you release them, you cannot retrieve them."

I have been appalled at seeing how hateful and hurtful some guests can be on afternoon TV talk shows. I am further appalled when I realize that literally millions of Americans find their words "amusing" or "entertaining!" We need to regain our sanity as a nation. Not only are hateful and hurtful words wrong, but also it is wrong to be amused by them, to encourage them in other people, or to sit by idly and say nothing to counteract them.

Critical, judgmental, and faultfinding words

My friend Joyce Meyer claims that she once was a very critical, faultfinding person. Her husband, Dave, was not the type of man to buy flowers on special occasions. He was, however, a man who was friendly and easy to get along with. Joyce admitted that she was critical of Dave because he didn't buy her flowers on special occasions like her birthday, their anniversary, or for Valentine's Day. Dave, however, would always tell her that he would buy her anything they could afford—he just needed to know what she wanted. Joyce finally came to the realization that she could be miserable about what Dave was not doing, or she could begin to be grateful for what he did do and say.

Jesus said, "Judge not, and ye shall not be judged: condemn not, and ye shall not be condemned" (Luke 6:37, KJV). To judge means to be critical of another person. To condemn means to be so critical that we no longer see any value whatsoever in the person—we are willing to "write them off" as worthless and unredeemable.

People who are critical and judgmental often resort to the use of single words to convey their disgust: "stupid," "idiot," "jerk," "pig." They become experts at name-calling.

Rude and inconsiderate words

We live in a discourteous world. We hear rude comments often; in fact, we seem to hear them so often that we no longer expect to hear a display of good manners. When was the last time you heard "yes, sir," "no, sir," "yes, ma'am," "no ma'am," "please," and "thank you" from a child or teenager? Far more often we hear "yeah" or "nah."

Good manners are not learned in a day. They are a product of training, which requires repetitive behavior.

"But," you may be asking, "why are good manners important? What do they have to do with stress?"

Manners are an outward visible sign of respect from one person to another, and especially a sign of respect to those who are in authority. Manners show honor to parents and to others who are worthy of esteem. The Bible says, "Be kindly affectionate to one another with brotherly love, in honor giving preference to one another" (Rom. 12:10). To honor or "give preference" to another person means to show respect in an outward and visible way.

Manners are a way in which we infuse both order and respect into our relationships. The opposite of order and respect are "chaos" and "scorn." Both are directly related to stress.

A disorderly, out-of-control, and chaotic environment—or relationship—produces stress. As human beings, we need a certain degree of order, harmony, and structure in order to feel peaceful, safe, and confident. When our world seems confusing or out of control to us, we easily become frustrated and stressed.

I vividly remember one teenage boy who came to my office suffering from depression. He had been seen by a psychiatrist who had put him on an antidepressant medication. Actually, this boy had already been through several different medications in search of the best one for his depression. His mother was especially upset because he was failing in school, seemed to get into fights quickly, and had already been in juvenile detention center on two occasions because of drugs and burglary. She feared her son was headed for a life of addiction and prison.

When I entered the examination room, I noted that he was giving his mother a hateful, angry look as he listened to music through the headphones he was wearing. I introduced myself, and he glared at me with the same angry, hateful expression. I asked him what he was listening to, and he murmured the name of a group I didn't know. I then asked him if I could listen to the music for a few seconds, and he agreed, but hesitantly. As I put the headphones to my ears, I was horrified at what I heard. The heavy metal music was grating, and the singer was screaming obscenities in pure hate and anger.

Psychologists have known for years that approximately 40 percent of any spoken message is communicated by "tone of voice." The tone of this singer's voice was a reflection of the look I had seen in this boy's eyes.

I asked his mother privately if he listened to this kind of music frequently. She said, "All day long." She told me he also watched DVDs of this music. I asked her how long he had been doing this, and she told me a couple of years. I then asked how long he had been depressed, had problems at school, was involved with drugs, and had been rebellious against the law. She said, "Two years."

I opened my Bible and read these two verses to his mother:

> Out of the abundance of the heart the mouth speaks.
> —MATTHEW 12:34

> Keep your heart with all diligence, for out of it spring the issues of life.
> —PROVERBS 4:23

I explained to her that we need to guard very carefully what we allow to enter our minds—garbage in, garbage out. I asked her, "Would you allow a garbage truck to pull up in front of your house and begin unloading all its contents into your home?" This got her attention. I went on to say, "These kinds of music, television programs, movies, books, magazines, and certain Internet sites are dumping a tremendous amount of garbage into the minds of your son and other young people."

I then made a deal with the boy. He was about to go before a judge on drug charges, and he faced the possibility of going to the juvenile detention center for a year or longer. I told him that if he would do something for me, I would do something for him. I told him that he needed to stop listening to heavy metal rock and rap music and begin listening to Christian music—I recommended Michael W. Smith, the Newsboys, and the Katinas to him. He had to stop watching movies and television programs that had violent content. He had to start reading his Bible on a daily basis, as well as one chapter a day of Rick Warren's book *The Purpose-Driven Life*. He had to attend youth service at a local church twice a week. If he would agree to do those things, I would write a letter to the judge on his behalf.

The boy hesitated, but he finally agreed. He further agreed to hand over all of his CDs to his mother that very night.

The boy and his mother returned to my office a month later. The mother was overjoyed. She had gone with him to his appointment with the psychiatrist the week prior to our appointment, and the psychiatrist had been amazed at his improvement. The boy was fulfilling his end of our "deal," and he was making new friends at church.

Within a few months his life had changed in ways that were profound. I then wrote a letter to the judge, and also asked the boy's pastor to write a letter, on his behalf. The judge miraculously dropped the drug charges against him.

Watch closely what your children put into their minds. If they are wallowing in lewd, crude, rude, and hateful emotional garbage, they will adopt those same behaviors.

Complaining and whining words

We are the wealthiest nation in the world, but we are also a nation of whiners. If you listen to most Americans, you would conclude that we are a nation that has nothing for which to be thankful and that we live in a society where nothing is right.

I have been on a number of missionary trips to third world nations, including nations in Africa and South America, that often do not have any comforts of life. I always return home with renewed gratitude for an abundance of hot water in which to bathe, clean water to drink, a comfortable bed, adequate space in which to live, and air conditioning. My list of things for which to be thankful is long.

I've noticed, however, that as grateful as I am in the forty-eight hours after I return home, I tend to take for granted many of these luxuries within a few weeks. We all seem to have a fairly short memory when it comes to our blessings.

Complainers and whiners have developed a mental filter through which they see and hear stimuli from the outside world. They may be given a compliment, but their filter distorts it to a complaint. They may be asked a question, but their filter warps it into a statement of doubt. They may see a person's expression and automatically jump to the conclusion that the expression is negative, and more specifically, that it is negatively aimed at them!

Philippians 2:14 says, "Do all things without complaining." Note that word *all*.

One of my colleagues was seeking to hire a registered nurse and finally found an extremely qualified person. Her résumé was one of the best he'd ever seen. She had worked in a hospital ICU unit for a number of years and was very skilled in various procedures, including giving intravenous fluids and medications. His entire staff was excited about her joining their team.

After the first day, however, one of his staff members came to him and said that she had never heard anyone complain, grumble, murmur, or whine as much as this nurse. She said that this new employee murmured under her breath every time he asked her to do something. She complained when one of the other nurses returned from her lunch break a few minutes late and when she couldn't find supplies she wanted. It quickly became apparent that she was whining and complaining to his patients, so much so that they were starting to ask for a different nurse. After just one month with them, she had poisoned his entire staff.

His wife was in charge of hiring and firing at his office. She personally was never around this particular nurse very much, but she did notice that her husband was coming home more and more exhausted at the end of the day. They discussed this situation, and he finally recognized that this woman was sapping his strength and energy with her negativity. His wife sat down with this nurse and explained to her that while she had excellent nursing skills, her whining attitude was a constant distraction. Rather than ask what she might do to turn the situation around, this woman immediately began to whine about her assessment. In the end, they had to let her go.

WORDS CAN RELIEVE STRESS

The Bible says, "Pleasant words are like a honeycomb, sweetness to the soul and health to the bones" (Prov. 16:24). Mother Teresa had a saying, "Let no one come to you without leaving happier and better." There are words and phrases we can use that soothe and calm—not only the person who hears them, but also the person who speaks them.

Two of my patients—a husband and wife—were having marital problems. They had seen a marriage counselor a few times, and I noticed a change in the way they related to each other. They were no longer critical of each other, but were kind, loving, and respectful toward one another. I was rather amazed at this fairly sudden turnaround, and I asked them about it. They told me that the marriage counselor had told them to change their speech. The counselor had asked them a simple question that had jarred each one of them to their core: "If you were on your deathbed and only had a few minutes left to live and only one phone call you could make, whom would you call, and what would you say?" The couple had been stunned at this question. The counselor quickly went on, "And why are you waiting?"

The couple turned to each other and each one apologized for saying hateful, critical things to the other. They reaffirmed their love for each other and agreed to begin speaking encouraging, kind, and gentle words from that day on.

The change in their relationship was tremendous. The stress they had produced in their relationship as a result of their contentious, angry, and quarrelsome speech began to evaporate. The environment of their relationship became one of peace and harmony.

Proverbs 21:23 says, "Whoever guards his mouth and tongue keeps his soul from troubles." Colossians 4:6 tells us, "Let your speech always be with grace, seasoned with salt, that you may know how you ought to answer each one."

We need to think before we speak and weigh what we say so that we truly do know the most beneficial thing to say to each person in each situation.

Look for ways in which to reinforce the good behaviors of other people. Look for attributes and behaviors about which you can give sincere compliments—phony compliments are perceived as manipulative. Only compliment what you can compliment with a genuine heartfelt sincerity.

One day I was standing in the customer service line of a major department store after Christmas. The line was quite long, and I brought a book along because I had thought this might be the case. I had to stop reading, however, because I was so startled by what was happening in the line ahead of me. Customer after customer blasted the poor clerk behind the counter with angry, hostile, hateful words. I felt like shouting, "It's the day after Christmas!" I knew that in shouting, however, I would just be adding to the chaotic, turbulent atmosphere. I also noticed that the clerk responded to these hateful people with a kind, gentle voice. She told each one that she understood their anger and was sorry for their inconvenience. I truly was moved by her incredible diplomacy at disarming one angry customer after another. Angry customers would later apologize for their initial outbursts. When it was my turn at the counter, I complimented this clerk for her kind and gentle manner. I told her I was amazed at how she handled herself and that she was a wonderful example of true "customer service." I also told her that I felt that she would probably be promoted because of the outstanding attitude and mannerism she had. Sure enough, the following year I happened to find myself back in that same line. This woman was now the manager of the department!

John Hagee once said, "Watch your thoughts, for they will become your words. Choose your words, for they will become your actions. Understand your actions, for they become habits. Study your habits, for they will become your character. Develop your character, for it becomes your destiny."

Speak positive affirmations to yourself daily.

Nobody can preach to you like you can preach to yourself! If others try to coax you into action, you are probably going to think they are nagging you. If you coax yourself into action, you will see yourself as a disciplined, motivated person. One of the ways to speak in a way that will relieve your own stress is to speak positive affirmations to yourself on a daily basis.

A positive affirmation is a statement that begins with "I am..." and ends with a positive character trait, attribute, or even an attitude or behavior that you desire to build into your life. Examples might be:

- "I am a loving person."

- "I am a patient person."

- "I am trusting God to show me how to organize my time in keeping with His plans and purposes for my life."

- "I am pursuing what I need."

- "I am willing to give up some of my 'wants' in order to have less stress."

- "I am building margin into my life."

As you review the previous chapters, come up with a list of positive affirmations you might speak to yourself on a regular basis. I recommend that you list these on a separate sheet of paper or on three-by-five-inch cards. Carry the list with you, and speak these affirmations to yourself several times a day.

Always make sure your affirmations are in line with God's Word. Seek to build character traits that He desires to see in your life. Galatians 5:22–23 gives us a wonderful list of these traits: "love, joy, peace, longsuffering [patience], kindness, goodness, faithfulness, gentleness, self-control."

Praise and thanksgiving go to God. Our offering of praise and thanks is a way of "giving" to God the honor and glory due Him.

Affirmations are really reaffirmations of what God says He desires to see as our character, values, and beliefs. See Appendix B and Appendix C for examples of positive and scriptural affirmations.

The Bible says, "The tongue has the power of life and death, and those who love it will eat its fruit" (Prov. 18:21, NIV). Jesus said in Matthew 12:36–37, "For every idle word men may speak, they will give account of it in the day of judgment. For by your words you will be justified, and by your words you will be condemned." What rolls off your tongue can become a weapon for destruction or a tool for edifying a life. Choose carefully what you say, and I guarantee you that stress will diminish in your life and the lives of those around you.

1 2

Building "Margin" Into Your Life

Years ago when I first encountered patients, friends, and acquaintances, I would ask them, "How are you doing?" The response was nearly always, "Fine." Now, I find that people tend to respond to my question with answers such as "Busy," "Tired," or "Exhausted."

I have met several people who genuinely believe being "busy" is a sign of success. A few take pride in being busy. They tend to push themselves to the point of exhaustion, trying to cram more and more activities, meetings, commitments, and friendships into an already tight schedule.

As a nation, we seem to be trapped in a work-and-spend cycle. This can be a vicious cycle because people who work more tend to want more and then to buy more. The more they owe, the more they must work, and so it goes. Author John de Graff calls this "afluenza"—a painful, contagious, socially transmitted condition of overload, debt, anxiety, and waste resulting from the dogged pursuit of "more."[1]

A few years ago we joined several friends for a vacation time in Colorado. One day we were all playing putt-putt golf, and during the entire eighteen holes of the game, one of my friends was on his cell phone. That was nearly three hours of talk time! He called various people, including his accountant, and several people called him. I quickly realized that he took pride in his "busyness." I did not take either a cell phone or beeper with me on this vacation. To me, that degree of "busyness" is not relaxing! I couldn't help but overhear some of his conversation as we played golf together, and I discovered that most of the conversations were little more than "small talk." There was nothing major that needed discussing and very little "business" being conducted. Nevertheless, he just had to take these important calls. It was as if every minute of every waking hour had to be spent "doing" something that was perceived as being productive. Most people who try to cram more and more into their hours feel "shocked" at how quickly time passes. They aren't enjoying the minutes as they are lived, and then one day, they awaken to realize with sadness that they have missed out on a great deal of enjoyment.

DO YOU HAVE A TYPE A PERSONALITY?

Many years ago, two San Francisco cardiologists, Dr. Meyer Friedman and Dr. Ray Rosenman, while doing research discovered a link between certain personality traits and coronary artery disease. They came to identify traits such as impatience, competitiveness, a chronic sense of urgency, and hostile anger as what we know today as a "type A" personality. Typically these individuals are multitaskers, highly aggressive, ambitious, hard workers, and easily annoyed by delays and interruptions. If they relax, then they feel guilty. They tend to finish other people's statements. They, in essence, suffer from "hurry sickness."

A number of medical research studies have found that people with type A personality have a higher incidence of coronary artery disease. Research has also revealed that type B personalities can be pushed into type A behavior if they are given too many responsibilities or feel too great a job-related pressure. The demands of urban life, deadlines, financial pressures, traffic problems, and the general "busyness" of schedules tend to press people into the type A behavior mold, even if those individuals don't already have a predisposition to that behavior style.[2]

In his book *The Overload Syndrome*, Dr. Richard Swenson accurately paints the picture of overload in our society. He contends that a concept he calls "margin" is necessary as a space between vitality and exhaustion. "Margin" is where we experience breathing room or reserve energy. Having sufficient margin is necessary to keep from overload.[3] In order to overcome overload, a person must intentionally seek to increase a healthy "margin" in their lives.

Let me give you an example of this. If a person is flying from New York to Los Angeles with a change of planes in Dallas, would that person leave himself only five minutes to make the connection between the two flights? No. For that matter, no travel agent would ever allow such a connection. If the person did attempt a five-minute change, there would be a very high probability that the person would miss the second leg of the flight. Very likely he would be very impatient, anxious, and frustrated for the first half of the trip, wondering if he was going to miss the second flight and eager to be first off the plane in Dallas. The point is, such a traveler has not left himself sufficient "margin" for an enjoyable journey.

Ray was a forty-five-year-old patient who had a massive heart attack that left him with only about a quarter of the original strength of his heart. The day after his heart attack, I explained to him this concept of margin using the example I gave above, and I was shocked when he said that he was a person who routinely gave himself only a few minutes between flights as he traveled! He had no trouble at all understanding the concept, and I had no trouble determining that one of the major reasons for his heart attack was this overload pressure he had placed on his own life.

I live in Orlando, Florida, and one of the main attractions besides the Disney parks and Universal Studios is a water park called "Wet 'N' Wild." This water park has a giant water slide, and a person must wait until the previous "slider" has gone down the slide before he begins his descent. This is closely governed by the slide attendants to ensure a good "margin of safety." We all know about a margin of safety when we drive. If a person is tailgating a driver at sixty miles an hour in rush hour traffic, there is little margin for error! Having sufficient "margin" is necessary in every area of life.

A question we each are wise to ask is this: "Have I allowed enough margin for what I am doing?"

A personal trainer (let's call him Rick) worked at a health club and also worked part-time for an electronics chain store. He had crammed too many obligations into his life in too short a time span, and he had no "margin." As a result, he was always running late. He was usually a few minutes late for work. He also ran late when his children had a ball game or recital. He was always late to church and social events, even weddings and funerals. For his part, Rick didn't seem to be very frustrated at being perpetually "behind schedule." But other people in his life were certainly frustrated by his behavior! It was their frustration that eventually caused Rick to become frustrated. Even if you don't feel the need for greater margin in your life, you are wise to build it in for the sake of those you love.

THE DO-MORE, HAVE-MORE TREADMILL

Countless people today are on a "do-more-so-I-can-have-more" treadmill. The more some people have, the more some people want, and therefore, the more they "do" so they can have their desires. It's a no-win, uphill climb because a person who is afflicted with this type of greed never has enough; therefore, they never feel they are doing enough.

God's Word tells us, "Do not love the world or the things in the world. If anyone loves the world, the love of the Father is not in him" (1 John 2:15). This passage goes on to define what is meant by "love the world." The Bible says, "For all that is in the world—the lust of the flesh, the lust of the eyes, and the pride of life—is not of the Father but is of the world. And the world is passing away, and the lust of it; but he who does the will of God abides forever" (vv. 16–17).

We need to recognize that everything we "own" really owns us. The more things we own, the more time and energy they consume.

Years ago I bought a lake house. I saw it as a place to relax and spend time with my family. We built a boathouse for our boat and jet skis, and also a seawall around most of the two-and-one-half-acre property. I mowed the grass with my riding lawn-mower, but every month or so it seemed that I ran over a root or a tree stump and had to have the mower repaired. It took time and energy to haul it to the shop and have it fixed—repeatedly.

The year after I bought the house we had a drought, and the lake receded so much that I couldn't even get the boat or jet skis out of the boathouse. The drought went on for three years! By then the portion of the lake closest to our home had produced weeds that were taller than I am. I had to buy a hand-pushed swamp mower just to cut the weeds in the lake. It was a grueling job. I got to the point where I dreaded going to the lake house because I knew that it would drain all my time and energy just dealing with the lawn, the lawn mower, and the problems associated with the lake. I finally sold the house, but not before I had to repair the boat and jet skis since they had not been used for so many years. Today when I look back, it seems more like that house, the boat, and jet skis owned me more than I owned them!

Too many of us seem to be seeking to own this earth, which we can never do. We are guests on this earth and stewards of it while we are here. The only thing we take from this life is our relationship with God. If we don't have a relationship with Him, we have nothing to take with us as we leave this life.

Jesus told a tremendous parable about a rich man who experienced a great harvest from his crops and didn't have room to store all the crops. Rather than give the excess away, he tore down his barns and built bigger barns. He concluded that he could take it easy and eat, drink, and be merry. God said to him, "You are foolish. This night you are going to die, and nothing that you have chosen to value is going to matter in eternity." (See Luke 12:16–22.)

Do you suffer from Pakhom's syndrome?

Leo Tolstoy, the famous Russian writer, told a story that has become famous. The story asks, "How much land does a person need?" In the story a peasant named Pakhom heard about a great deal on land in a faraway country. He traveled to the land of the Bashkirs, and there, he bargained with an elder in the village, who he thought was a fool. The elder told Pakhom that he could have all the land he wanted for only a thousand rubles a day. Pakhom didn't understand what he meant by that and asked how many acres that included. The elder told him that the land was sold "by the day" and that whatever Pakhom could walk around in one day—from sunup to sundown—would be his. The only catch was that he had to return to the starting point by sundown, or the money was forfeited. Pakhom said that a man could walk around a great deal of land in one day, and the elder burst out laughing, saying, "Then all of it would be yours!"

Pakhom was so excited that night he could hardly sleep. He arose at dawn and went with the villagers to the top of the hill where the elder put down his hat. Pakhom placed a thousand rubles on top of the hat and then began walking and digging holes as he went to mark out the boundaries of his land. It was going so well that he thought he could travel another few miles and then turn left. The land was so beautiful he hated to miss out on claiming as much of it as possible.

Pakhom hurried through the morning to add more and more land. At noon, he looked back at the hill where he started and found it difficult to see the villagers. He worried that he perhaps had gone too far and decided to cut down on some of his goals. The heat was exhausting as the afternoon wore on. By late afternoon, his bare feet were cut and bruised, and his legs were weak. He wanted to rest, but he couldn't allow himself that luxury.

Pakhom struggled on, walking faster and finally running. As he ran, he worried that perhaps he had been too greedy. His shirt was soaked, and his throat was parched. His lungs were breathing like a blacksmith's bellows, and his heart was beating like a hammer. He was terrified at the thought that he had overextended himself and might die before he got back to the starting point.

Even though he feared death, he raced on. He feared even more than death the likelihood that the people would call him an idiot. Finally he was close enough to hear the Bashkir villagers cheering him on. He summoned his last ounce of strength and kept running. As he reached the hill, suddenly the skies became dark, and he groaned as he realized that the sun had set. And then, he realized that the sun had not set yet from the top of the hill; it only appeared to have set where he was in the valley.

He took a deep breath and struggled to get to the top of the hill. There he saw the elder sitting by the hat laughing. Pakhom was exhausted and fell forward as his legs gave way, and he grabbed the cap. The elder complimented him, telling him how well he had done. He had earned a lot of land.

Pakhom's worker tried to lift Pakhom to his feet, but Pakhom had died. So they picked up Pakhom's body, dug a grave, and buried him at the top of the hill. He was given six feet of land—which is exactly the amount of land Pakhom needed to be buried from head to toe.[4]

Wanting too much of anything can drive a person to an early grave. The Bashkirs knew that Pakhom's body had limits, but Pakhom's greed did not. Wanting too much and striving to attain can be deadly.

JESUS WASN'T IN A HURRY!

I have read through the Bible a number of times, and I have noticed that none of the Gospel writers ever refer to Jesus as being in a hurry. Rather, Jesus spoke against a "hurried and harried" mind-set. While Jesus was visiting in the home of Martha and Mary, the sisters of a man named Lazarus, Martha was busy preparing and serving food to Jesus and those who were traveling with him. Mary sat at the feet of Jesus, listening intently to what He was teaching. Martha became so frustrated that she was having to do all the kitchen work by herself that she said to Jesus, "Lord, don't You care that my sister has left me to serve alone? Therefore tell her to help me." Jesus replied, "Martha, Martha, you are worried and troubled about many things. But one thing is needed, and Mary has chosen that good part, which will not be taken away from her." (See Luke 10:38–41.)

Jesus knew that Martha was worried and troubled about far more than preparing and serving a meal. She very likely was a woman who felt as if the weight of the whole world was on her shoulders. She was like many people I encounter who seem to believe, "If I don't do it, it just won't get done."

Some things don't need to be done

The truth is, many things don't need to be done! At least they don't need to be done immediately, under pressure, or as a top priority. Many things in life are not only unnecessary; they are also counterproductive to the things we truly value: our family, our friendships, our health, and our own peace and joy.

Jesus said to Martha that her sister Mary had the right perspective on life: put Jesus first. It's a relationship with Him that is going to last forever and that is truly the most important thing in life. If that relationship is in right order, all other necessities of life will fall into place. He will enable us to use our time and energy in wise ways so that we get done all that we need to do in any given day, week, month, or year.

When we become too busy we lose our joy. People irritate us. We become frustrated, anxious, and critical. We complain too much. How can we break out of the trap of being too busy and practice keeping a healthy "margin" in our lives? One of the foremost ways is to become a better steward of our time. For most people, that means "organizing" their time and cutting out anything that is not in line with their top priorities.

CONTROL STRESS BY TAKING CONTROL OF YOUR TIME

Time is ultimately your most precious possession. How you spend your time determines, in many ways, how you will spend eternity. Many people stay stressed because they fail to organize their time. This is so simple to do, but some people don't know where to begin. I recommend these steps:

1. Purchase a calendar "organizer" or a PDA. Put key dates—such as birthdays and anniversaries, as well as deadlines and the dates of major events—onto the calendar.

2. Organize your desk at work and home—the place where you do your paperwork, pay bills, and so forth. The average office worker spends about thirty-six hours a week at his "desk" and another three hours a week sorting piles trying to locate which project to work on next![5]

3. Throw away junk mail daily.

4. Buy a filing cabinet or organizing system for storing important papers, articles, warranties,

documents, deeds, wills, and other valuable items that may currently be stuck in various drawers throughout the house.

5. Organize your kitchen. Countless hours are spent searching for items in the kitchen as one prepares meals. Stay organized, and meal preparation will be easier and faster.

6. Prevent nuisance phone calls by telemarketers. Get call block or caller ID, or simply unplug the phone during certain hours to avoid taking calls that are a total waste of your time.

7. Declare one day a week, or perhaps one weekend a month, as a media "fast" time. That means no computer, no television, no radio, no news, and no videos or DVDs. Use this time to connect with your family or friends. As a general rule, choose to cut back on your television-watching time. In the average American home, the television set is turned on for seven hours a day, and the average viewer watches between twenty and thirty-six hours of television a week.[6] Most of that viewing is a total waste of time! If you think you are watching television just for "escapism" or "fun," ask yourself what you are trying to escape from and why you are looking for "fun" on the media rather than being with people and creating your own "fun times."

8. Make the most of your "waiting" times. Everybody, even physicians, finds themselves in waiting rooms from time to time. It may be a doctor's office or a dentist's office, an appointment at the bank, or at the airport. Always have a book, magazine, tape, or piece of handwork available to fill this time with something positive and productive. "Shouldn't I just chill out and relax?" you may ask. These environments are not places of relaxation—you may as well make good use of

your time and do something productive! Taking a five- or ten-minute mini vacation in your mind is a good use of a "waiting" time, but most people find themselves waiting for longer periods. Have something positive to do.

9. Make a conscious and intentional decision to limit the amount of time you spend with negative, pessimistic people. They not only will sabotage your goals, but they will also drain energy from you. I call these people "energy vampires" or "energy leaches" because no matter what you do, they seem to make you "tired" by their endless whining, complaining, and bickering. Avoid this frustration by avoiding or limiting your time spent with such people.

10. Refuse to be distracted if you are focused on a work project. Turn on the answering machine or have somebody answer your calls. Close your door. Don't allow for interruptions. You can generally get more done in an hour of totally focused time without interruptions than in three hours of time that has only a few interruptions.

Individuals with type A personalities are prone to multitasking (doing more than one thing at a time). Focusing on just one thing at a time will take discipline. It requires doing fewer things. Stick with one task until it is finished, and then move on to the next.

11. Make a to-do list each evening before you go to bed. This way you don't need to continue to mull things over in your mind all night. You know the list is made and waiting for you in the morning. Once the list is made, refuse to think about it until morning! As part of your to-do list, set a specific time to exercise, have your daily devotional and prayer time, and eat your meals. Make sure you have a little "margin" for relaxation

and for emergencies or unavoidable interruption. Remain flexible, and do not let interruptions unnerve you.

12. Make dining an experience by tasting, smelling, and savoring every bite of food instead of wolfing it down. (This is the main reason why the French people have significantly fewer problems with obesity than Americans even though they eat small portions of rich desserts and pastries.) I recommend that you give yourself at least thirty minutes to connect with family members. Do not scold or reprimand children at mealtime. Also, avoid arguments and stressful topics at mealtime.

    Avoid eating on the run or as you drive your car. You need to be able to relax, chew every bite thirty times, and give your body's digestive system an opportunity to do its work. A great deal of stress can be eliminated if a person will simply use mealtimes as opportunities to relax, daydream a little, and rest.

I know some people who spend as much as two hours a day commuting to and from work. I recommend that these people listen to books on CD or tape, perhaps take an audio college course, learn a new language, or expand their awareness of classical music. Choose to be a good steward of your time, and as a part of your stewardship, build in a healthy margin that is totally unscheduled. This time is likely to fuel your creativity and energy, and defuse your stress level simultaneously.

13
_____

Sleep—God's "Stress Buster"

According to the International Labor Organization, Americans now work more hours in a year than any other people in an industrialized nation of the world. A very high percentage of Americans are burning the candle at both ends by staying up late and getting up early. Instead of working to live, many Americans are living to work.

More than a third of Americans—38 percent—say they are working fifty hours or more a week. The vast majority of these people say that working this much cuts into their "sleep time."[1] When a person cuts short his sleeping time, he may be adding more hours to a day, but he is probably subtracting hours from his life.

Many individuals routinely watch programs such as heart-pounding television programs and adrenaline-pumping ball games before going to bed—including fear-invoking nightly news that is often steeped with news about war, terrorist threats, a weak economy, and local crime.

Then, after getting "worked up" by television images, they go to bed in a heightened emotional state—generally speaking, a negative emotional state. They can't fall asleep readily, don't sleep soundly, awaken frequently, and usually don't feel fully rested when the alarm clock jolts them into starting a new day. Why? Stress hormones have flooded their body right before they retired for the night.

In the early 1900s, Americans got an average of nine hours of sleep a night. Today, the average American reports seven hours of sleep a night. The result is that we as a nation are sleeping fewer hours and with less restful sleep.

The cycle is a cortisol-related cycle: elevated cortisol levels cause insomnia, and insomnia and fatigue create stress, which causes more cortisol production. Cortisol is the stress hormone.

What reverses this cycle? Getting at least eight hours a night of restful, uninterrupted sleep will help bring cortisol levels back to normal. Let's focus first on how we can increase the quality of our sleep time.

RECOGNIZING OUR NEED FOR SLEEP

First and foremost we need to recognize that God designed our bodies to *need* sleep. We need this "down time" every night to restore, remove, and replace worn-out and dead cells in the body. We also need adequate sleep to give the brain an opportunity to "sort out" the information of the day in ways that are intricately designed by our Creator and are far too complex to begin to explain here. In extremely simplified terms, we need a sufficient break from sensory input in order to categorize and store information for use as "memories" that guide future behavior.

As part of recognizing that we need sleep, we must come to value sleep. A majority of Americans, however, don't seem to value sleep enough to get the sleep they need. A National Sleep Foundation poll revealed that the majority of Americans—63 percent—do not get eight hours of sleep a night, and nearly a third of Americans—31 percent—get fewer than seven hours of sleep a night.[2] An estimated sixty million Americans suffer from insomnia and other sleep disorders. About 40 percent of these people link stress or emotional factors to their insomnia. Nearly two-thirds of Americans—62 percent—experience a sleep problem a few nights a week or more. As a result, this same percentage of the population reports "daytime drowsiness."[3]

A good night's sleep is not a luxury. It is a necessity for health. Several things that are highly beneficial to the human body happen during sleep:

1.   *Important hormones are secreted during sleep.* Growth hormone is one of these hormones secreted while a person sleeps. This is a very important hormone for the growth of children, but it is also important in regulating muscle mass and controlling fat in adults. As men and women age, growth hormone production decreases. A lack of sleep further lowers secretion of growth hormone. This could be one of the reasons approximately two-thirds of Americans are overweight or obese. In addition, the hormone leptin is also secreted during sleep. This hormone has a direct influence on appetite and weight control—it is the hormone that tells the body when it should feel "full." A person who doesn't have this regulating hormone in his body is likely to have difficulty curbing appetite and is prone to overeating at any given meal.

2.   *Adequate sleep slows the aging process and the visible effects associated with aging.* We have all heard the term "beauty rest." It's true! Sleep slows the aging process, and some say it is the most important "secret" for averting wrinkles. How well a person sleeps is one of the most important predictors of how long a person will live.

3.   *Sleep boosts the immune system.* We all know that when a person is sick, sleep is often the most therapeutic remedy. There is good reason for this.

     Individuals who sleep nine hours a night instead of seven hours have greater than normal "natural killer cell" activity. Natural killer cells destroy viruses, bacteria, and cancer cells.

4. *Adequate sleep lowers cortisol levels.* Elevated cortisol levels are associated with many diseases. Sufficient sleep helps reduce the levels of this stress hormone.

5. *Adequate sleep improves brain function.* Prolonged exposure of neurons (nerve cells) to high cortisol levels—which occur as a result of too little sleep and too much stress—decreases a person's ability to take up glucose, and in turn, the neurons shrink in size. The result can be impaired memory or memory loss.

    Elevated cortisol levels disrupt neurotransmitter balance in the brain—this can cause individuals to become more irritable and to be more prone to depression and anxiety.

Other consequences from a lack of sleep

A number of medical research studies have revealed what happens when a person doesn't get sufficient sleep. Here are just some of the negative situations and diseases associated with insufficient sleep:

- *An increased risk of developing type 2 diabetes.* One study published by the prestigious medical journal *Lancet* revealed that even in young healthy individuals, a sleep deficit of three to four hours a night over the course of a week affected the body's ability to process carbohydrates. Over time, this resulted in impaired glucose tolerance and insulin resistance, which is associated with a prediabetic state.[4]

- *Impairment of cognition and motor performance.* People who were awake for up to nineteen hours without sleep scored significantly worse on performance tests and tests of alertness skills than those with a blood alcohol level of .08, which is legally "drunk."[5]

• *Lowering of sex drive in both men and women.* Elevated cortisol from sleep deprivation blocks the normal response of the testicles to testosterone and causes a decrease in the production of hormonal precursors to testosterone. This is one of the reasons why young men in boot camp for the armed services generally have a lower sex drive.[6]

WHAT ELSE MIGHT CAUSE INSOMNIA?

Apart from stress and the resulting increase in cortisol levels, there are a number of other causes for insomnia. They include chronic pain (especially arthritis), chronic back pain, fibromyalgia, degenerative disc disease, and any other painful medical condition. Benign prostatic hypertrophy (BPH)—an enlarged prostate—can cause frequent trips to the bathroom at night, with resulting insomnia. Hot flashes as well as painful menstrual cramps can cause insomnia. So can heartburn from gastroesophageal reflux (which occurs when stomach acids flow up into the esophagus) and nighttime coughing.

Psychological problems, such as anxiety and depression, can cause insomnia. Individuals with anxiety usually have problems both getting to sleep and staying asleep, whereas patients with depression usually have trouble staying asleep. Depressed persons tend to wake up around two or three o'clock in the morning and find they are unable to fall back asleep.

The top seven conditions associated with insomnia in a recent sleep poll were depression, nighttime heartburn, diabetes, cancer, hypertension, heart disease, and arthritis.[7]

Medications can also cause insomnia, especially ones that contain caffeine. A number of headache medications, such as Excedrin, are high in caffeine. Decongestants, appetite suppressants, asthma medications (such as theophylline), prednisone, thyroid medications, estrogens, some pain relievers, some blood pressure medications, and certain antidepressants may all cause insomnia.

The impact of caffeine

Caffeine is an extremely common cause of insomnia. It is found in coffee, tea, many sodas, and chocolate. This stimulant increases the stress hormones adrenaline and cortisol. Caffeine can remain in the body for up to twenty hours. More than 80 percent of all Americans consume caffeine regularly, and the average American drinks about three cups of coffee a day. Below are some examples of products that contain caffeine and their caffeine content.[8]

CAFFEINE-CONTAINING BEVERAGES	
Quantity and Substance	**Amount of Caffeine**
8 ounces brewed coffee	135 mg
8 ounces instant coffee	95 mg
Starbucks coffee, grande (16 ounces)	550 mg
12 ounces Coca Cola	34.5 mg
12 ounces Mountain Dew	55.5 mg
8 ounces black tea	50 mg
8 ounces green tea	30 mg
2 Excedrin capsules	130 mg

"But," you may be saying, "I can drink caffeine and still go to sleep." That's true for some people. Other people can have severe insomnia from only a little caffeine. If you are suffering from insomnia and simply must have your morning coffee for a caffeine infusion, try to limit your coffee to one cup a day and drink it early in the morning, or at least before noon.

Nicotine and alcohol

Both nicotine and alcohol can interfere with sleep. Some people think alcohol helps a person fall asleep, but what they often don't recognize is that alcohol can disrupt the stages of sleep, causing a person to sleep lighter and to awaken feeling less refreshed. Nicotine from cigarette smoking is a stimulant that causes adrenaline to be released, which often causes insomnia.

Hypoglycemia

Excessive sugar and highly processed carbohydrates can also lead to insomnia. Many people consume too much sugar and highly processed foods at night, such as having a big bowl of ice cream or a piece of pie or cake before going to bed. Foods high in sugar and processed carbohydrates stimulate excessive insulin release from the pancreas. The result is a sugar "high" of energy. Later, however, blood sugar hits a "low." When blood sugar hits a low, it triggers the adrenal glands to produce more adrenaline and cortisol, which causes a person to awaken and stay awake.

Low-carb diets can result in your going to bed hungry—and this too can create a low-blood-sugar reaction. If you are having sleep interrupted because of excessive sugar or carb intake, or lack of carb intake, there's a simple solution: eat a light evening snack that is correctly balanced with proteins, carbohydrates, and fats. This snack will help stabilize blood sugar through the nighttime hours.

A person who has adrenal fatigue, with low salivary cortisol levels, will be more prone to low-blood-sugar symptoms, nightmares, anxiety attacks, and restless sleep between the hours of one and four o'clock in the morning.

UNDERSTANDING OUR CIRCADIAN RHYTHMS

Our bodies are hormonally designed to stay in sync with the cycles of nature. When the sun goes down and the sky turns dark, we have been designed by our Creator to go to bed and sleep! When the sun comes up and the sky turns light, we are to get up! This natural rhythm of the body linked to nature is called the "circadian rhythm."

Very few people, of course, go to bed when it becomes dark or get up when the sky turns light. We have tricked our bodies with light at night and draperies over windows during the day.

Biologically speaking, here is what happens. Melatonin is a hormone produced by the pineal gland that produces feelings of relaxation or "mellowness," even to the point of being drowsy and sleepy.

The amount of light that reaches the eyes determines the amount of melatonin produced by the pineal gland. The greater the light, the less production of melatonin. This is why some people feel far more alert and energetic on sunny days and more lethargic on cloudy days—the less light, the greater the "mellowing out" amount of melatonin released into their bodies. In the evening, the pineal gland gradually starts secreting more and more melatonin. Melatonin is secreted throughout the night, but when light begins to hit the eyes in the morning, melatonin production decreases dramatically, and a person awakens.

Simply looking at a bright computer screen or watching television can prevent melatonin from rising to levels that induce sleep. I recommend that if you want to induce natural sleep, you put dimmer switches on some of the main lights in your home and keep those lights dimmed during the evening hours. Consider installing room-darkening curtains to make your bedroom nice and dark.

When a person keeps a regular schedule of going to bed and awakening at the same time every day, the body's internal clock becomes "set." Having regular mealtimes and regular exercise times also impacts this setting of a person's body clock. The more "set" a person's body clock, the greater the likelihood the person will be able to get to sleep and stay asleep all night.

WHAT ABOUT EXERCISE AND SLEEP?

Aerobic exercise, such as brisk walking, is one of the best things a person can do to improve the quality of his or her sleep. Regular aerobic exercise has been shown repeatedly to help people fall asleep faster and sleep longer and sounder. Those who exercise regularly spend a greater amount of sleep time in stage 3 and stage 4, which are the most restorative stages of sleep.

Those who exercise within three hours of going to sleep, however, may actually be interfering with sleep by temporarily raising the levels of stress hormones.

FACTORS THAT AID SLEEP

There are a number of things that a person can do to aid sleep; here are a few.

Comfortable temperature

Keep your bedroom at a temperature that is comfortable for you. Many people prefer a ceiling fan to improve airflow. You should feel as if the room is "comfortable"—neither too hot, too cold, or too humid. If your feet get cold, wear warm socks rather than increase the temperature of the entire room. Some of the best sleep I have ever had has been in the mountains during winter months in which I slept with an open window under a warm comforter. I slept soundly even though the outside temperature was thirty to forty degrees Fahrenheit.

A good mattress

If you are going to spend a third of your life asleep, do so on a good mattress! The mattress on your bed is the most important piece of furniture you own when it comes to health.

A mattress that is too firm does not adequately allow for the right alignment of the spine. A mattress that is too soft will allow the spine to sag and may cause a backache. When you shop for a mattress, don't just lie on your back; also lie on your side and your stomach. Slide your hand, palm down, between the mattress and the small of your back as you try lying on your back. If you are able to get your entire hand through the small of your back, the mattress is too hard. If while lying flat on the bed the base of the spine is lower than your heels, the mattress is too soft.

A good pillow

If your pillow is too hard, too soft, too large, or too small, your quality of sleep is likely to be affected. Select the right pillow for you. A pillow should be soft enough to conform to the contours of your head and neck, but also thick enough to support the head and neck in a neutral position.

Coping with snoring

Snoring can be a sign of sleep apnea, which may require a medical evaluation. Those who snore often have anatomical differences, such as an obstructed nasal passage, an elongation of the uvula (the soft tissue that hangs down the back of the throat), or a sagging soft palate. Enlarged tonsils or adenoids can also cause snoring, as can poor muscle tone in the tongue and throat. Most snorers tend to be overweight. They typically have increased girth of their neck and poor muscle tone of their tongue and throat. Simply losing weight and exercising may be their best cure for snoring. A weight loss of only ten to fifteen pounds can make a big difference.

Snoring can also be helped if a person avoids using alcohol, muscle relaxants, tranquilizers, or sleep medications. These tend to relax the muscles of the throat and can worsen snoring. Snorers who have nasal congestion might try products such as Breathe Right strips or nasal steroids such as Flonase or Nasonex to open nasal passages.

Changing positions while sleeping can also help. People who sleep on their sides or stomachs snore less. There are special throat sprays and dental appliances, as well as "snore alarms," that can help.

To help a spouse who doesn't snore, I often recommend a sound generator or soft earplugs.

SLEEPING PILLS OR NATURAL REMEDIES?

Most people don't seem to know this important fact: sleeping pills are approved by the FDA for treating insomnia, but they should only be used for two weeks or less. They have never been approved for *perpetual* use over long periods of time. Unfortunately, most patients become addicted to sleeping pills and find they are unable to sleep well without them. Sleeping pills tend to promote tolerance and dependency.

I recommend that a person try to find the root cause of the insomnia—such as excessive stress, depression, anxiety, or chronic pain—rather than resort to medication. For information on natural treatments to treat insomnia, please refer to my book *The Bible Cure for Sleep Disorders.*

TRUSTING IN GOD AND MEDITATING ON SCRIPTURE

One night Jesus and His disciples got into a boat to cross the Sea of Galilee—actually a lake about nine miles wide—and as they sailed, Jesus fell fast asleep. A great windstorm came up on the lake, and the seas were so rough that the boat in which they were sailing began to take on water. All aboard were in danger of drowning should the boat capsize. Jesus remained asleep, even though the rocking of the boat must have been violent and rain was pouring down. The disciples, in fear, finally awakened Jesus by crying out to Him. (See Luke 8:22–24.)

Jesus very likely was in stage 4 sleep, which is the most refreshing and rejuvenating stage. The Bible tells us about the Lord, "You will keep him in perfect peace, whose mind is stayed on You, because he trusts in You" (Isa. 26:3). I have no doubt

Jesus was able to sleep so soundly because He completely trusted in His heavenly Father and had His mind stayed upon the Father. His "perfect peace" also meant perfect sleep!

So many people today are far from experiencing "perfect peace" because they do not trust God and their minds are not fixed on Him and His ability to protect them, provide for them, and guide them into every good path. They spend their days and nights worrying about the past or fretting about the future.

This passage tells us that perfect peace comes as we trust God and keep our minds "stayed" on Him. How can we do that? I believe one of the best ways is to memorize entire chapters of Scripture, and then to meditate on these if and when we awaken in the night. A person who is reciting and meditating on Scripture is not a person who can think simultaneously about problems or worries.

The Bible says that the weapons of spiritual warfare are not carnal, but mighty in God. I believe these weapons are, first and foremost, our identity in Christ Jesus and the Word of God. (See Ephesians 6:11–18.) These weapons are "for pulling down strongholds, casting down arguments and every high thing that exalts itself against the knowledge of God, bringing every thought into captivity to the obedience of Christ" (2 Cor. 10:4–5).

To "pull down" a stronghold means to take authority over anything that has gripped the mind with a strong hold. To "cast down" arguments and thoughts does not mean that a person stops thinking about problems and worrisome situations simply because he tries to stop thinking about them. It means that the person actively chooses to think about something other than the problem or worrisome situation. The only way to stop thinking about something is to think about something else. The best thing a person can think about is God's Word, which reveals to us the loving, infinite, merciful, protecting, providing, safeguarding nature of our heavenly Father.

DON'T JUST CARRY AN EMOTIONAL LOAD—
CARRY IT TO GOD!

Trusting God means that we carry all of our emotional burdens to God...and lay them at His feet. We may be carrying a heavy load of responsibility, which includes *feeling* responsible for certain people and tasks. We are wise if we carry that load some-where and to someone—the only One truly capable of helping us to carry our burdens all the time in every situation of life is our heavenly Father. Jesus said, "Come to Me, all you who labor and are heavy laden, and I will give you rest" (Matt. 11:28).

God's rest is a vital factor in walking out God's divine health for your body, mind, and emotions.

OBEYING GOD'S LAW OF REST

In addition to trusting God with our whole heart, we also must obey God's law of rest. We need to keep the Sabbath. God's Word strongly admonishes us to set aside a day each week to rest and worship God. The Bible commands:

- "Remember the Sabbath day, to keep it holy. Six days you shall labor and do all your work, but the seventh day is the Sabbath of the LORD your God. In it you shall do no work: you, nor your son, nor your daughter, nor your male servant, nor your female servant, nor your cattle, nor your stranger who is within your gates. For in six days the LORD made the heavens and the earth, the sea, and all that is in them, and rested the seventh day. Therefore the LORD blessed the Sabbath day and hal-lowed it" (Exod. 20:8–11).

- "Six years you shall sow your land and gather in its produce, but the seventh year you shall let it rest and lie fallow, that the poor of your people may eat; and what they leave, the beasts of the field may eat. In like manner you shall do with your vineyard and your olive grove. Six days you shall do your work, and on the seventh day you shall rest, that your ox and your donkey may rest, and the son of your female servant and the stranger may be refreshed" (Exod. 23:10–12).

- "Work shall be done for six days, but the seventh is the Sabbath of rest, holy to the LORD. Whoever does any work on the Sabbath day, he shall surely be put to death. Therefore the children of Israel shall keep the Sabbath, to observe the Sabbath throughout their generations as a perpetual covenant. It is a sign between Me and the children of Israel forever; for in six days the LORD made the heavens and the earth, and on the seventh day He rested and was refreshed" (Exod. 31:15–17).

Some people believe these laws of rest were only for Old Testament times, but let me point out in the last passage cited above, God says His covenant about the Sabbath is a *perpetual covenant*, one that is to be observed throughout the generations.

Certainly as Christians we are not subject to all the laws of the Old Testament. Jesus purchased for us the fulfillment of all the laws related to sin and sacrifice. Nevertheless, rest remains a spiritual principle that we cannot disregard when it comes to our health and well-being. We may not be "put to death" by others if we fail to infuse enough rest into our lives, but we may very well be putting ourselves to an earlier death by failing to trust God and follow His commands about resting. Hebrews 4:9 says very clearly and simply, "There remains therefore a rest for the people of God." Throw off stress, and rest, knowing that God is taking care of you and He is in control.

14

A Diet to Reduce Stress

John was a thirty-five-year-old junior executive for a major corporation. He came to see me for a complete physical examination required by his employers. At the time he came, he had not been to see a physician in more than ten years, and he believed that his physical exam would be normal. In the last decade, however, John had gained approximately fifty pounds. He reasoned that this gain wasn't all that bad—only five pounds a year. Blood tests showed that his blood triglycerides and cholesterol were elevated, his blood sugar was elevated into the prediabetic range, and his good cholesterol number was very low. Furthermore, he had high blood pressure. John was suffering from Syndrome X, which is a cluster of symptoms including insulin resistance, hypertension, elevated cholesterol, and abdominal fat. Individuals with Syndrome X are very prone to developing diabetes and heart disease.

Syndrome X has become extremely common in our nation. One study has concluded that as many as one in every two adults has this syndrome. That's an epidemic! Most people, however, don't even know they are in danger of serious disease.

The most common causes of obesity and the other symptoms related to Syndrome X are very simple: a diet high in sugar and refined carbohydrates, a lack of exercise, and chronic stress.

FOODS THAT BAIT THE CORTISOL TRAP

When cortisol levels are raised—as a result of a mental or physical stress reaction—a person craves sugar as well as carbohydrate-rich foods, such as breads, pasta, potatoes, corn chips, crackers, and so forth. These foods calm the emotions temporarily by increasing blood sugar levels and serotonin levels in the brain. Two to three hours after eating these foods, however, a person's insulin level skyrockets, causing blood sugar to drop. If insulin levels remain elevated, the body continues to store fat. Elevated insulin prevents the body from burning stored fat for energy. In other words, chronically elevated insulin levels from eating excessive amounts of sugar or carbohydrates on a frequent basis literally program the body to be in a fat storage mode and unable to burn stored fat for energy.

Most obese people can't break out of this cycle because they are constantly craving sugars and carbohydrates throughout the day, and they mindlessly seek to satisfy those cravings with readily available "snack" foods.

The average person can store about 300 to 400 grams of carbohydrates in the muscles and about 90 grams in the liver. The stored carbohydrates are actually a form of glucose called glycogen. Once these two major storehouses are filled, any excess carbohydrates are converted into fat and stored in fatty tissues.

Hypoglycemia raises cortisol levels.

In the aftermath of a person eating a doughnut or drinking a soft drink, blood sugar rises, and the pancreas responds by secreting insulin to lower the sugar level. If too much insulin is secreted and the blood sugar level drops too low, a person develops hypoglycemia. This is potentially dangerous to health because the brain needs adequate glucose (blood sugar) to function normally. If the brain doesn't get the glucose it needs, it sends out warning signals that include carbohydrate cravings, extreme hunger, mood swings, fatigue, and problems concentrating. These signals cause individuals to reach for something sweet or a highly processed carbohydrate such as chips or crackers as a "quick energy fix" in order to raise blood sugar levels to normal.

The brain also sends a signal to the adrenal glands to increase cortisol levels. Elevated cortisol causes the release of stored sugar or glycogen from the liver and muscles. Muscle cells may begin to break down their proteins to amino acids to eventually convert them into sugar. The net effect is that blood sugar levels rise again. Elevated cortisol may stimulate the appetite by causing neurotransmitter imbalances, affecting levels of the neurotransmitters serotonin and dopamine. These imbalances may cause cravings for sugars and carbohydrates; low dopamine and serotonin levels are also linked to depression. With the eating of sugars and carbohydrates, blood sugars rise, insulin production soars, blood sugar levels may plunge, and the entire cycle is repeated.

Several major research studies have demonstrated that excessive stress, obesity, and elevated cortisol go hand in hand.[1]

A number of years ago I met a man from a small town in the Northwest who said that his town actually passed a city ordinance to ban policemen from stopping at doughnut shops while on duty. People in the community were advised to report officers who were parked in front of a doughnut shop. What was the reason for this crackdown? The policemen were treating their fatigue and the frustrations of their job with sugar and coffee, and the result was an overall increase in obesity and decrease in physical activity on the part of the policemen, which tended to create a less energetic and less capable police force. The policemen were also less alert while on the job as the result of periodic "sugar lows."

Refusing the ever-available "snack"

America is on a sugar and highly processed carbohydrate merry-go-round, fueled by advertising from the fast-food and processed-food industries. Fast foods and processed foods are generally high in sugar or highly processed refined carbohydrates, salt, food additives, and unhealthy fats. The average American consumes 150 pounds of sugar a year! The Center for Science in the Public Interest, a consumer organization, has described soft drinks as "liquid candy." The processed food industry actually hires brilliant chemists to create the most appealing taste, smell, texture, and visual appeal for their processed food items, and then they hire psychologists to consult on the advertising so that the consumer is unable to eat just one. The result is something of an addiction to foods that raise our insulin levels, increase cortisol levels, and cause an imbalance in neurotransmitters. We literally are craving foods that are destroying our health.

In addition to the blood-sugar-insulin problems, we have an epidemic of obesity in our nation. Two-thirds of Americans are either overweight or obese.

Obesity is directly linked to hypertension (high blood pressure) and heart disease. One out of four adult Americans has hypertension.

Excess weight also contributes to inflammation in the body since fat cells secrete chemicals including C-reactive protein and interleukin-6, both of which promote inflammation. Inflammation causes the pain of arthritis and underlies heart disease, many forms of cancer, and Alzheimer's disease.

Caffeine contributes to the negative cycle.

Countless American adults are addicted to caffeine. Coffee, tea, and soda are staples to the American diet. I have heard of people refusing to move to another town because it didn't have a Starbucks coffee shop. A Starbucks "card" for the purchasing of coffee is one of the hottest gift items on the market today.

It takes only about 200 mg of caffeine—equivalent to one and one-half to two cups of coffee—to raise blood levels of cortisol by 30 percent within one hour. A Starbucks coffee, grande, has 550 mg of caffeine; imagine what that is doing to a person's cortisol level!

Caffeine is not the only stimulant, of course, that raises cortisol. A number of stimulants used to promote weight loss, increase energy, relieve pain, and act as a decongestant also elevate cortisol. Stimulants such as ephedra, which includes ephedrine and pseudoephedrine, can be found in decongestants. The herb ma huang, used in many dietary supplements or weight-loss supplements, is a strong stimulant. Guarana is an herbal form of caffeine commonly used in supplements to increase energy.

Yohimbe is commonly promoted as a natural way to increase testosterone and is used by weight lifters and bodybuilders to build muscle and lose fat. Yohimbe supplements can also raise blood pressure and cause heart palpitations, headaches, anxiety, and even hallucinations. This supplement raises cortisol levels.

The stimulant herbs are even more potent than caffeine in elevating cortisol. These stimulant herbs can stimulate the adrenal glands to secrete both adrenaline and cortisol. With continued use, the very supplements that a person is using to lose weight can in fact cause weight gain in the truncal area and a loss of muscle mass in the arms and legs. Adverse side effects of these herbal supplements include insomnia, irritability, headaches, elevated blood pressure, heart palpitations, and even arrhythmias (abnormal heart rhythm).

I recently went on a cruise, and the ship had to make an emergency stop at an island not on our itinerary because a fifty-year-old man had taken a weight-loss supplement that contained ephedra. He had developed a dangerous arrhythmia (abnormal rhythm of his heart), and the situation could have been fatal. Fortunately, physicians were able to stabilize him and transfer him to the island safely.

I strongly recommend that you eliminate stimulant herbs such as ephedra and that you begin to decrease your consumption of caffeine or eliminate caffeinated beverages completely. If you are drinking a few cups of coffee a day and stop suddenly, you may experience a caffeine-withdrawal headache. So, take it slowly, and gradually wean yourself off caffeine.

THE IMPORTANCE OF THE RIGHT BREAKFAST

When a person awakens in the morning, his blood sugar is generally low because he hasn't eaten for eight to twelve hours. What a person eats for breakfast is extremely important. The typical American breakfast consists of coffee and a bagel or doughnut. Or it may be a glass of juice with a bowl of cereal or pancakes, waffles, pastry, or toast. These high-sugar, high-carb foods generally lead to hypoglycemia. They are precisely the *wrong* foods to eat!

The bread and white-flour items I listed above are all foods that convert quickly into sugar. Juice is very high in sugar.

Orange, grape, and apple juices are all high in fructose, a fruit sugar. Grapefruit juice and cranberry juice are better choices, but even then, I recommend only 4 ounces of juice or less. It is far better to choose whole fruits. The whole fruit is less likely to raise insulin levels.

Many people skip breakfast and eat a small lunch, then have a large dinner in the evening. I find this is very common among my patients, and especially among my stressed-out and overweight patients.

If you skip breakfast, you will have fasted (gone without food) for twelve to sixteen or more hours by the time you eat lunch. You probably have put your body into a temporary hypoglycemic state by that time. Every time you do this, your adrenals are stimulated to produce more cortisol and your cravings for sugar and carbohydrates will increase. By the time a person reaches the dinner hour, that person will most likely have experienced many episodes of "hypoglycemia" during the day since they likely have snacked on sugar and highly processed carbohydrate foods. Their insulin levels are usually elevated, and they are in "fat-storage" mode.

While in this fat-storage mode, they eat a large dinner with bread, meat, a vegetable, a starch, and a dessert! They go to bed a couple of hours later. The elevated insulin tells the body to store the sugars and carbohydrates as glycogen in the liver and muscles, and the excess carb and sugar calories as fat. So the person awakens the next morning having "stored" all that excess food. And the process begins all over again.

STAYING OFF THE PATH THAT LEADS TO DIABETES

A prolonged cycle of eating excessive amounts of sugar and high-glycemic carbohydrates can cause the body to become resistant to its own insulin. The cells of the liver and muscles have simply been exposed to too much insulin for too long a period. The liver begins to convert excess blood sugar into fat to be stored in fatty tissues. Syndrome X develops, and the person is predisposed to developing type 2 diabetes.

THE BEST WAY TO EAT: THE RIGHT FOODS IN BALANCE

How then should a person eat? A person ideally should eat mainly low-glycemic carbohydrates balanced with healthy fats and lean, free-range, or organic protein foods. A person should "graze" throughout the day, eating three well-balanced meals and two to three smaller and well-balanced snacks—one between breakfast and lunch, one between lunch and dinner, and sometimes a bedtime snack.

For years I have told my patients to eat breakfast like a king, lunch like a prince, and dinner like a pauper. The most important meal of the day is breakfast. By choosing the right foods in proper balance at breakfast, as well as other meals, a person can greatly lower his or her insulin and cortisol levels to normal and greatly assist any weight-loss plan.

THE RIGHT KINDS OF PROTEIN

A simple way to calculate your protein requirement is to take your weight in pounds and divide it by two. That is the amount of protein a person should have per day in grams. As an example, if a person weights 170 pounds, he needs 85 grams of protein a day.

If you are morbidly obese, your protein requirement should be based on your lean muscle weight and not on your total body weight. For obese patients I use a special instrument designed to measure lean body mass and percent body fat.

One ounce of chicken, turkey, beef, pork, lamb, or venison has approximately 7 grams of protein. A 4-ounce portion, therefore, has 28 grams of protein. One cup of yogurt, 1 cup of skim milk, and one egg each have about 7 grams of protein. Fish generally has 4.5 grams of protein per ounce.

Men generally need no more than 4 to 5 ounces of protein per meal, and women 3 to 4 ounces per meal. Men can generally eat 5 to 8 ounces of fish at a meal, and women 4 to 6 ounces.

Choose the leanest piece of meat you can, with little or no marbling, and trim off any visible fat. It is important to peel off the skin and cut away any visible fat from chicken and poultry. Choose white meat rather than dark meat. Grill, bake, or broil your meats rather than frying them. If you grill your food, be sure to avoid charred meats since they contain a chemical called benzopyrene, which is carcinogenic (cancer causing). I strongly advise against deep-frying any food since these fats create a tremendous amount of free radicals in the body. Free radicals are highly reactive molecules that damage cells and tissues. They are produced in the body and have an unpaired electron in their outer field. If you must fry a food, lightly stir-fry it at the lowest temperature possible, with a little organic butter or cold-pressed macadamia nut oil. Macadamia nut oil is better than olive oil for frying since its smoke point is greater than four hundred degrees Fahrenheit, whereas olive oil's smoke point is only about two hundred degrees Fahrenheit. You can find cold-pressed macadamia nut oil at most health food stores.

I also recommend that you limit or avoid highly processed meats such as hot dogs, bologna, sausage, cold cuts, ham, bacon, and most packaged luncheon meats. They are generally very high in sodium content, very high in fat, and usually have nitrites and nitrates added. Nitrites and nitrates are converted in the digestive tract to nitrosamines, which are associated with an increased risk of cancer.

Limit foods that contain significant amounts of arachidonic acid. These include beef, pork, lamb, high-fat dairy products, egg yolks, shrimp, lobster, clams, as well as most shellfish. Omega-6 oils such as corn, safflower, sunflower, peanut, cottonseed, and soybean oil are also converted to arachidonic acid. Arachidonic acid is converted in the body into a variety of very powerful inflammation-causing compounds known as eicosanoids, including prostaglandin E2. Prostaglandin E2 is an extremely inflammatory substance. Excessive inflammation can lead to numerous diseases.

Inflammation is generally associated with pain, swelling, redness, and warmth. Common inflammatory diseases include osteoarthritis, rheumatoid arthritis, and chronic tendonitis and bursitis. Inflammation is also a major factor in coronary artery disease, most cancers, Alzheimer's disease, as well as psoriasis and eczema, Crohn's disease, and ulcerative colitis. Inflammation generally raises cortisol levels since it stresses the body.

THE RIGHT KINDS OF CARBOHYDRATES

Not all carbohydrates are bad—a person needs a sufficient quantity of "good" carbohydrates. Proteins, fats, and carbohydrates need to be in the right balance. Understanding which carbohydrates have a favorable glycemic index is a key to preventing hypoglycemia and keeping insulin and cortisol levels normal.

High-glycemic carbohydrates—which are rapidly converted to sugar—may cause an insulin spike. A large quantity of medium glycemic index carbohydrates can also cause a spike. It is best to stick to low glycemic index foods and to greatly curtail those that are high or even moderately high glycemic.

Low-glycemic carbohydrates include most green vegetables such as lettuce, zucchini, squash, spinach, cabbage, and so on. It also includes low-glycemic fruits such as berries, kiwi, Granny Smith apples, and grapefruit. Whole grains rich in soluble fiber are also low glycemic and include old-fashioned oatmeal (not instant), oat bran, and other high-fiber foods.

High-glycemic carbohydrates include starches and most processed grains (such as white breads, processed pastas, and white rice), starchy vegetables (such as potatoes and corn), and high-glycemic fruits (such as dried fruits). For more information on this topic, refer to *The Bible Cure for Weight Loss and Muscle Gain*.

CHOOSE HEALTHY FATS

Fats are extremely important for good health. They help form cell membranes and regulate what enters and exits the cells. They are a critical part of most body tissues. More than 60 percent of the dry weight of the brain is fat!

Fat forms the myelin sheath in nerve cells, which is similar to electrical wire insulation. Fat is required for the synapses or connections between the nerves, which allow information to be transmitted. Fat forms the building blocks for the body's pro- and anti-inflammatory compounds.

The important thing about dietary fat is this: not all fats are created equal! Healthy fats include the omega-3 and omega-9 fats.

Omega-3 fats supply the building blocks for powerful anti-inflammatory compounds in the body. Alpha-linolenic acid is a powerful omega-3 fat that is found in flaxseed and dark green leafy vegetables. The most potent omega-3 fat is eicosapentaenoic acid (EPA), which is found in cold-water fish and fish oils (which may be taken as supplements in capsule form). This omega-3 fat assists in the body's production of inflammation-suppressing substances. High-quality fish oil has been linked to significant reduction of inflammation in the body.[2]

Fish with the highest concentrations of omega-3 oils are mackerel, Pacific herring, king salmon, Atlantic salmon, anchovies, and lake trout. Wild salmon contains higher omega-3 fat than farm-raised salmon.

Monounsaturated fats, which are the omega-9 fats, have no direct effect on insulin or inflammation, but they are still considered very healthy fats. These fats include olive oil (extra-virgin is preferred), avocado, and nut oils—including almond and macadamia nut. I personally enjoy extra-virgin olive oil and balsamic vinegar as a salad dressing. I recommend that you use almond butter in place of peanut butter for omega-9 benefit.

Use these omega-9 fats in moderation, and they will help create the correct fuel mixture to lower both insulin and cortisol levels.

AVOID CERTAIN FOOD ADDITIVES

There are two main food additives that are extremely popular but also potentially dangerous. Both may elevate cortisol levels. They are aspartame and MSG.

Aspartame

Aspartame is made of three components: methanol, aspartic acid, and phenylalanine. Methanol is also known as "wood alcohol," and it is 10 percent of what is released from aspartame when this substance is broken down in the human digestive tract. In the body, methanol is converted to formaldehyde—yes, embalming fluid—and formic acid. Methanol and formaldehyde in high amounts can cause blindness, eye damage, or neurological damage.

When broken down in the digestive tract, 40 percent of what is produced from aspartame is aspartic acid. This is known in scientific and medical circles as an excitatory amino acid and also as an excitotoxin. An excitotoxin is a substance that over-stimulates or excites nerve cells and may cause permanent damage to the nervous system. Aspartic acid has been linked to brain abnormalities, including brain tumors in research animals.[3]

Side effects of aspartame include headaches, confusion, depression, dizziness, convulsions, nausea, diarrhea, and shortness of breath.

MSG

Monosodium glutamate (MSG) has become controversial in the past thirty years as reports of adverse reactions have come to light. Research related to the role of glutamates—a group of chemicals that includes MSG—has raised serious questions about the chemical's safety. Even so, MSG continues to be used in a widespread manner as a flavor enhancer. It is commonly used in Asian restaurants and in many processed foods. It is present in hydrolyzed vegetable protein and in autolyzed yeast extract. It is also found in many salad dressings, gravy mixes, soups, croutons, and batters for breaded foods.

The amino acid in MSG acts as an excitotoxin in the brain— it can overstimulate nerve cells to the point of nerve death. MSG stimulates the pancreas to increase its output of insulin just minutes after eating foods that contain MSG. This usually causes a drop in blood sugar to the point that a person may feel both tired and hungry soon after eating foods with MSG.[4]

Much more research needs to be done when it comes to aspartame and MSG. Hundreds of complaints have been filed with the FDA Center for Food Safety and Applied Nutrition since these products were introduced to the marketplace. What we presently know puts these chemicals on my "high risk" list. I strongly suggest that you avoid consuming products that have them, especially if you are planning to dine at an Asian restaurant.

CHOOSE THE RIGHT FUELS FOR THE BEST MILEAGE
AND BEST PERFORMANCE

I drive a Hummer, and it uses regular unleaded gas. When I use the right fuel, it runs great. I also have a Harley Davidson truck, which has a high-performance engine and requires premium unleaded gasoline. When I first purchased this truck, I mistakenly put in regular unleaded gas instead of premium unleaded. The truck didn't run well at all. It sputtered, stalled, and rattled. Then I realized that I hadn't used the correct fuel. When I switched, I had no problems with the truck. Not only did the vehicle run better, but also I got the miles per gallon I had hoped for.

The fuel mixture that you put in your body is critically important for preventing inflammation and hypoglycemia, and for lowering insulin and cortisol. Not only do you need to choose the best forms of protein, carbohydrates, and fats, but you also need to choose the proper ratio and balance of proteins to carbohydrates to fats. The "mix" is critically important.

I have a weed trimmer that uses a mix of gasoline and oil. If I put too much oil in the mixture, the machine smokes. If I don't put in enough oil, I can destroy the machine. If machines are this sensitive to fuel mixture, our bodies are even more so!

A WORD ABOUT FOOD ALLERGIES AND FOOD SENSITIVITIES

I treat many patients with chronic disease, and through the years, I have been surprised at how many of these individuals have food allergies or food sensitivities that create tremendous stress in their bodies overall. Generally I find that the very food they crave the most is usually the food to which they are allergic or have a sensitivity.

As I have shared with you earlier in this book, I once had severe psoriasis, and I also had a strong craving for tomatoes, salsa, and potatoes at that time. I thought my body needed these foods, so I had potatoes at breakfast and again at dinner. I enjoyed salsa or tomatoes at lunch nearly every day. As my psoriasis got worse, I had a food allergy test. It revealed that I was very sensitive to nightshades. Nightshades are a group of foods that include potatoes, tomatoes, and peppers! The foods I craved were the foods that fueled my disease. When I eliminated these foods from my diet, the psoriasis began to clear up.

Many times a food allergy or sensitivity can go undetected for many years. If you suspect that you might have a food allergy or sensitivity—or if you seem to have a strong craving for a particular food—I recommend that you have a food allergy test. The one I prefer is the ELISA/ACT test, which identifies all three pathways related to delayed allergy/hypersensitivity reactions. Many people don't realize they are reacting to specific substances because the onset of symptoms is often delayed. This test measures sensitivity to more than three hundred foods, food additives and preservatives, environmental chemicals and toxic minerals, molds, medications, herbs, and dander. See Appendix D for more information on ELISA/ACT.

CHANGE YOUR DIET AND CHANGE YOUR STRESS LEVEL!

It isn't enough to change your perceptions, reactions, and ability to cope with stress. Often you need to change your diet! Eat three small meals, have two to three high-quality snacks a day, and by all means, eat a nutritious breakfast. Limit high glycemic foods, and choose a mix of healthy proteins, carbohydrates (with an emphasis on low-glycemic vegetables, fruits, and whole grains), and healthy fats. Avoid foods that trigger inflammation, avoid aspartame and MSG, and identify any food allergies or sensitivities so that you can avoid these items.

In following these simple principles, you will not only feel better physically and have a greater peace of mind, but you will also be doing a great deal to prevent disease and painful ailments. By preventing hypoglycemic reactions, you will lower your cortisol levels—and therefore lower your stress!

15
_____

Nutrients for Coping With Stress

The American Medical Association recently issued an advisory recommending that every adult take a multivitamin on a daily basis.[1] While this may be a step in the right direction, the AMA recommendation falls far short of what is actually required by the human body.

There are thirteen vitamins: The four fat-soluble vitamins are vitamins A, D, E, and K. The water-soluble vitamins are vitamin C and eight B vitamins (B_1, B_2, niacin, B_6, folic acid, B_{12}, pantothenic acid, and biotin). The ideal way to get these vitamins into our bodies is through the food we eat. Unfortunately, many of the essential vitamins are destroyed by the way we store, cook, and process our food. To make sure a person gets an adequate amount of these essential vitamins, they need to take them in supplement form—and usually as individual or combined supplements.

The human body also needs twenty-two essential minerals on a daily basis. Many people are deficient in several of these minerals. There are seven macro-minerals (which are the major minerals): calcium, phosphorus, sodium, chloride, magnesium, potassium, and sulfur. People usually get plenty of phosphorus, sodium, chloride, potassium, and sulfur, but many people do not get enough calcium or magnesium. In addition, we need fifteen trace minerals: boron, chromium, cobalt, copper, fluoride, iodine, iron, manganese, molybdenum, nickel, selenium, silicon, tin, vanadium, and zinc.

Minerals tend to make their way into food through mineral-rich soil in which foods are grown. Unfortunately, much of the soil in our nation has been depleted or is lacking in the minerals that our ancestors took for granted. The vast majority of Americans also need to take minerals in supplement form.

Stress and high cortisol levels also cause depletion of certain nutrients in the body. People who are under excessive stress nearly always need to have an increase in the B vitamins, vitamin C, magnesium, zinc, copper, chromium, selenium, and vitamin E.

THE B VITAMINS: KEY TO STRESS RELIEF

For many years the B vitamins have been known as the "stress relief" vitamins. The B vitamins provide the greatest benefit when they are supplemented together, such as a balanced B "complex." Some B vitamins actually require other B vitamins for activation. The B vitamins are especially important for elderly individuals since B vitamins are not absorbed as well as a person ages. The B vitamins are associated primarily with the brain and nervous system function.

Thiamin (B₁)

Thiamin helps in nervous system function and is needed for the release of energy from carbohydrates. Deficiency of B_1 creates a condition known as beriberi, and the symptoms include confusion, loss of balance, weakness, and heart damage. A severe deficiency leads to disturbances in the musculoskeletal as well as the nervous system. A large percentage of elderly people are deficient in this vitamin.[2]

Food sources for thiamin include beans, peas, nuts, seeds, and whole grains.

Riboflavin (B₂)

Riboflavin is essential for converting proteins, fats, and carbohydrates into energy. In a study of monkeys, a deficiency of riboflavin led to adrenal cortex dysfunction.[3] The elderly population has a high rate of marginal deficiency of riboflavin.[4]

Riboflavin is found in most vegetables, nuts, legumes, and leafy greens.

Niacin (B₃)

Niacin is important for normal mental function. It is also needed for the release of energy from foods, and it aids in the function of the nervous system. Pellagra is a disease caused by a niacin deficiency. Its symptoms include loss of appetite, diarrhea, skin rash, mental changes, beefy tongue, and digestive and emotional disturbances. Marginally low levels of niacin may lead to depression, apprehension, emotional instability, hyperirritability, and memory impairment.[5]

Food sources for niacin include bran, nuts, seeds, wild rice, brown rice, whole wheat, almonds, and peas.

Pantothenic acid (B₅)

Pantothenic acid is known as the "anti-stress" vitamin because it plays such a vital role in the production of adrenal hormones. A deficiency of pantothenic acid leads to a decreased resistance to stress.[6] Pantothenic acid provides critical support for the adrenal glands as it responds to stress and adequate supplementation is very important for the health of adrenal glands in most people.

Pantothenic acid can be found in salmon, yeast, vegetables, dairy, eggs, grains, and meat.

Vitamin B₆

Vitamin B_6 is vital for the utilization of amino acids (which are the building blocks for proteins). A vitamin B_6 deficiency is often marked by depression, irritability, nervousness, muscle weakness, dermatitis, slow learning, numbness, and cramping in the extremities. B_6 is required by the nervous system and is needed for normal brain function. It is needed to produce dopamine, serotonin, and GABA (gamma-amino butyric acid). These are very important neurotransmitters for promoting feelings of well-being, relaxation, and calmness.

Vitamin B_6 is especially important for women using oral contraceptives (birth control pills) and experiencing bouts of depression, irritability, moodiness, fatigue, and decreased sex drive. Many of these symptoms can be reversed with B_6 supplementation.[7]

Food sources for B_6 include lentils, lima beans, soybeans, sunflower seeds, bananas, avocados, buckwheat, and brewer's yeast.

Vitamin B₁₂

A vitamin B_{12} deficiency has been related to peripheral neuropathy, anemia, paresthesias, demyelination of the dorsal columns and corticospinal tract of the spinal cord, depression, dementia, and heart disease. A deficiency has also been associated with low energy, poor memory, problems in thinking, low stomach acid, and elevated homocysteine levels.[8]

A study conducted at Tufts University found that nearly 40 percent of those studied had a B_{12} blood level in "low normal" range, which is where neurological symptoms begin to occur. The individuals between the ages of twenty-six and forty-nine were discovered to have the same high risk for B_{12} deficiency as those over the age of sixty-five.[9]

Vitamin B_{12} is also important for maintaining the myelin sheaths that cover and protect nerve endings. Subclinical or borderline B_{12} deficiency is rather common, especially among the elderly.[10]

Foods rich in B_{12} include liver, trout, salmon, and beef. Vegetarians usually need to take B_{12} supplements.

Folic acid

Folic acid is needed for DNA synthesis. It is extremely important in pregnancy in preventing most neural tube birth defects, such as spina bifida. Some researchers have suggested that an increase of folic acid intake could potentially prevent an estimated 13,500 deaths from cardiovascular disease each year.[11]

Folic acid deficiency is especially common in alcoholics, indigent populations, the elderly, and individuals with malabsorption disorders. One study conducted at the Massachusetts

General Hospital in Boston found that people with low folate levels were more likely to have melancholic depression and were significantly less likely to respond to Prozac, a very popular anti-depressant medication.[12]

Symptoms of a folic acid deficiency include irritability, weakness, forgetfulness, megaloblastic anemia, weight loss, apathy, hostility, paranoid behavior, palpitations, headaches, gastrointestinal disturbances, and diarrhea. Taking birth control pills may increase the likelihood of a folic acid deficiency.

Good food sources for folic acid are dark green leafy vegetables, oranges, most fruits, brown rice, beans, asparagus, soybeans, and brewer's yeast.

We know from nutrition-related research that much of vitamins B_6, B_{12}, and folic acid are destroyed in the processing and refining of foods. With so many Americans hooked on highly processed foods, fast foods, and foods that contain high amounts of sugar, it is probable that countless American adults are suffering from borderline or frank deficiency in these B vitamins. This may be one reason cardiovascular disease is escalating at such a great rate.

Overall food sources for B vitamins

B vitamins are generally found in grains, vegetables, fruits, seeds, and nuts—all of which are typically under-consumed in the American diet. The United States National Academy of Sciences has recommended that every person eat five to nine servings of fresh fruits and vegetables a day to maintain health. A summary of 1999 data released by the U.S. Department of Health and Human Services Centers for Disease Control and Prevention included the following information:

- Less than one quarter of adults in the United States reported eating the recommended amount of fruits and vegetables per day in 1998.

- Those not eating the recommended amounts of fruits and vegetables ranged from 68 percent not eating the daily recommendation in Minnesota to 91 percent not eating the recommended amounts in Arizona. This means that only one in ten people in Arizona eats the recommended amount of nutrients daily!

Sprays and sublingual forms of the B vitamins are better absorbed and are better choices for older people and those who have difficulty absorbing these vitamins.

VITAMIN C: A KEY ANTISTRESS ANTIOXIDANT

Vitamin C is an extremely important vitamin and antioxidant in the battle against stress. It is more concentrated in the adrenal glands than almost anywhere else in the body.[13] The adrenal glands use more vitamin C per gram of tissue weight than any other organ or tissue in the body.

A number of research studies have confirmed that vitamin C has a great ability to decrease stress. An example is:

- A study at the University of Alabama concluded that vitamin C supplementation significantly decreased stress hormone levels in laboratory rats. The vitamin C also decreased other typical indicators of physical and emotional stress, such as enlargement of the adrenal glands and reduction in size of the thymus and spleen.[14]

Vitamin C is an antioxidant, and as such, it has indirect benefits related to stress. As we have noted previously, chronic stress raises both cortisol and adrenaline in the body. These hormones increase free-radical production, which creates "oxidative stress."

Antioxidants are compounds that help protect the cells from free-radical damage. They are able to disarm free radicals.

Antioxidants work synergistically, or as a "team," in the body. For example, vitamin C helps to restore vitamin E to its full potency. Other water-soluble antioxidants that help protect the cells from free-radical damage are pine bark extract, grape seed extract, green tea extract, quercetin, and most phytonutrients. (Phytonutrients are found in fruits and vegetables and are also readily available in supplement form.)

The current RDI (Reference Daily Intake) for vitamin C is 75–90 mg a day to prevent disease. Dr. Balch, author of *Prescription for Nutritional Healing*, recommends 1,000–3,000 mg a day for optimal daily intake. As a water-soluble vitamin, any vitamin C that is consumed and isn't needed by the body will be flushed out through the bloodstream and kidneys.

Medications such as aspirin and oral contraceptives deplete vitamin C in the body. People who develop kidney stones or are on numerous medications should consult their physician about taking additional vitamin C.

ANTISTRESS BENEFIT FROM MAGNESIUM

Magnesium is involved in the activation of more than three hundred different enzymes in the body. It is vital to health.

Magnesium is one of the few essential nutrients for which deficiencies are fairly common. One survey showed that 72 percent of women and 42 percent of men between the ages of nineteen and fifty did not take in the daily recommended amount of magnesium. The same study showed that 89 percent of females between the ages of sixteen and eighteen did not meet the daily requirement.[15]

Approximately 99 percent of magnesium in sugar cane is lost when the cane is refined to white sugar, and between 80 and 96 percent of magnesium in wheat is removed when it is refined to white flour.

When cortisol and adrenaline levels are elevated, there is also an increase of urinary excretion of magnesium. This indicates that in times of stress, our bodies have an increased need for magnesium.

The characteristic signs and symptoms of a magnesium deficiency include muscle cramps, muscle spasms, hyperventilation, and weakness. Low levels of magnesium in the diet increase a person's risk for developing a wide variety of diseases and ailments, including high blood pressure, heart disease, insomnia, kidney stones, multiple sclerosis, headaches, and menstrual cramps. Laboratory animals that were deficient in magnesium even showed an increased risk of damage related to noise stress and noise-induced hearing loss.[16]

I have found in my medical practice that a person may register a "normal" blood-serum magnesium level, but may actually have a deficit in intracellular magnesium. Therefore, I commonly check for RBC magnesium levels, which is a more reliable test for magnesium in the body.

Good dietary sources of magnesium include wheat bran, wheat germ, nuts, blackstrap molasses, legumes, and whole grains. The dietary recommendation for magnesium is 300 mg. I commonly recommend 200 mg of magnesium two times a day.

Magnesium, as well as other minerals, is necessary for sustaining bone density and cellular metabolism related to digestion, adrenal function, and liver function.

SUPPLEMENTS THAT HELP CONTROL OR MODULATE CORTISOL

There are several herbal products and nutritional products that can help control or modulate cortisol levels in the body. We have seen that stress and high cortisol levels can deplete our bodies of essential vitamins and minerals, which need to be supplemented back into our diets. But now let's look at specific herbs, adaptagens, supplements, and amino acids that help to control excessive cortisol secretion and lower our stress.

Magnolia bark

Magnolia bark, *magnolia officinalis*, is a traditional Chinese medicine that has been used for thousands of years to help with low energy, emotional distress, digestive problems, cough, diarrhea, and asthma. Magnolia bark comes from the stem, root, or branch of the magnolia tree. It is known in Chinese medicine as *Hou Po*. Modern research has focused on magnolia for its sedative and muscle relaxant properties. Magnolia does not cause motor impairment, physical dependency, loss of coordination, or memory loss—all of which are potential side effects from typical antianxiety agents such as benzodiazepines. Nevertheless, magnolia has a sedative and relaxing effect. In a recent study, mice were treated with magnolia and diazepam before going through a maze. The magnolia group was more relaxed and finished without any loss of motor activity or muscle tone. The diazepam group had side effects that included drowsiness, disruptive learning and memory, and withdrawal symptoms.[17]

In summary, magnolia extract has the potential to decrease stress, create a calming effect for the nerves, and make a person sleepy.

Magnolia also has strong antioxidant properties. Numerous studies have revealed that magnolia extract protects mitochondria from free-radical damage in the liver, heart, and brain.[18]

Some research has found that magnolia extract is even more potent than vitamin E in preventing lipid peroxidation, which is a contributor to heart disease and atherosclerosis.[19]

Phosphatidylserine

Phosphatidylserine, or PS, is an essential component in every cell membrane in the body. It is found in high concentrations in the brain, and it may help prevent a decline in mental function. One study has shown benefits from PS supplements for early Alzheimer's disease patients—in the study, PS supplements were given for three to twelve weeks at a dose of 300 mg a day.[20] PS has also been shown to buffer the overproduction of cortisol, especially after intense exercise. In one study, healthy European men were given 800 mg of PS a day for ten days prior to cycling to the "near exhaustion" point. They were found to have a 30 percent decrease in cortisol production even after strenuous exercise compared to those who did not receive the PS supplements.[21] Athletes may benefit from taking up to 800 mg a day either prior to training or immediately following training.

The average dose of PS is 100 mg in capsule form and compared to many supplements, PS is quite expensive. Those who are undergoing significant physical stress—such as competitive weight lifters, marathon runners, and others—may find the cost well worth the results. Salivary cortisol levels can be checked prior to and after strenuous exercise to assist you in adjusting your dose of PS.

Phytosterols

Phytosterols, or plant sterols, were first described chemically in 1922. Phytosterols are simply plant-derived compounds that are very similar in structure to cholesterol. Their purpose, however, is to inhibit cholesterol absorption from the diet—this was first described in 1983. Medical uses are not limited to the treatment of high cholesterol, however. Phytosterols are also used to treat benign prostatic hypertrophy, rheumatoid arthritis, HIV, fibromyalgia, lupus, psoriasis, allergies, and viruses. Unrefined plant oils typically contain high concentrations of phytosterols. Nuts and seeds also have significant amounts of phytosterols. Most fruits and vegetables contain some phytosterols. A great deal of research into these plant sterols has been done in the last fifteen years, and these compounds have been shown to have very important antiviral, anti-inflammatory, anticancer, antidiabetic, and antiulcer properties.[22]

Recent studies are showing that a blend of plant sterols can help protect marathon runners and other athletes in intensive training from excessive inflammation and suppression of the immune system, both of which are common to those who train intensively.[23]

I have used a sterol/sterolin mixture for years in my practice to help people with a variety of stress-related disorders with significant results. Two of the products that I recommend are Moducare and Natur-Leaf. They are also used to treat benign prostatic hypertrophy, as well as to help lower cholesterol. Other sterol spreads sold over the counter, such as Benecol and Take Control, have also been shown to help lower cholesterol levels.

ADAPTAGENS

An adaptagen is a substance that will help the body adapt to stress by balancing the adrenal gland's response to stress. The end result is that cortisol levels will be neither too high nor too low, but will be balanced. The term adaptagen was first used by a Russian scientist, Dr. Nicolai Lazarev, in 1947. The "father of adaptagens," however, is considered to be Dr. Israel Brekhman, who worked at the Far East Science Center of the USSR as head of the Department of Physiology and Pharmacology. He holds forty patents related to the discovery of adaptagenic herbs and applications. Dr. Brekhman describes adaptagens as having these qualities: (1) completely nontoxic to the human body—with no harmful or negative effects no matter what amount or how long they are used; (2) helpful to the body's mental and physical performance while providing resistance to stressful insults at the cellular level;

(3) balance and normalize the body's systems, leading to homeo-statis and health.[24]

Rhodiola

Rhodiola rosea is also known as "golden root" or "Arctic root." This herb is native to the mountainous regions of Asia, parts of Europe, and the Arctic. Rhodiola is an adaptagen that is said to stimulate the nervous system, decrease depression, eliminate fatigue, increase work performance, enhance immunity, increase exercise capacity, increase memorization skills, and prevent high-altitude sickness. It has been studied in the former Soviet Union nations for more than thirty-five years, but much of this research has not been available for review in the West. In more recent studies, rhodiola was reported to have a "clear anti-fatigue effect" without any side effects when given to subjects who were experi-encing a moderate level of fatigue and stress.[25] In another study, researchers concluded that rhodiola was helpful in increasing energy and decreasing mental fatigue.[26] Researchers speculate that rhodiola works by influencing key central nervous system neurotransmitters, including dopamine and serotonin.

I recommend a product that uses a standardization of 2 to 3 percent rosavin, which is the active ingredient of rhodiola used in clinical studies. The common dose is 100–200 mg three times a day.

Ginseng products

Ginseng is another adaptagen that helps the body adapt to stress. A number of different products are available under the general umbrella of ginseng. Know the ginseng you are consider-ing taking!

Korean ginseng

Korean ginseng, also called Panax ginseng and Chinese gin-seng, has long been used in Chinese medicine to help the body adapt to stress. (Korean and Chinese ginseng are the same plant, grown in different areas.) The name "Panax" was given to this herb from the Greek word for "cure-all." Ginseng is an adaptagen that reportedly increases physical and mental energy, enables athletes to adapt to stress, and may be used to improve memory, prevent senility, and to increase longevity.

A quality ginseng product should have at least 25 mg of gin-senoside, calculated as ginsenoside Rgl. The standard dose for a standardized Panax ginseng extract that contains 14 percent saponins would be 200 mg. Ginseng is typically taken one to three times a day, and the usual regimen is three weeks on and two weeks off.

Siberian ginseng

This product, also known as eleuthero, or SG, was actually introduced by Soviet scientists who were seeking a cheap, abundant substitute for Panax ginseng. The herb is native to the southeastern part of Russia, northern China, Korea, and Japan. The main active compound in Korean ginseng is ginsenoside, as noted above, but there are no ginsenosides in Siberian ginseng! Its active compound is eleutherocide. Nevertheless, clinical trials with SG have shown it to increase capacity for mental and physical work and athletic performance; decrease recovery time from work and injury; and improve tolerance of environmental stimuli such as noise, heat, and work load increase.[27] SG has been given to Russian cosmonauts and athletes to increase energy, to normalize elevated blood pressure and blood sugar, to stimulate activity, and in response to sports and performance-related stress.[28]

SG has been shown to provide many of the benefits of caffeine, but without the post-caffeine "let down." It seems to improve the use of oxygen in exercising muscle tissues, which means a person might exercise longer and recover quicker from aerobic exercise.[29]

Standardized extracts of eleutherocides B and E are generally recommended in a dose of 300–400 mg a day. It should be taken continuously for six to eight weeks, followed by a one- to two-week break. Siberian ginseng is available in many forms, including tablets, capsules, extracts, teas, chewing gum, and drinks.

Ashwagandha

This product is known as "Indian ginseng." The use of the root of this plant can be traced back three thousand years. It is a strong, vigorous plant that thrives where many other plants wither and die. The Indian *Materia Medica* recommends using ashwagandha for impotence, general debility, brain fatigue, low sperm count, nervous exhaustion, as an aphrodisiac, and in any case in which vigor must be restored. The chemical compounds in ashwagandha are similar to those found in ginseng—studies, however, have shown it to be superior in relieving stress when compared to Chinese ginseng. In one study involving laboratory mice, ashwagandha was able to prevent stress-related gastrointestinal ulcers. It has also been shown to increase physical endurance and prevent the depletion of vitamin C and cortisol in subjects undergoing exercise stress.[30]

Epimedium

Epimedium functions similarly to an adaptagen by reducing cortisol levels when they are elevated and by increasing epinephrine, norepinephrine, dopamine, and serotonin when they are low. It is known in Chinese medicine as *Yin Yang Huo.* It has also been translated as "licentious goat plant." The supplement companies have renamed it "horny goat weed." It has been used for more than two thousand years in Chinese medicine as a sexual rejuvenation tonic.

In one study done by Chinese researchers, high-dose synthetic cortisol, which suppresses immune function and accelerates bone loss in both humans and animals, was administered to test subjects, followed by an epimedium extract. The extract reduced levels of cortisol and improved immune function in humans, and it slowed bone loss and strengthened bones in animals.[31] Increased cortisol levels are known to cause both decreased sex drive and fatigue, so it is little wonder this herb is used to increase libido.

One study has also shown that epimedium can raise low levels of thyroid hormone and testosterone to normal levels.[32]

No adverse effects have been associated with the traditional preparation of epimedium, which is a tea. The suggested dosage is 200–1,000 mg a day in two to three divided doses.

The Brekhman Elixir

As noted earlier, Dr. Israel Brekhman has been the leading researcher on adaptagenic herbs for more than forty-five years. He has formulated a liquid elixir, which consists of seven Siberian adaptagenic herbs, from plants that grow in the eastern Siberian forests. This elixir has been given to world-class

Russian athletes as well as cosmonauts in the Russian space program. Top Soviet athletes, including Olympic athletes, have routinely included adaptagenic herbs in their training programs. These products help them achieve maximum performance but without the harmful side effects of anabolic steroids.[33]

The main herb in this elixir is Siberian ginseng. The product also has Chinese magnolia vine, maral root, golden root (rhodiola), Manchurian thorn tree, ural licorice root, and cinnamon rose. This blend of herbs has been found in studies to be more effective than any single herb alone.

THE USE OF AMINO ACIDS TO RELIEVE STRESS

Chronic stress interferes with neurotransmitters. If stress persists too long, there will eventually occur a lowering of serotonin, which is a neurotransmitter. Low serotonin levels are associated with impatience, aggression, irritability, and anxiety—all of which are readily associated with being "stressed out." Low brain serotonin levels have also been associated with depression, anxiety, obesity, PMS, violent behavior, suicide, alcoholism, compulsive gambling, insomnia, carbohydrate craving, seasonal affective disorder, and migraine headaches. In contrast, adequate brain serotonin levels are associated with feelings of calmness, well-being, security, confidence, concentration, and relaxation.

Approximately nineteen million Americans suffer from depression, and another nineteen million suffer from anxiety. Approximately two-thirds of Americans are overweight or obese, and about 20 percent of American adults suffer from a diagnosable mental disorder in any given year. Approximately 50 percent of American adults suffer from insomnia at least a few times a week. I have a strong hunch that low brain serotonin levels or altered neurotransmitters may be at an epidemic level in our nation!

Some people are born with low brain serotonin levels, and thus, they are more easily stressed and more prone to develop depression. Serotonin levels can also be lowered by traumatic life experiences, such as the death of a loved one, a major accident, or a major illness. Brain serotonin levels are also decreased during periods of chronic stress. I recommend targeted amino acid therapy (TAAP) to correct neurotransmitter imbalances. See NeuroScience in Appendix D.

5-HTP

The body manufactures serotonin from the essential amino acid L-tryptophan. This amino acid is converted into 5-hydroxy-tryptophan (5-HTP). Supplementation with 5-HTP has been shown to raise brain serotonin levels. In a study done in Europe, 5-HTP was found to be more effective than medications similar to Prozac, with fewer side effects.[34]

The usual dose of 5-HTP is 150–300 mg a day in divided dosages. I typically start patients on 50 mg, three times a day. If they do not notice improvement after four weeks, I typically increase the dose to 100 mg three times a day. Individuals who are taking prescription antidepressants, herbal supplements for depression, or weight-loss medications should not combine these with 5-HTP supplements without consulting a physician first.

Do not confuse 5-HTP with L-tryptophan. The FDA ordered a recall of L-tryptophan, an amino acid nutritional supplement, in the fall of 1989, stating that it caused a rare and deadly flu-like condition. In March 1990, the FDA banned the public sale of dietary L-tryptophan completely. The ban continues today. The ban was caused by a single batch of contaminated tryptophan from a single Japanese producer. Nonetheless, it is considered a banned substance. 5-HTP supplements are readily available and are just as effective.

L-theanine

L-theanine is another amino acid and is commonly found in green tea. L-theanine was initially discovered in 1950 and was approved as a food additive by the Japanese minister of health and welfare in 1964. Only 1 to 2 percent of the dry weight of tea leaves consists of L-theanine. Because of this, a patented enzymatic process was developed in Japan to synthesize 100 percent pure L-theanine. This product has been shown to decrease stress, promote relaxation, calm nervousness, and decrease restlessness. It is nonsedating and promotes concentration in students. I have used this supplement widely and with significant success in treating ADHD children and stressed-out adults.

L-theanine helps increase the production of alpha waves in the brain. An EEG (electroencephalogram) monitors brain wave patterns, and four main patterns are possible: beta, alpha, theta, and delta. The main brain waves during deep sleep are the slow delta waves, and in twilight sleep, the pattern is theta. Beta waves occur primarily when we are stressed. When awake and relaxed, the pattern is alpha, which makes alpha the preferred pattern. A person with alpha waves is able to concentrate and be more creative.[35]

L-theanine is able to cross the blood-brain barrier, and it supports the activity of certain neurotransmitters in the brain. L-theanine does not cause daytime drowsiness and is an excellent alternative for benzodiazepines, which are found in many antianxiety medications.

I recommend this substance commonly in my practice. A person can take 100–300 mg a day or more of L-theanine supplement, or consume three to four cups of green tea a day. Be aware, however, that decaffeinated green tea contains little to no L-theanine since the majority of L-theanine is lost during the decaffeination process.

MONITORING A PERSON'S LEVEL OF ADRENAL STATUS

Many physicians do not understand the importance of measuring cortisol levels, and those who do measure cortisol levels often measure blood levels of cortisol rather than salivary levels. Cortisol is the main stress hormone associated with chronic stress. Typically when a person has been under long-term stress, the cortisol levels in the blood or saliva are elevated. However, taking the specific herbs, adaptagens, supplements, or amino acids mentioned in this chapter can help lower cortisol levels.

Cortisol levels need to be measured throughout a day—the level may appear normal during one part of the day and be high or low during another part of the day. My preferred tests to measure adrenal function are the BioHealth Adrenal Panel, Neuro Stress Inventory by NeuroScience, and the ZRT Adrenal Salivary Panel. These tests measure the fluctuations of "salivary" cortisol during the circadian cycle. Four saliva samples are spaced through the day to evaluate hypothalamic-adrenal function and rhythm under real-life conditions. Circadian abnormalities, which are generally observed with this form of testing, help to diagnose subtle and often undetected problems.

If your physician is not familiar with salivary testing, you can refer him to the information in Appendix D about the tests above.

A SUMMARY ABOUT SUPPLEMENTATION

Supplementation should always start with a strong foundation of a comprehensive multivitamin. I recommend adding to this vitamin C, magnesium, and sublingual B_{12}, B_6, and folic acid. If you have your salivary adrenal hormones tested and you have elevated cortisol levels, I recommend starting with magnolia extract. I occasionally add phytosterols to a patient's regimen, usually Moducare or Natur-Leaf—two capsules in the morning and two in the evening on an empty stomach. For my patients with high cortisol who exercise, I usually recommend phosphatidylserine, 400–800 mg, to lower cortisol after exercise.

In extremely stressful periods during your life, you will probably need an adaptagen. I usually start patients with rhodiola at a dosage of 200 mg three times a day, though on occasion some will benefit from a combination of adaptagens. In these cases, I commonly recommend a product called Prime One, or Russian Gold, a powerful combination of seven adaptagenic herbs.

For individuals who have chronic stress and have developed depression, chronic anxiety, carbohydrate craving, or any of the other symptoms listed in the section on serotonin earlier in this chapter, I recommend 5-HTP at a dosage of 50 mg three times a day. These patients generally benefit greatly from L-theanine, 100–200 mg three times a day as needed.

In addition to supplementing with the abovementioned products, I also commonly perform salivary hormone testing to check male and female sex hormones, including testosterone, estrogen, and progesterone. I believe it is important to balance these hormones using natural hormone replacement therapy. I also commonly check thyroid blood tests, and if levels are low, I suggest using a natural thyroid hormone such as Armour Thyroid.

USE CAUTION IN SUPPLEMENTATION

I strongly recommend that a person seek the advice of their medical practitioner prior to taking any nutritional supplement. Some supplements, as well as some foods, negatively interact with prescription medications.

Supplementation is critically important for reducing cortisol levels and helping to prevent the harmful effects of chronic stress. See Appendix D for more information on these supplements.

16

Exercises That Relieve Stress

Most people think they exercise for the sake of their body—generally to stay lean and strong physically. The greater truth is that exercise is also good for the mind and emotions.

The benefits of exercise are far-reaching. They are not only "external" in the form of appearance, flexibility, and manifestations of strength. They are also "internal" at the cellular level. Several types of exercises are directly related to stress reduction.

There are many forms of exercise that, if done correctly, can be great stress reducers. Many exercises from ballroom dancing to Tai Chi to aerobics can help you overcome the stress factor in your life. Let's begin by taking a look at aerobic exercise.

AEROBIC EXERCISE CAN LOWER STRESS

Aerobic literally means "in the presence of air." Aerobic exercises increase the oxygen-carrying capacity of the body as a whole. The muscles and cardiovascular system both become stronger and more efficient if a person is exercising aerobically on a regular basis.

Aerobic exercises are generally those that exercise the large muscle groups of the body in repetitive motions for a sustained period of time. Such exercises include brisk walking, jogging, cycling, swimming, rowing, aerobic dance routines, stair stepping, skating, and cross-country skiing. Active sports, such as singles tennis, racquetball, and basketball, also produce an aerobic effect.

Aerobic exercise has been shown in countless studies to decrease the risk of cardiovascular disease and cancer, decrease body weight, lower blood pressure, and lower triglycerides and LDL (bad) cholesterol. It also helps raise HDL (good) cholesterol, helps prevent diabetes, and improves glucose tolerance. It increases a person's energy level and promotes more restful sleep.

Aerobic exercise increases the release of endorphins and norepinephrine in the brain. Endorphins are hormone-like substances that elevate mood and give a person a sense of well-being. In this way, aerobic exercise has an antidepressant effect. You may have heard of something called a "runner's high"—those who exercise vigorously and regularly often feel euphoric as they exercise. They are getting "high" on their own release of endorphins.

Even moderate aerobic exercise has a calming effect on the body and diminishes the response to stress for up to four hours after the exercise session. Aerobic exercise that is enjoyable to the person doing it—such as a dance class—decreases the stress response to an even greater extent than aerobic exercise that is less enjoyable and more of a "chore" to the person doing it. Therefore, choose an aerobic exercise that you like doing. Not only will you do it more consistently and for longer periods, but also you will experience greater health and emotional benefits.

Moderate aerobic exercise reduces cortisol levels, but aerobic exercise that is too intense or prolonged may raise cortisol levels. Few people need to worry about whether they are exercising too intensely or for too lengthy a period—the vast majority of people don't get enough aerobic exercise.

One study looked at aerobic exercise as a means of treating clinical depression. An aerobic exercise program was compared to standard medication in a group of older adult patients. The experiment lasted sixteen weeks. Medication relieved symptoms of depression more rapidly at the outset, but aerobic exercise was shown to be equally effective to medication over the course of the four-month study. Since some medications for depression have adverse effects or cease to be as effective with prolonged use, this was an important finding—aerobic exercise may be a very viable long-term therapy.[1]

The greatest benefits of aerobic exercise tend to occur if a person exercises early in the morning. This is especially true if a person is attempting to lose weight. However, the time a person does aerobic exercise is not nearly as important as the frequency and duration of the exercise. A person should do aerobic exercises three to four times a week for twenty to thirty minutes each time.

FINDING YOUR TARGET HEART RATE RANGE

When starting an aerobic exercise program, you need to determine your training heart rate range. If you are exercising at too high a heart rate, you are probably overstressing your body and producing excessive amounts of cortisol. On the other hand, if you are exercising at too low a heart rate, you are not going to obtain the tremendous health benefits of aerobic exercise. Your heart rate should be between 50 and 80 percent of your maximum heart rate. To determine this, subtract your age from 220. Multiply that number by 0.5 (50%), and then multiply that same number by 0.8 (80%). For example, if your age is 40, subtract that number from 220, which gives you 180. Fifty percent of 180 is 90, and 80 percent of 180 is 144.

1.   220 - 40 = 180

2.   180 x 0.5 = 90

3.   180 x 0.8 = 144

So your training heart rate range is 90 to 144 beats per minute.

As you begin your exercise program, keep your heart rate range between 50 and 60 percent of the maximum. In this example, that would be between 90 and 108 beats per minute. After a month or two, increase the intensity to 60 to 70 percent of the maximum. In the example above, that would be between 108 and 126 beats per minute. After several more months, increase the intensity of your exercise to 70 to 80 percent. Again, in our example, that number would be 126 to 144 beats per minute.

Increasing heart rate during exercise beyond the 80 percent threshold is usually more harmful than beneficial. Too many free radicals are released, and cortisol levels rise.

The so-called "weekend warriors"—those who try to do a week's worth of exercise on a weekend—tend to assume that they can do two to three hours of solid exercise to make up for failing to do thirty minutes of exercise four to five times a week. That's just not true! Weekend warriors have more pulled muscles, aches and pains, shin splints, foot problems, and other musculoskeletal problems than regular exercisers. They also increase their risk for heart attack. A sedentary fifty-year-old male who suddenly begins to do extensive strenuous physical activity—such as shoveling snow from the front walk—is 10,000 percent more likely to have a heart attack than an individual the same age who exercises regularly and is well-conditioned.[2]

ADD STRETCHING AND RESISTANCE EXERCISES

It is important to add stretching exercises as well as resistance exercises, also called weight training, to your aerobic exercise.

As we discussed in an earlier chapter, when a person is stressed, that person's muscles are nearly always tense. Stretching exercises can help relieve tension and loosen uptight, tense muscles. Stretching promotes flexibility and can help greatly in reducing injuries. It also helps reduce symptoms of arthritis. Stretches are simple to do, but they should be accompanied by proper breathing techniques.

It is best to stretch muscles after they are warm—in other words, after you have done some aerobic exercising. Exercising a cold muscle is like pulling a rubber band that has been in the refrigerator and isn't warm. An optimal approach for reducing musculoskeletal injuries is to walk for ten minutes at a moderate pace, stop to do a series of stretching exercises for fifteen minutes, and then continue with more vigorous walking for twenty minutes. Give your muscles a cool-down period of another five minutes of relaxed walking.

Never stretch a muscle to the point where you feel prolonged pain. At the first sign of pain, back off to a "stretch point" where you feel no pain.

Resistance exercises are also very important to preserve muscle mass and prevent osteoporosis. You can benefit greatly in this by joining a gym, going regularly, and working with a certified personal trainer who can help you set weights and develop a program that is right for you.

START WITH A MEDICAL EXAM

Most exercise physiologists and physicians recommend that a person undergo a thorough medical exam prior to starting an exercise program. The medical exam should include an exercise treadmill test conducted by a qualified physician. This is especially recommended for persons over thirty years of age and for those who have cardiovascular risk factors such as hypertension, elevated cholesterol, or who smoke.

CONSIDER ALTERNATIVE FORMS OF EXERCISE

A number of alternate forms of exercise also have been shown to have excellent benefits in reducing stress and improving overall health. Although as a believer I don't condone the practice of Eastern religions, I do, however, believe the various forms of exercise that they have introduced to the Western world are highly beneficial to most people. If people only knew how helpful these exercises can be in overcoming stress and other health issues, they would be less likely to label it a taboo subject. We can participate in the exercises and breathing techniques without getting involved with the religion.

Yoga

Yoga is a form of exercise that combines stretching and breathing to relax the body.

There are several types of yoga. "Hatha" yoga is the most popular type practiced in the United States. More than eighteen million Americans now practice yoga, which is up from six million people just a decade or so ago.[3]

Yoga is more than five thousand years old and is an ancient Eastern practice initially designed to bring the body, mind, and soul into harmony. It was and is considered an alternate form of physical activity. Yoga is "low impact," and Hatha yoga concentrates on these three activities: controlled breathing, posture, and meditation. The slow breathing promotes relaxation, and the various "postures" of yoga promote flexibility by gently stretching the body into different positions.

Other forms of yoga include Ashtanga, or power yoga, generally preferred by athletes to develop strength and stamina. Bikram yoga is done in a hot room that is thirty-eight degrees Centigrade or higher, and it is recommended only for extremely fit individuals; otherwise, it can elevate stress hormones. Kundalini yoga is a more meditative form of yoga and incorporates meditation, visualization, guided imagery, and mantras. There are several other forms of yoga beyond these. I encourage you to recognize that when doing yoga, you do not need to meditate on a mantra, but instead, you can meditate on the Scriptures or on the name of Jesus and perhaps His various attributes and titles in the Bible.

Medical research done on various groups of people by the Physiology Department of Lady Hardinge Medical College in New Delhi, India, and Sucheta Kripalani Hospital concluded that Sahaja yoga produced a decrease in tension, stress, anxiety, depression, and hypertension. Physicians studied the effect of Sahaja yoga on blood pressure, heart rate, levels of blood lactate, levels of VMA, which is a metabolite of the stress hormone epinephrine in the urine, and the galvanic skin resistance test, which indicates whether the patient is tense or relaxed. The group that practiced yoga showed improvement in all of these parameters.[4]

Yoga is different from most other forms of exercise in that it is not concerned with how many repetitions are performed or how well a person performs a particular exercise. Instead, yoga focuses a person's attention on how the body is structured and how to move the body without aggravating an injury or causing pain. It teaches a person how to breathe properly and how to integrate breathing with positions of the body. A person doesn't strain or "force" the body in doing yoga, but rather, gently stretches various muscles. With practice, yoga can improve a person's strength, flexibility, endurance, and help reduce stress. A recent study reported in the *Journal of the American Medical Association* reported that daily yoga practice could reduce the pain associated with carpal tunnel syndrome.[5]

Tai Chi

Tai Chi is an ancient Chinese martial art that involves slow, smooth, and fluid movements. As a martial art, Tai Chi has been practiced for many centuries.

Tai Chi emphasizes diaphragmatic or abdominal breathing. It is an exceptionally good exercise for older people who have arthritis, peripheral vascular disease, chronic obstructive pulmonary disease, osteoporosis, or other physical problems. The Arthritis Foundation recommends Tai Chi for individuals with arthritis.[6]

Research has shown that Tai Chi may improve muscle mass, tone, flexibility, strength, stamina, balance, coordination, posture, and well-being. It can also provide similar cardiovascular benefits to modern aerobic exercise. One of the most beneficial effects of Tai Chi is its ability to reduce stress. The regular practice of Tai Chi was shown in one study to increase noradrenaline excretion in the urine, as well as to decrease salivary cortisol concentrations. These two effects are directly related to the lowering of stress. Subjects reported feeling less tension, depression, anger, fatigue, confusion, and anxiety, and they felt more vigorous.[7]

Tai Chi is practiced slowly with smooth, low-intensity, graceful movements, which are accompanied by rhythmic abdominal breathing. A typical exercise session is a series of gentle, deliberate moves or postures combined into a sequential "choreography" of sorts. These movements are called "forms," and each form has between twenty and one hundred moves. The exercise typically requires up to twenty minutes to complete a basic form. Tai Chi relies totally on technique rather than power or strength.

Tai Chi lowers stress hormones, reduces tension, increases energy, and helps clear the mind. It can be practiced by a person at any age and by individuals who have a wide range of chronic diseases. The calming effect of Tai Chi changes the brain's frequency from "beta," which is the normal waking wave pattern, to "alpha," which is associated with an improved ability to learn and remember. Tai Chi calms the mind, promotes flexibility, and exercises and tones the body, including the cardiovascular system—all at the same time. Tai Chi, like yoga, includes meditation. However, I encourage my patients to practice the exercise and to only meditate on God's Word.

To learn more about Tai Chi, you can watch videos or DVDs, read books, or attend classes. See Appendix D for more information.

Pilates

Pilates exercises were developed by Joseph Pilates approximately one hundred years ago. As a child, Pilates suffered from rheumatic fever, rickets, and asthma. He was determined to overcome his ailments, and he began studying anatomy at a young age. He also studied both Eastern and Western forms of exercise, including yoga, gymnastics, dance, and self-defense. When he was fourteen years old, he became a successful gymnast, boxer, skier, and diver.

During World War II, Pilates worked as a nurse, and it was then that he began to develop equipment to help rehabilitate the war injured. He would take bedsprings and attach them to the ceiling so that bedridden patients might exercise and gain strength. Eventually Pilates moved to the United States and opened an exercise studio in New York City, where he trained many great dancers.

Pilates exercises are designed to target deep postural muscles, to help correct alignment, and to strengthen and rebalance the body. Pilates also helps to reduce tension and stress. Many health clubs now offer Pilates exercise classes.

Ballroom dancing

Ballroom dancing is an excellent alternative for those individuals who do not enjoy exercising but do enjoy dancing! Ballroom dancing provides most of the benefits of aerobic exercise, plus it adds the "enjoyment factor" that produces even greater stress-reduction benefits.

The roots of ballroom dancing go back to the Renaissance period with the very structured dances created by and for the upper classes.

Ballroom dancing can help a person develop coordination, balance, and rhythm. It is usually associated with a very pleasant environment, with soothing music, an opportunity for creative expression, and social interaction. Among the more common dances are the fox-trot, swing, cha-cha, tango, waltz, rumba, mambo, samba, and merengue. Most of the dances come from Europe, South America, and the Caribbean—with the exception, of course, of the fox-trot and swing dancing, which are purely American.

Ballroom dancing is typically a good low-impact aerobic exercise that uses the large muscle groups of the body. It can be done for thirty minutes to an hour or for an entire evening. People who become bored with exercising on a treadmill or exercise bike usually find ballroom dancing a fun alternative. Classes are often offered at a college, university, or in private studios. The basic steps for most dances can be learned from videos, DVDs, or books. An inexpensive way to explore the possibility to doing ballroom dancing is to rent or buy a basic dance video.

One of the great advantages of this form of exercise is that most people who participate in ballroom dancing rarely think of their activity as exercising. They simply see it as a fun way to spend time with other people. This means, of course, that they tend to do more of the dancing for more decades of their life. That makes it an especially good exercise in my opinion!

REGULAR EXERCISING VS. OVERTRAINING

Regular exercising is exercise that is done in moderate amounts on a regular basis for a prolonged period of time. Even ten minutes a day of exercise has been shown to have beneficial effects on both the body and mind. Longer periods of exercise done regularly and in moderation have been shown to decrease appetite, decrease body fat, build muscle and bone, stimulate the immune system, and improve a person's mental and emotional well-being. Regular exercise enhances neurotransmitter production, leading to an increase of both serotonin and dopamine (which also relieves symptoms of anxiety and depression).

Raising the levels of neurotransmitters to normal levels also helps lower cortisol levels.

Overtraining is different from "regular" exercising. Overtraining is an extreme amount of exercise, usually in a short period of time. Researchers at the University of Colorado have found that extremes of exercise—usually performed by endurance athletes—can actually elevate cortisol levels.[8] Overtraining can suppress the immune system, increase the risk of injury, increase a person's body fat, and interfere with emotional and mental function.

Overtraining can occur in stressed-out individuals who go to a gym and spend hours grinding it out on the treadmill. They may think they are doing themselves a favor with the intensity of their exercise, even though they are fatigued and "stressed," but they may actually be doing themselves harm. They are overtraining and causing their cortisol levels to rise.

Any time a person is lifting weights and working out longer and harder only to find that his strength is diminishing, he is overtraining. He is putting himself into a position to lose muscle mass and gain abdominal fat. Excess cortisol affects tendons and ligaments as well as muscles, and the person who overtrains also tends to be far more susceptible to tendonitis, ligament sprains, and muscle strains. As cortisol levels increase, testosterone, DHEA, and androgenic hormones decrease. Resistance training and aerobics training—when they move into levels of overtraining—can cause as much stress to the body as trauma, surgery, infections, and anxiety. In one study, increased cortisol levels caused an increase in protein breakdown by 5 to 20 percent—this was protein stored in muscles and major organs, including the heart muscle.[9]

MIX IT UP!

Find a good balance of regular exercise that is tailored to your fitness level, sleep pattern, nutritional status, weight, stress level, and busy schedule. Make it personal, and make it fun! A variety of exercises can help keep you motivated.

I advise my patients to schedule a workout at least every other day and to put that workout time in their appointment book—and then keep the appointment, just as if they were making an appointment with a physician or a business consultant. I also encourage my patients to have a "training partner" to whom they are accountable for sticking with a regular exercise program. On days when you are simply too exhausted or too stressed, or after nights in which you have not slept well, don't push yourself to exercise. Listen to your body, and learn when to exercise and when to rest.

Keep in mind, however, that an exercise program that includes a balance of stretching, resistance, and aerobic exercises will do far more to reduce stress than choosing not to exercise at all. Even people with severe fatigue benefit from mild exercise, such as stretching and a leisurely walk.

17

Cultivating Happiness and Joy as a Lifestyle

How many *happy* people do you know—I mean really happy, smiling, cheerful people who make others smile when they come into a room? Are you happy? If your answer is no, what would it take to make you a happy person? Where does joy come from? Is it possible to cultivate happiness as a *lifestyle*? If so, how would happiness affect your stress levels?

You may already have answers to these questions. But if even one of them caught your attention, you may find some help you need in this chapter that could result in your becoming a happier person. As I discussed in chapter two, we do have control over much of our lives even though we live in a world that seems out of control. I explained that it is possible to control our thoughts, our words, our social situations, our reactions, and even our physical environments. In these ways, we can increase our happiness quotient, if we know how to think about it.

We've discussed the importance of controlling negative emotional reactions in order to keep chronic stress from ruining our emotional and mental health. It is impossible to harbor negative feelings of anger, rage, resentment, and bitterness—even disappointment—and expect to be a happy person. Negative emotions and happiness cannot coexist.

While we cannot live life without enduring some negative situations, we can choose to respond to them in a positive way that will not be destructive to our emotional well-being—our happiness. If you are realizing that you have a problem with some long-term negative emotions, I encourage you to read my book *Deadly Emotions*. There I discuss in more depth the effect these negative emotions can have on your overall well-being, as well as the hope available to be freed from their destructive power. We must determine to conquer negative emotions if we hope to be truly happy.

WHAT DOES HAPPINESS LOOK LIKE?

For millions of people in the world, happiness is derived from satisfying basic living needs like clean water, enough food, and a simple hut to live in. Working hard, raising a family, celebrating community traditions, and living in peace define the goals of their lives. Survival is still the number one priority for millions of people around the world today.

However, people who are born into affluent countries of our Western civilization have often taken life's basic needs for granted from birth, being offered so many choices of food, clothes, toys, and other amenities as they grew up that their expectation for happiness involves much more than "survival needs." Living in the abundance of our nation's wealth has changed the definition of happiness for most Americans, even those who consider themselves to be poor. It is, in large part, this heightened expectation that makes happiness elusive for many. According to recent research, Americans feel happy just 54 percent of the time. They say they feel neutral about 25 percent of the time. And Americans have the blues 21 percent of the time.[1]

If you don't clearly define happiness, it is unlikely that you will ever consider yourself to be happy. And what makes one person feel happy does not necessarily make another feel the same. If your happiness is dependent on waking to a sunny, warm day, then you can expect your emotional state to change as quickly as the weather. If you live for Friday afternoons to begin your "happiness time," you have decided to be unhappy the rest of the week. And even long-term happiness goals, like the satisfaction of raising your children, can end abruptly when you begin to experience the empty-nest syndrome, making your happiness evaporate. You may argue, "No one can be happy all the time." While that is certainly true, there are scientific, as well as spiritual, guidelines that can help you cultivate a lifestyle of happiness. If you choose to follow these proven protocols for happiness, you can develop a happy state of mind and heart that will effectively reduce the stress of your life.

Defining happiness

Webster's dictionary defines *happiness* simply as "a state of well-being and contentment; a pleasurable satisfaction."[2] And *happy* is defined as "fortunate; enjoying or characterized by well-being and contentment."[3] By definition, a happy person is one who has reason to be content and is satisfied with at least much of what life has offered. Of course, we have to deal with the issue of perception, as we discussed earlier. Knowing that you are living in a state of well-being and being grateful for that depend on how you perceive your life's goals. There are wealthy people who, despite having have all the toys life offers, great success in career and family, and positive community recognition, nevertheless admit to being extremely unhappy. Their problem is one of perception.

Martin Seligman, in his book *Authentic Happiness,* presents three categories of positive emotions of happiness, i.e., *past, present,* and *future*:[4]

- Past: feelings of satisfaction, contentment, pride, and serenity.

- Present (examples): enjoying the taste of food, glee at listening to music, absorption in reading.

- Future: feelings of optimism, hope, trust, faith, and confidence.

What is joy?

While Webster's dictionary lists *joy* as a synonym for happiness, it also defines the differences between them. In defining joy, Webster states that it is "the emotion evoked by well-being, success, or good fortune, or by the prospect of possessing what one desires."[5] While happiness is a *state* of being, joy is the *emotion* expressed as a result of that state. In cultivating a lifestyle of happiness, we express our contentment and pleasurable satisfaction through joyous speech, laughter, and other joy-filled responses.

Where do we get joy? Is such a positive emotion dependent on the circumstances of our life? Again, to answer this question honestly, we have to deal with the issue of *perception*. It is possible to control our state of happiness as we educate our perspective. In other words, we can *choose* to be grateful for the many good things in our lives. On the other hand, if our perception demands an expectation that we are entitled to have more than we do, we will lock ourselves into a syndrome of resentment and unhappiness that will not allow us to experience joy.

Divine source

The Bible tells us where to find true joy. The psalmist declared of God, "You will show me the path of life; in Your presence is fullness of joy; at Your right hand are pleasures forevermore" (Ps. 16:11). God made us to be happy people, filled with joy and love for life.

There are many levels of joy described in the Bible, including *gladness, contentment,* and *cheerfulness.* Each instance where joy is recorded, it involves a positive attitude or pleasant emotion of delight. Though even wicked people are described as experiencing a perverted joy for the evil deeds they do (which could translate today to the alcoholic who finds destructive pleasure in the bottle), the joy the people of God should have is holy and pure. This joy rises above circumstances and focuses on the very character of God. (See Notes section for biblical examples.[6])

Many people could begin at this moment to overcome their sense of unhappiness and become happy people if they would choose to alter their perspective of who they are and begin to consider the reasons they have to be content. However, if they are determined to keep up with the Joneses, always wanting more and never stopping to enjoy what they have, they will never perceive themselves to be in a state of well-being—happy and joyful.

It's sad to me that many people never enjoy their health until they lose it. Others miss so many delightful moments with their children, failing to laugh and play with them, realizing too late that they have grown up and gone on their way. Spouses caught in the busyness and stress of their daily duties overlook the opportunities for tenderness, a kind word, a smile, or a word of encouragement. In these and many other ways the daily joys of life escape many people who are, ironically, focused on their own pursuit of happiness.

In order to gain a proper perception of the happiness available in life, we need to change our thinking, to obsess less over what we don't have and begin to be thankful for what we do have. Gratitude is a virtue that unlocks many doors to happiness. Of course, there is a greater reason for happiness than even the blessings of life we enjoy.

GOD'S DESIGN FOR HAPPINESS

God's intention for mankind was that we live in a state of happiness and contentment, enjoying relationship with Him and fulfilling the purpose for which He made each of us. The New Testament declares, "Every good gift and every perfect gift is from above, and comes down from the Father of lights" (James 1:17). God never intended that the world be filled with murder, violence, disease, and suffering of all kinds; those are a direct result of the disobedience of the first couple against God. Since that time, God has been carrying out His plan to redeem mankind from the terrible power of sin and its consequences.

According to Scripture, God is the giver of life and all that pertains to it. When Jesus walked on the earth, He declared, "I have come that they may have life, and that they may have it more abundantly" (John 10:10). About what He had taught His disciples, He said, "These things I have spoken to you, that My joy may remain in you, and that your joy may be full" (John 15:11). God's design for your life is to restore the joy He created you to know.

BENEFITS OF HAPPINESS

For hundreds of years psychologists and other medical professionals have studied the *negative* forces that affect the physical, emotional, and mental health of their patients. Only in recent years have studies begun to focus on the *positive* forces that make people healthy and happy. Here are a few of the measurable benefits that happiness exerts for living a healthy life.

Better health

King Solomon, the wisest man who ever lived, understood the benefits of a happy heart. He declared, "A cheerful heart is good medicine" (Prov. 17:22, NIV). He must have observed how cheerfulness and positive emotions affected the health of lives around him. Perhaps he also saw the destructive results worked in people's minds and bodies by negative emotions. Could he even have known what a preventive "drug" a cheerful heart could be against sickness and disease?

The great philosopher Voltaire wrote, "The art of medicine consists of keeping the patient amused while nature heals the disease."[7] The healing power of happiness was referred to as a medicine by Solomon and as an art by Voltaire. Thousands of years later, scientists are proving the validity of both as they have learned to measure the physical, mental, and emotional value of living in a state of happiness. Rich Bayer, PhD, CEO of Upper Bay Counseling and Support Services, Inc., writes:

> Happiness is good for us. It brings us physical, mental, and emotional health.... People who are happy do better in social relationships, use their intelligence more efficiently, are more optimistic, have better physical health, [and] are more creative.[8]

Healthy relationships

According to Bayer, happy people have more social contact and better social relations than their unhappy counterparts. Studies of positive people show that they rate high on having good relationships with themselves and with others. Their love life is better off as well. Happy people tend to be kinder to others and to express empathy more easily. They also have the ability to use their intelligence more effectively. Some studies show that people become better students when they are feeling happy.[9]

Optimism

Optimism is a result of living in a state of happiness. Happy people are not exempt from tragedy and hardship, but studies show that happy people have learned to think on the positive side of life more often. They remember the good events in their lives more readily, and when tragedy happens, they believe things will eventually be all right. They have hope. Studies also show that happy people actually have fewer health problems.[10]

Longevity

Want to live longer? Be happy. Research among older people indicates that folks with positive emotions outlived their negative counterparts. Happy people were shown to be half as likely to become disabled as sad people in the same age bracket. It is also very interesting that, according to scientific studies, happy people have a higher pain threshold than those who are sad.[11]

LAUGHTER REFLECTS HAPPINESS

Surely no human being has a corner on learning to live a happy life. So why do some people attain it and others don't? I believe all people can enjoy the wonderful, healthful benefits of living in a state of contentment and happiness if they follow the guidelines discussed here. Grappling with negative emotions to overcome them, allowing your perception of life to dwell on the positive, defining what makes you happy without trying to keep up with the Joneses, and, of course, considering your relationship with God, the eternal source of happiness, are all keys to unlocking your own happiness.

As you work to cultivate a lifestyle of happiness, laughter will play an important role. Laughter is the result of happiness.

Laughter is innate.

One of the key reasons happiness reduces stress is that happiness produces laughter. A happy person knows how to laugh. You may be aware of stories that have been highly publicized of people who have healed themselves from terminal illnesses through the power of laughter. "Throughout the centuries court jesters have been hired to relieve royalty's stress from governmental duties," writes Lynn Shaw.[12] In her article "A Prescription to Laugh: Healing Through Humor and Laughter," Ms. Shaw differentiates between laughter and humor:

> Laughter is innate, and you are born with your giggles. You have unique sounds of laughter. Your laughter may sound similar to another's laughter, but your sound is brilliantly yours. Laughter exists on its own merit. You do not have to "get the joke," hear a story, or decipher a code in order to laugh....In summary, laughter is innate and can be shared. Humor is learned and isn't always appreciated by more than the interpreter. There must be an intellectual connection as well.[13]

All of us have experienced the scenario of being in a room with other people who hear something and begin to laugh uproariously while we look around quizzically wondering what's so funny. That could be because we have different perceptions of what is humorous. Or it could be that we need to practice seeing the humorous in the everyday events around us. It is a fact that a sense of humor is developed from childhood. Lynn Shaw writes:

> Your sense of humor begins forming during your early life lessons of what is appropriate to laugh about or inappropriate (such as ridicule or teasing). Once the perception is processed in your mind, then your mind informs your body to push the laughter button and let your laughter sounds begin.[14]

Since I have become aware of the powerful healing therapy that laughter offers, I have asked my patients about their laughter patterns. Some have confessed that they have not laughed for years; they can't remember the last time they laughed. If you relate to that scenario, you need to do some "emotional work," taking stock of where your happiness quotient is at this stage of your life. Learning to laugh again can help to improve your health and your happiness.

Applying the salve of laughter

It is a simple fact that healthy laughter is not going to be released from a heart filled with depression, anger, resentment, bitterness, or even fear. Healthy laughter is an expression of delight and joy, and it springs from a sense of well-being and peace. Yet even if you are struggling with serious unhappiness, you can learn to apply the "salve" of laughter, which can release stress and unlock healing for you: body, mind, and spirit. In Lynn Shaw's article, she offers a prescription for using laughter and humor for healing:

> For the purpose of applying laughter to your daily life and the healing of your mind, body and spirit, think of humor as the brain waves jumpstarting your laughter. Become aware of what you interpret as funny. For example, next time you purchase a card, discover which ones elicited laughter. Read cartoons, bumper stickers, billboard signs to enhance your awareness of what generates laughter. When people tell stories, pay attention to how you felt afterwards. Did you laugh?... Finally, spend time daily practicing laughing out loud. Maybe smiling first, then leaning into a giggle, then outright belly laughs. Now move beyond thinking about laughter and humor. Go ahead... it's safe... you can do it... ready, get set, laugh![15]

I tell my patients that laughter is as powerful as a drug, very inexpensive, and has absolutely no side effects, except for the proverbial bursting your sides from laughing so hard. Even the worst negative life events don't seem so bad when we can find something about them to laugh at. Shakespeare said, "Nothing is good or bad. It is thinking that makes it so."[16] He understood something of the power of perception that controls our attitudes about life events.

Laughter is contagious

> The sound of roaring laughter is far more contagious than any cough, sniffle, or sneeze. Humor and laughter can cause a domino effect of joy

and amusement, as well as set off a number of positive physical effects. A good hearty laugh can help:

- Reduce stress
- Lower blood pressure
- Elevate mood
- Boost immune system,
- Improve brain functioning
- Protect the heart
- Connect you to others
- Foster instant relaxation
- Make you feel good[17]

According to the Association for Applied and Therapeutic Humor, "without humor one's thought processes are likely to become stuck and narrowly focused, leading to increased distress."[18] One of the delights of childhood is the spontaneous giggles of laughter that simple new discoveries elicit. Just listening to a child's uninhibited, unpretentious giggling brings smiles to the faces of adults who observe them. "Science of Laughter," on the Discovery Health Web site, asserts, "By the time a child reaches nursery school, he or she will laugh about 300 times a day. In comparison, adults laugh an average of 17 times a day."[19]

Perhaps this laughter phenomenon is one of the childlike characteristics Jesus had in mind when He "called a little child to Him, set him in the midst of them, and said, 'Assuredly, I say to you, unless you are converted and become as little children, you will by no means enter the kingdom of heaven. Therefore whoever humbles himself as this little child is the greatest in the kingdom of heaven'" (Matt. 18:2–4). Childlike trust in the Father to meet all our needs gives us freedom to enjoy everything He gives to us. Delight and joy are part of a healthy child's emotional expression.

Later, the apostle Paul described the kingdom of heaven as "righteousness and peace and joy in the Holy Spirit" (Rom. 14:17). Christ, who is our healer as well as our Savior, gives us His joy and expects us to nurture it as one of the vital elements of His kingdom. He understands the power of joy to ensure our peaceful state of well-being. The opposite is also true: our peaceful state of well-being elicits a joyful response.

MANAGING A SMILE

There are people who cannot even "manage" a smile even while others around them are laughing in delight. When posing for a formal photograph, they can only muster a toothy "grimace," which seems painful even for a few seconds. This is an outward symptom of an inner emotional struggle. Worry, fear, anger, and even "hurry" can make you incapable of smiling. A peaceful, positive, and confident emotional state is that which can manage a smile.

In psychology, there is a theory entitled the facial feedback hypothesis. It states that involuntary facial movements can drive emotional experience. In other words, you may actually be able to improve your mood by simply smiling![20] Clinical research shows that seeing a smile can give more pleasure than sex or eating chocolate. Receiving a smile from a friend or relative generates much higher levels of stimulation to the brain and the heart than being given money, according to clinical tests. But the amount of pleasure depends on who is smiling: a child's face or that of a celebrity has a much better effect than that of a politician. The research, carried out by the computer giant Hewlett-Packard, suggests that simple human interaction is still worth far more than material pleasure.[21]

Have you noticed how disarming a genuine smile can be? A person whose eyes light up and whose face is wrinkled into a toothy smile can hardly be feared. And it is difficult to be angry with someone you love who is beaming back a reconciliatory smile. Children learn early the power of their smile over their parents. Who can resist the plea of an enthusiastically smiling child, as opposed to a whining one?

It is true that some people learn to mask their inner turmoil and pain with their smile. Yet for many, the "required" smile in social situations can be as painful as the emotional turmoil they carry inside. It is an outward symptom of an inner need for healing.

Having trouble forcing a smile? Here are a few suggestions that may help:

- Jump on the bed.
- Make faces at yourself in the mirror.
- Dance around the house.
- Find your baby pictures.
- Hug someone you love.
- Watch cartoons you loved as a kid.
- Imitate a well-known comedian—with exaggeration.
- Visit a pet store.[22]

It takes some effort to break habit patterns that continually energize our negative emotions, but the results are worth the effort. Practice smiling every day. It's a very cheap prescription for lifting your mood and affecting your attitude in a positive way.

MAKING HAPPINESS A HABIT

Consider again our discussion in chapter nine of the fact that *attitude* is your best friend or your worst enemy. I listed in that chapter several attitudes that turn off the stress response, including contentment, appreciation, forgiveness, joy, love, and compassion. These positive attitudes are all conducive to happiness. And the good news is that they can be *practiced*; they can become a habit. You can decide every day not to display negative attitudes and to adopt positive ones. In that same way, laughter can be a choice; you can practice cultivating a smiling countenance and learn to include healthy laughter in your life every day. I tell my patients that they need ten belly laughs a day to ensure health.

Of course, we do not live in a vacuum, and no one element of health is a cure-all. But if you decide to cultivate a lifestyle of happiness and joy, applying the principles we have discussed here, you will be well on your way to living a healthy, *stress less* life. And you will be able to bring lightheartedness and joy to others as you allow empathy and compassion to fill your heart for them.

Create a habit of happiness instead of a habit of worry. Develop a habit of laughter instead of a habit of complaining. Determine to make the right choices that will change your perception of life forever. Gratitude and thanksgiving for the good things of life will begin to fill your thoughts instead of obsession over the things you don't have. It's up to you. Your happiness is not at the mercy of other people or life circumstances and events. You can increase your happiness quotient if you are willing to change your habit patterns and enjoy God's design for your lifestyle.

As you allow your perspective of life to be changed and you begin to experience less stress, you will realize that not only are your mind and emotions experiencing relief, but your body is becoming more relaxed as well. In the next chapter we will discuss ways you can enhance relaxation in your life as you determine to *Stress Less*.

18
_____

Learning to Relax

Muscle tension is nature's primary way of informing you that you are under stress. The body registers stress before the conscious mind does. When the stress response is triggered in the body, muscles automatically contract in preparation to either "fight" or "flee." When we don't fight or flee, however, these muscles remain tense. The tension may be expressed as a furrowed brow, a clenched jaw, pursed lips, clenched fists, or a curling of the toes. It can be felt as tightness of the neck, shoulders, or back, or as tension in any other muscle group, such as the buttocks or abdominal muscles.

Most people don't realize they are developing tense muscles, and therefore they don't recognize the first warning sign of stress. They are unaware of the slowly contracting and tightening of muscle tissue until that tension reaches the point where they have a full-blown headache, sore neck, or backache.

Jessica was a forty-two-year-old female patient who told me she had suffered from tension headaches since she was in her teens. She had been to numerous doctors through the years, including family practitioners, neurologists, and chiropractors, but she had experienced only minor relief. She had taken numerous mediations, but again with only minor relief. The headaches generally started midmorning and persisted throughout the day and even into the night.

Jessica had always been an intense, highly motivated person. She excelled in school, making almost straight As. She strove for perfection in her life and had forged a very successful career in real estate. She had three children and a loving husband who was an appliance salesman at a major department store.

Her children, unlike Jessica, were very laid back and made mostly Bs and Cs on their report cards. They rarely cleaned their rooms, and this frustrated her. Her husband was even more laid back and had never even attempted to earn a promotion at his job. This also frustrated Jessica.

After examining Jessica, reading her case history, and talking to her about her life in general, I explained to Jessica that I believed the root reason for her headaches was her perfectionist attitude and the resulting frustrations she felt toward the "imperfections" of other people. I taught her how to scan her body for muscle tension throughout the day. That scan begins by asking five basic questions:

1. Are you furrowing your brow?
2. Are you clenching your jaw?
3. Are you pursing your lips?
4. Are your shoulders and neck tense or tight?
5. Do you have discomfort anywhere in your body?

When Jessica began to scan her body for muscle tension and learned how to release that tension as it started to develop, her headaches simply did not materialize. She no longer needed medication. She was ecstatic!

Not every person is the same when it comes to the amount of tension he or she experiences, or how that tension is expressed in the body. One person might have a clenched jaw and another person a furrowed brow. Some people wear their tension on their shoulders or neck. We also need to remind ourselves that not everybody has the same distortional thought patterns—every person has a different set of mental and emotional habits and internal "software" that trigger stress.

No matter how we accumulate stress, it is a scientific fact that nearly all people can use the same basic relaxation techniques to identify their particular expressions of tension and the underlying mental and emotional reasons for it. In this chapter I want to introduce several practical techniques that are available and effective for enhanced relaxation. You will find complete instructions for these helpful exercise programs in the resources listed with them.

MINDFULNESS

Let's begin with a technique designed to alleviate a primary cause of stress, which we have discussed—our thinking patterns. In the late 1960s Herbert Benson, MD, president of Mind/Body Medical Institute (MBMI), was the first person to describe the physiologic reaction called the relaxation response. The relaxation response is a physical state of deep rest that changes the physical and emotional responses to stress. It has been effective in decreasing heart rate, blood pressure, and muscle tension. If practiced regularly, it can have lasting effects when encountering stress throughout the day and can improve health. You can find complete instructions at their Web site, www.mbmi.org.[1]

This relaxation response includes a concept called mindfulness. According to Dr. Benson:

> Mindfulness is the practice of learning to pay attention to what is happening to you from moment to moment. To be mindful, you must slow down, do one activity at a time, and bring your full awareness to both the activity at hand and to your inner experience of it. Mindfulness provides a potentially powerful antidote to the common causes of daily stress such as time pressure, distraction, agitation, and interpersonal conflicts.[2]

This definition of mindfulness reminds me of the words of Jesus: "Therefore do not worry about tomorrow, for tomorrow will worry about its own things. Sufficient for the day is its own trouble" (Matt. 6:34). The apostle Paul's exhortation to "[forget] those things which are behind" is another instruction to focus on what is at hand.

So many people do not live in the present moment. They are wishing for a "different" moment—either past or future. They go through the motions required to function in the present moment, but mentally they are thinking thoughts such as:

- "I wish I could sleep later."
- "I wish I could get a promotion."
- "I wish I had gone to college."
- "I wish my children would behave."
- "I wish I was already home and not stuck in this traffic."
- "I wish I was on vacation."

Mindfulness means letting go of any thought that is unrelated to the present moment and finding something to enjoy in the present—continually. Dr. Benson offers some practical ways to cultivate mindfulness:

- As you awaken in the morning, bring your attention to your breathing. Instead of letting your mind spin off into yesterday or today, take *mindful* breaths. Focus on your breathing, and sense the effects of breathing throughout your body.

- Instead of hurrying to your usual routine, slow down and enjoy something special about the morning: a flower that bloomed, the sound of birds, the wind in the trees.

- When stopped at a red light, pay attention to your breathing and enjoy the landscape.

- As you go to sleep, let go of today and tomorrow, and take some slow, mindful breaths.[3]

Dan was a colleague of mine—a very goal-oriented man. When he was a teenager, he couldn't wait to graduate from high school and go to college. He worked hard and graduated from college a year early. Then he entered medical school and finished near the top of his class. His next goal was to finish his surgery residency, which he did in five years. Then he entered a group practice where he was on call every fourth night, which meant he was usually up all night. By that time he had driven himself so hard for so long that he had forgotten how to enjoy his life.

Dan was an extremely fun-loving guy when he was on vacation, but the vast majority of the year he was driven. He rarely spent quality time or had fun with his spouse and children, and one by one through the years, his wives left him. He divorced and remarried three times and had one child with each of these three wives. His children ended up on drugs, using alcohol, or were in total rebellion. Dan seemed to live and work for his two-week vacation each year.

Every time Dan reached a goal, he quickly set a new one. Over the years, "vacation" became his top goal. He focused his attention on that future time and regretted his past. He lived with a great deal of tension and stress. Dan had become a chronic worrier.

I discussed with Dan his need to focus on the present moment and learn to enjoy "now." I explained that it wasn't necessary or mentally healthy to think about and entertain every thought that pops into one's head, and that he could choose what he was going to think about. Even though Dan was a physician and surgeon, he had never been confronted with these ideas.

Dan began to learn how to live in the present moment. He replaced his old thought patterns and perceptions with new ones as he practiced mindfulness. He is now happily married and enjoys spending quality time with his children, who come to visit him regularly. They turned from most of their rebellious ways once their father began to show genuine affection toward them and to express a desire to spend time with them. He no longer lives for vacation, but he enjoys his life. His tension and stress levels are greatly reduced.

Mindfulness can become a way of life, a continual pattern for practicing relaxation during the day. Like any other habit, good or bad, it must be practiced to become an accepted part of everyday life. Your mental and physical health will prosper from this habit.

Praise and thanksgiving: a spiritual form of mindfulness

Voicing gratitude and praise to God is a way to practice mindfulness. The Book of Psalms is filled with the poetry of thanksgiving and praise to God:

> Bless the LORD, O my soul;
> And all that is within me, bless His holy name!
> Bless the LORD, O my soul,
> And forget not all His benefits:
> Who forgives all your iniquities,
> Who heals all your diseases,
> Who redeems your life from destruction,
> Who crowns you with lovingkindness and ten-
>   der mercies,
> Who satisfies your mouth with good things,
> So that your youth is renewed like the eagle's.
> —PSALM 103:1–5

I recommend that you start each day by saying aloud, "I thank You, Lord, for..." or, "I praise You, Lord, for..." and identifying at least twenty or thirty specific things, great and small, for which you are grateful. Psalm 118:24 declares, "This is the day the LORD has made; we will rejoice and be glad in it."

You can encourage your children and spouse to join you in this activity. Spend some time at the breakfast table praising the Lord for the ways you are trusting Him to help you through the coming day. Express your thanks for the food you are eating, the clothes you are wearing, the school you are attending, or the workplace where you are going that day.

Thank the Lord for teachers, friends, colleagues, patients, clients, vendors, customers, and neighbors. Thank Him for the police and fire departments that stand guard over the community's safety. Thank Him for elected officials who set policy for the city, state, and nation. Thank Him for church leaders who give moral and biblical guidance and teaching. You won't run out of things to thank the Lord for as a family. Take turns around the breakfast table voicing thanks. Even if you express only a dozen or so specific things of thanksgiving and praise, you will have established a mind-set of being in the moment of today with gratitude.

Teach your children to be thankful for the little luxuries they have that they don't even know are luxuries. As your child emerges from a warm bath or shower, remind your child that warm water is a gift from God to your family. If you lived in parts of Africa where I have traveled, you would have to walk a mile—or more—to reach water. Then to bathe in it would mean going into cold and very possibly polluted water and facing the risk of parasites, dysentery, and even crocodiles as part of a bath.

Learn to be thankful not only for a meal that is set before you, but also for each bite. Appreciate the food's taste, aroma, and appearance.

Look closely at the world around you.

When you walk with a spouse, friend, or child, focus on the beautiful scenery, the chirping of the birds and crickets, and the feel of the warm sunshine or the chill in the air. Focus on the way your body feels as you move your muscles during a brisk twenty-minute walk. Refuse to think about goals, projects, or tasks that are not part of the present moment. If a stressful thought comes to mind, choose to move on to a thought that is related to what you are presently seeing, hearing, smelling, or feeling.

You may also benefit by assigning an otherwise irritating sight or sound to become a signal to you to practice mindfulness. For example, if you encounter a red light while driving to work, rather than become frustrated, consider this a prompt to take in all the sights around you as you voice thanksgiving and praise. Show your gratitude for the privilege of having an automobile to drive, music to hear in your car, air conditioning or heating for the car, and so forth. If you are usually irritated by the sound of a ringing phone, use that ringing sound to signal mindfulness—begin to thank the Lord for at least one person as you make your way to the phone. If the phone is in a different room from where you are in your home, you may have time to thank the Lord for several people!

As people practice mindfulness, their muscles generally begin to relax. Mindfulness is the foundation on which other muscle-relaxation techniques should be based. It simply focuses your attention on the present moment. Gratitude is an easy way to practice mindfulness because it generally focuses your mind on what is good at present.

BREATHING

Thich Nhat Hanh, author of *The Miracle of Mindfulness*, states: "To master our breath is to be in control of our bodies and minds."[4] You may never have thought about the simple physiological activity of breathing as a means of relaxation. Becoming conscious of how you breathe can have a powerful effect over the well-being of your entire psyche.

You have been breathing about sixteen times per minute all of your life, breathing faster when you exercise, and using your breath to speak and shout as you wanted.[5] The physical function of breathing is one of the most subconscious activities of the physical body; that is, until a health crisis or panic attack or other trauma interferes with its normal function. Perhaps the first bodily function that is changed when you face a fight-or-flight situation is your breathing. If you can become aware of the marvelous mechanisms that are involved in your natural breathing, you can use them as one of the most effective relaxation techniques available.

Biblical significance

Breathing has always had not only a natural, physical function in the body, but also a link to man's emotions and spirit. In both Hebrew and Greek, the original languages of the Bible, the word for *breath* has a double meaning. It refers to natural breathing and also to the spirit. In Genesis, God created Adam by breathing into his nostrils the breath of life, and Adam became a "living soul" (Gen. 2:7, KJV). After His resurrection, Jesus appeared to His disciples and "breathed on them, and saith unto them, Receive ye the Holy Ghost" (John 20:22, KJV).

Creating awareness

Most people take breathing for granted so long as it is normal. An exception to that fact may be vocalists or musicians who have been taught to use their breath for specific purposes that require endurance and skilled control. I will help you to learn some of these same principles of breathing as a relaxation technique.

The practice of "deep breathing" is an intentional process—it is breathing with a mental awareness and discipline. The good news is that deep breathing is one of the easiest, simplest, and best ways to decrease muscle tension and relieve stress. With each deep breath, you are delivering life-sustaining oxygen to the cells of your body, while at the same time you are eliminating carbon dioxide, a waste product.

There are two main types of breathing: chest breathing (thoracic breathing) and abdominal breathing (diaphragmatic breathing). As an infant, you were an abdominal breather. Have you ever observed a toddler wearing only his diaper and watched his ribs move in and out as he breathes? He is still breathing deeply, as adults do only when they sleep. Most adults, unless trained otherwise, use their shoulder and upper chest muscles to inhale and exhale. However, the normal pattern for breathing is when our abdominal muscles force air out of our lungs and allow air to enter our lungs, commonly referred to as deep breathing.

Discovering your diaphragm

It is fun to watch newborns discover their hands and toes; it is all part of their development. It is just as necessary, for relaxation purposes, for adults to discover their diaphragm. It is not difficult, but it will take some effort. First, try this experiment:

> See how much air you can push out of your body. Squeeze your ribs in on both sides, using your elbows to help. At the same time, pull in your abdominal muscles and hold this position for three or four seconds. Then, relax, allow air back into your lungs, and think about the wonders of your breathing mechanism.[6]

Though you may have felt like you were out of air, there is always some air left in the lungs: residual air. If you tried to keep the air out of your body for more than a minute, the body would relax involuntarily and air would rush in; you would not faint. When you finished this experiment and decided to breathe again, was it hard to get air? No; air rushed in automatically.

Before trying another experiment, consider these facts about your breathing mechanism. Air is stored in the lungs, which are merely sacs, subdivided into thousands of tiny sub-compartments. They have no muscles of their own; rather, they adhere to the ribs, growing smaller when the ribs move in and larger when they move out. To exhale completely, you used a number of different muscles, but there are two principal muscle groups involved: the intercostal muscles, which are between the ribs, and the abdominal muscles, which support the tummy. Strengthening these between-the-ribs muscles will be very helpful in controlling breathing for relaxation purposes. To do so, try this exercise:

- Try to widen your rib cage from side to side. As high as you can reach with your hands, grip your rib cage on both sides. Press your hands against your ribs, and then inhale (breathe in), at the same time pushing your ribs out against the pressure of your hands.

- Now relax your abdominal muscles so that your tummy wall moves gently outward, opening up space so that air rushes into your lungs. Hold this position for three or four seconds, then let your abdominal muscles pull in again, pushing the breath out, while the ribs return to their relaxed position.[7]

Becoming an abdominal breather

Are you a chest or abdominal breather? To find out, simply lie on your back and place your right hand on your abdomen at your waistline (or on your belly button). Then place your left hand on the center of your chest. Now simply breathe normally and notice which hand rises more when you inhale. For most people, the hand on their chest will rise more. This means you are a chest breather. If the hand on your abdomen rises more, you are an abdominal breather.

To become an abdominal breather, you have to control your diaphragm, which is the muscle separating the chest cavity from the abdominal cavity. As you inhale, the diaphragm flattens downward, allowing the lungs more space to fill. By flattening this muscle, you allow more oxygen into the body and more carbon dioxide out of the body. To do this, I recommend that you lie on your back on a bed, carpet, or rug. Put your legs straight out and mildly apart, with your toes pointed outward. Place one hand on your abdomen over the belly button and the other hand at the center of your chest. Slowly inhale through your nose, making sure the hand on the abdomen rises. Intentionally push out your abdomen; the hand on the chest should move only a little. As you inhale through your nose, count to yourself, "One thousand one, one thousand two, one thousand three." As you exhale through your mouth, count, "One thousand one, one thousand two, one thousand three." You should feel your abdomen falling as you exhale.

People sometimes wonder whether breathing exercises will thicken their waistlines. Quite the opposite! Good abdominal muscles are essential to a good figure. Incidentally, they also support the back muscles and help you avoid back pain.[8]

Some people take this exercise a step further. As they inhale, they say to themselves, "I breathe in the breath of relaxation," or they say, "Relaxation in" or "Peace in," to themselves. As they exhale, they say to themselves, "I breathe out tension," "I release the tension," "Tension out," or "Stress out."

Don't wait until you feel stressed to practice this breathing. Begin to practice deep breathing in the evening or morning when you are *not* feeling stressed. A basketball team doesn't wait until the end-of-the-season tournaments to begin practicing free throws. Likewise, you are wise to practice abdominal breathing on a daily basis, so that when stressful times occur, you can move quickly and easily into abdominal breathing.

Breathing to prevent hyperventilation

When a person experiences a panic attack, he usually gasps, breathes, and then holds his breath. This leads to rapid, shallow breathing. When a person starts to panic, if he will simply exhale first to open up the lungs, he may be able to abort a full-blown panic attack. The person then should begin to practice abdominal breathing, inhaling and exhaling through the nose. The exhalation should be longer than the inhalation. This slows down the breathing process, and it prevents hyperventilation.

MEDITATION

Most Americans—for that matter, most people in the industrialized Western cultures—have come to enjoy being busy, filling their lives with activity, people, and noise. Many do not even understand the art of quiet, solitary meditation; others consider it boring. I highly recommend meditation, however, and find it anything but boring!

In 1968, Dr. Herbert Benson and his colleagues at Harvard Medical School put meditation to the test and scientifically proved five major beneficial aspects of meditation:[9]

1. Heart rate and breathing rate slowed significantly.
2. The need for oxygen consumption fell by 20 percent.
3. Blood lactate levels dropped.
4. Skin resistance to electrical current increased fourfold (a sign of relaxation).
5. EEG tracings of brain-wave patterns indicated increased alpha activity, a sign of relaxation.

Meditation, in essence, involves a process of focusing one's attention on only one thing at a time and letting all other thoughts go. Simply put, meditation is "focused thinking." If a stray thought comes to a meditating person's mind, he should not resist that thought or judge it—rather, he should simply notice it and then immediately let it go. The conscious mind should remain focused on a word or phrase that the person has chosen to focus on through repetition.

For example, from ancient times God has instructed His people to meditate on His Word:

> This book of the law shall not depart out of thy mouth; but thou shalt *meditate* therein day and night, that thou mayest observe to do according to all that is written therein: for then thou shalt make thy way prosperous, and then thou shalt have good success.
> —JOSHUA 1:8, KJV, EMPHASIS ADDED

God promised a prosperous life of success for those who would quietly meditate on the Word of God continually. While there are many forms of meditation, my favorite is meditating on Scripture. You may call this reflecting on God's Word or contemplating God's Word. It doesn't take great skill to learn to meditate, just a decision to become quiet, control your thoughts, and center in on one idea. What better ideas than what the Word of God offers?

According to Rick Warren, the author of *The Purpose-Driven Life*, "If you know how to worry, you already know how to meditate."[10] Worry is also focused thinking—focusing on the problem. In meditation, the goal is to help a person gain and sustain a positive focus. For the Christian, what a person focuses upon is just as important as the focusing technique.

Meditation not only helps a person calm the mind and relax the body, but it also helps a person control thoughts, which is very important as he seeks to take control over distortional thought patterns and change them. Hebrews 4:12 (KJV) tells us:

> The word of God is quick, and powerful, and sharper than any twoedged sword, piercing even to the dividing asunder of soul and spirit, and of the joints and marrow, and is a discerner of the thoughts and intents of the heart.

The Word of God has the power to reveal our wrong thinking patterns and help us to change them so that we can be filled with peace and calm. The apostle Paul exhorted believers:

> Do not be conformed to this world, but be transformed by the renewing of your mind, that you may prove what is that good and acceptable and perfect will of God.
>
> —ROMANS 12:2

The unnecessary stressors this culture presses upon us can be overcome as we choose to meditate on God's Word. Jesus said, "The words that I speak to you are spirit, and they are life" (John 6:63). I choose especially to focus on the words of Jesus as I meditate. I repeat what I have memorized of the words of Jesus as I sit calmly. I train my mind to focus on His words, and I allow them to sink deep into my heart and soul.

Science affirms the power of prayer.

Prayer is a form of meditation, quietly focusing our hearts and minds on God. Many kinds of prayer are taught in the Bible, including thanksgiving, intercession for others, petition for our needs, and prayers for healing. Jeffrey Cram, PhD, has studied the extrasensory effects of prayer. He cites Larry Dossey's book *Healing Words*, which has an appendix with more than two hundred scientific studies done on prayer.[11]

Dr. Cram also refers to a review of randomized, controlled trials of healing that was published in the June 2000 *Annals of Internal Medicine*. More than half of the studies showed significant results. For example, coronary care patients who were treated with prayerful meditation required less ventilatory support, antibiotics, or diuretics. And AIDS patients had fewer new AIDS-defining illnesses, less illness severity, fewer physician visits and hospitalizations, and improved mood.[12]

Though Dr. Cram refers to these results as "phenomena," he concludes that scientists "need to be open to these phenomena. Consider how we can better use our instruments to document these extraordinary sensory experiences. Perhaps, by validating what we cannot see, hear or touch, we can refine our extra sensory experience and learn to grow more in these areas."[13]

Of course, the Scriptures teach clearly the power of prayer:

> Be anxious for nothing, but in everything by prayer and supplication, with thanksgiving, let your requests be made known to God; and the peace of God, which surpasses all understanding, will guard your hearts and minds through Christ Jesus.
>
> —Philippians 4:6–7

USE YOUR IMAGINATION IN A HEALTHY WAY

From our childhood, we have discovered and developed the art of daydreaming. We used our imagination perhaps to escape the circumstances we were in or to dream of what we would like to be or do. Unfortunately, as our minds take on more distortional thinking, hurt, pain, and worldly ideas, our imaginations become more negative and corrupt. People imagine catastrophes that will come to them and many kinds of unclean thoughts. From the beginning of mankind, after sin entered the world, our imaginations have been bent to evil: "And GOD saw that the wickedness of man was great in the earth, and that every imagination of the thoughts of his heart was only evil continually" (Gen. 6:5, KJV).

Christians, who have the power of God dwelling within, can completely change this negative inclination to an evil imagination. The apostle Paul, after instructing believers not to be anxious and to pray with thanksgiving, continues his instructions:

> Finally, brethren, whatever things are true, whatever things are noble, whatever things are just, whatever things are pure, whatever things are lovely, whatever things are of good report, if there is any virtue and if there is anything praiseworthy—*meditate* on these things.
> —PHILIPPIANS 4:8, EMPHASIS ADDED

Choosing to think about noble, just, pure, and lovely things will cleanse our mind of many stressful factors. Using our imagination in a healthy way can be a useful technique for relaxation. We all practice mental visualization on a daily basis, even if we're not aware that we do. Daydreaming and imagining are visualization techniques. There is great benefit in reducing stress by purposefully and consciously using visualization techniques.

Find a quiet place where you will not be disturbed, and lie down or sit in a comfortable chair. Think of an image, place, memory, or scene that relaxes you. Allow yourself to be immersed in your image by involving all five senses in the visualization. See the images, hear the sounds, feel the fabric or air temperature, smell and taste items related to your image, and so forth.

If your favorite vacation spot is the beach, imagine yourself walking along the beach on a bright, sunny day, experiencing the ocean breeze as it blows through your hair, the warmth of the sun on your skin, and hearing the slap of the waves on the shoreline; taste the salty air, and breathe deeply the relaxation all of that brings. Let your imagination be filled with the sights, sounds, and other comforting sensory perceptions you have experienced. Whatever your relaxing daydream is, spend five or ten minutes there, and see what relaxation effects it has on your psyche. And don't forget to return to mindful thoughts about the blessings of the present moment.

FREEZE-FRAME: MOVING FROM THE HEAD TO THE HEART

Researchers at HeartMath developed a system of techniques to relieve stress that helps people move their concentration from what's going on in their head to what's going on in their heart. One such technique is called "Freeze-Frame." The person who learns this technique tends to experience much greater appreciation, joy, compassion, and love. (You can learn more about this on their Web sites at www.heartmath.com or www.heartmath.org.)

Most of us are familiar with the general concept of freezing a frame. It is what we do when we are watching a video or DVD and decide to pause the video momentarily so we can do something else. Using the steps of Freeze-Frame as an emotional refocusing technique is very similar. A person practices this technique in the midst of a stressful event by "stopping" the processing of the event momentarily to gain a clearer perspective.

Becoming skilled at freeze-framing takes practice, but eventually it can become second nature. I frequently recommend the Freeze Framer Interactive Learning System computer program to my patients—this gives real-time heart rate variability feedback.

Most people have developed a habit of spontaneously reacting to experiences or events in their lives rather than responding consciously and deliberately. Although it may be difficult to stop this habit, the benefits are worth the effort!

There are specific steps to the Freeze-Frame technique to shift your negative or stressful thought process. You can learn these steps through books and other materials available from HeartMath. The first step is similar to pushing pause on a video. In other steps, you shift your attention away from what is causing you stress and focus on your heart. The key is to experience positive feelings in the moment and learn to follow your heart.

Overall, using HeartMath techniques can be an effective way to keep your reactive mind and emotions in check. Your "com-

monsense heart" is far more rational than most people know![14]
See Appendix D for more information.

THE TECHNIQUE OF PROGRESSIVE RELAXATION

The progressive relaxation technique was pioneered in the
1930s by Edmund Jacobson.[15] Jacobson believed that if people
could learn to relax their muscles through a precise method,
mental relaxation would follow. His technique involves tensing
and relaxing various voluntary muscle groups throughout the
body in an orderly sequence.[16]

Scientists today are learning the superior value this method
of relaxation offers. According to psychologists Robert Woolfolk
and Frank Richardson, "Despite the relative obscurity of this
method, progressive relaxation is perhaps the most reliable and
effective [relaxation] procedure of all."[17]

Progressive muscle relaxation (PMR), as it is called today, is
one of the most simple and easily learned techniques for relaxation. It works because of the relationship between your muscle
tension and your emotional tension; your emotional turmoil
causes you to tense your muscles, unknowingly. That muscle
tension causes other ailments, like headache and backache.

PMR teaches you to relax your muscles following two precise
steps: First, you apply tension to certain muscle groups, and then
you stop the tension and concentrate on how the muscles are
relaxing as the tension ceases. For a complete list of instructions,
please refer to my book *Deadly Emotions*.

Do not begin this procedure without your doctor's evaluation. People who have had injuries, surgeries, or other ailments
should not create tension in muscle groups that could cause
further damage. I always recommend that you do no exercise
program without your doctor's approval.

AUTOGENIC TRAINING HELPS THE
AUTONOMIC NERVOUS SYSTEM

Progressive relaxation works on the muscle groups in a conscious, deliberate fashion. But what about relaxing those muscle
groups that we unconsciously tighten and are unable to relax
long term using progressive relaxation or breathing exercises?
For those muscles and nerves, *autogenic* training can be very

helpful. *Autogenic* literally means "self-regulation." In essence, this system uses the mind to regulate stress and has been used for years, along with biofeedback, to reduce stress.

To engage in this technique, relax in a quiet, undisturbed environment in a comfortable position. You may lie down or sit, but make certain your head, back, and extremities are well supported. Develop an attitude of passive concentration, which means that you are focused and alert without falling asleep, but that you refuse to analyze, ponder, or allow your mind to work too hard. Simply relax and allow the suggestions you give to your body to flow in an easy way.

Concentrate your thinking on images of heaviness, followed by images of warmth in the limbs. Very specifically...

- Concentrate first on one arm and then on your other arm and then both arms at the same time. Say to yourself, "My arm is heavy." Keep repeating your statement for each arm for a minute or so. Do this several times a day. Always begin with your dominant arm—if you are right-handed, that is your right arm. Repeat this exercise for several days.

- Concentrate first on one leg and then on your other leg and then both legs at the same time. Again, say to yourself, "My leg is heavy." Do this several times a day and keep repeating the statement for each leg for a minute or so. Begin with your dominant leg. Repeat this exercise for several days.

- Then, as you concentrate on your arms and legs together, saying to yourself, "My arms are heavy" and, "My legs are heavy," begin to add statements about warmth: "My arms are warm," and, "My legs are warm." Repeat each statement for several minutes, and do this exercise several times a day. Repeat this exercise for several days.

- As you become skilled at feeling heaviness and warmth in your limbs, do these exercises for longer periods of time, up to ten to twenty minutes, three to six times a day. With practice, this exercise becomes easy.

In concentrating on images of heaviness, a person promotes the relaxation of the voluntary muscles, the ones that move the arms and legs. In concentrating on images of warmth, a person promotes peripheral vasodilation. There are other standard exercises in autogenic training—meditative and special exercises beyond the scope of this book. For more information, I recommend that you read *Autogenic: A Clinical Guide* by Wolfgang Linden and *The Relaxation and Stress Reduction Workbook* by Martha Davis, Elizabeth Eshelman, and Matthew McKay.[18]

USING BIOFEEDBACK TO DETERMINE YOUR FOCUS OF STRESS

Biofeedback uses instruments and machines that measure various biological parameters, such as heart rate, blood pressure, skin conductivity (sweating), skin surface temperature, muscle tension, and brain-wave activity. Each of these biological parameters can be controlled to some extent by working with a biofeedback trainer.

In a biofeedback session, a person works with a trained professional to identify which aspects of the nervous system are not relaxed. For example, a person's EEG may show alpha wave activity in the brain (a sign of relaxation), but the EMG shows muscle tension and the skin temperature is cool—both are signs of stress. Biofeedback helps a person identify what aspect of the body needs to be addressed with a relaxation technique.

Most large cities and major universities offer biofeedback training. To find a certified biofeedback practitioner, call (303) 422–8436. Some companies offer less expensive home biofeedback "trainers" that can be hooked up to a person's computer. You might ask a certified practitioner about these programs to determine which is best for you. Again, biofeedback is not a relaxation technique, per se. Rather, it is helpful in learning where and how to focus relaxation techniques.

THE HOLOSYNC TECHNIQUE CREATES BRAIN PATTERNS

Bill Harris started Centerpointe Research Institute in the late 1980s. He and his colleagues discovered modern technological methods of creating brain wave patterns associated with deep meditation, as well as other desirable mental states. They used audio technology they called "Holosync." This technology contains no spoken information or messages, but rather it uses certain precise combinations of sine wave tones. Holosync creates in the listener an electrical brain wave pattern in which the two sides of the brain communicate in a highly beneficial way.

According to Harris, Holosync stimulates the brain to make structural changes that help a person's ability to handle stress, meet challenges, tap into creativity, and experience personal feelings of joy, inner peace, and happiness.

The program works like this: Two soundtracks are played on a CD. This CD should be listened to using stereo headphones. One of the soundtracks is a half-hour soundtrack that gradually places a person into deep meditation. The second half-hour soundtrack holds the person in that state. After a few months of listening to the Holosync CD using stereo headphones, a person is able to add his or her own affirmations, recorded in the person's own voice. (See Appendix D for more information, or visit their Web site at www.Holosync.com.)

This is a new form of sound technology, and even though some of the advertisements for this sound New Age–related, the science of it is not. Take the science and spit out the New Age bones, replacing them with scriptural affirmations, such as the ones listed in Appendix C.

MASSAGE TO RELAX THE BODY

There are at least two hundred known massage techniques. From perhaps the oldest, acupressure, dating back five thousand years, to those forms of massage developed in the twentieth century, these techniques do benefit the relaxation process of the body. Massage is always a recommendation I give my patients, especially if their condition is exacerbated by stress. Even a handheld massage device can help to relieve tension in the muscles, thereby relieving stress. For an alphabetical listing and brief synopsis of many types of massage, refer to the Web site at www.AboutMasssage.com.

There are even massages that accommodate our hectic "airport" routines. The "chair massage" is designed to relax you as you are massaged in a special chair, fully clothed, waiting for your next flight. You could even invite a practitioner to bring his or her portable massage chair to your office or business, or to a party for your invited guests' benefit. This ten- or twenty-minute massage can bring moderate relaxation, wherever it is administered.[19]

The Bowen Technique is named after Australian Tom Bowen who in the 1950s introduced the concept of having rest periods between a series of massage movements, allowing the body to absorb the healing process before continuing the session. This technique involves gentle, soft tissue manipulations, which are precise and intended to create harmony within the body, allowing it to make its own adjustments and achieve its own cure.[20] This type of massage is able to balance the autonomic nervous system, relieving stress significantly. I routinely prescribe this type of massage for my patients.

SUMMARIZING THE BIG PICTURE OF RELAXATION

To relax, you first need to reprogram your mind by practicing mindfulness, which is simply focusing your attention on the present moment. As you learn to calm your mind, your muscles will relax. Allowing your mind to be renewed through meditation will help you to get rid of distortional thinking that causes tension.

You can combine mindfulness with specific techniques to further enhance the relaxation response. These techniques include deep breathing, progressive muscle relaxation (PMR), and autogenic training. Various forms of massage therapy and other relaxation techniques can be explored, which are like icing on the cake of relaxation.

The good news for stressed out people is that it is possible to move from a state of frustration and anxiety to a relaxed state fairly quickly. Even more importantly, it is possible to live continually in a much more relaxed state.

Adrenal Fatigue and Burnout

James was a schoolteacher in a small town in the Northwest. He and his wife were happily married. When they began to have children, Jim decided to supplement his income by becoming a firefighter with the fire department in his small town. James would work all day at school, come home in the afternoon, change his clothes, and head off to the fire department to work all night. He worked every other night and on some weekends. Occasionally James would get a nap between his school teaching job and his fire department job. On some nights he was able to sleep for several uninterrupted hours at the fire department, but many nights at the fire department he was up all night or a significant part of the night.

After a few years of this, James' wife noticed that James' health was changing. First he developed allergies that he had never had before. He was always tired and was also very irritable and short-tempered. His three young children seemed especially to irritate him, and he often snapped at them and then later felt remorseful. As James became more and more fatigued, he became more forgetful, lost all interest in sex, and became very sluggish. He no longer went to a gym to work out on days he didn't go to the fire department. He no longer played softball. He didn't have any recreational outlet.

Eventually James developed such severe fatigue that he was unable to go to work one week. He went to see his physician and was diagnosed with chronic fatigue, fibromyalgia, and depression. He was given an antidepressant, some sleeping pills, and some muscle relaxants. James, however, could still only work at school for a few hours. He was unable to perform his duties as a firefighter.

James returned to his physician, and his physician recommended a two-week vacation. During the vacation, James felt great! He was able to do many of the things he could not do before. Upon returning home from this vacation, James was able to return to teaching full time, but he could not do his job at the fire department. Within a few days, however, he again became extremely fatigued and had to go back to working only part time at the school. This continued for nearly a year.

It was at that point that James first came to my office. I performed salivary adrenal hormone tests on James, and the tests showed that his cortisol and DHEA levels were both extremely low. I diagnosed Jim with stage 3 adrenal exhaustion. I placed him on a comprehensive nutritional program, including a specific eating plan and nutritional supplements for his adrenal glands. I instructed him to sleep between eight and ten hours a night and to eat a well-balanced diet with healthy snacks between meals to avoid low blood sugar. I also recommended stress reduction as well as instructed him to build some "margin" into his life by limiting his daily activities.

Within six months, James was a different person. His energy was greatly improved—he felt he was about 75 percent back to the energy levels he once had. The chronic fatigue and painful fibromyalgia were both gone. His sex drive improved. So did his allergies. He was able to return to teaching full time.

Within a year and a half, James had 100 percent of his energy back, and he felt like a young man again.

ADRENAL FATIGUE IMPACTS MILLIONS OF PEOPLE

Adrenal fatigue or adrenal exhaustion has been recognized medically for more than one hundred years. Most physicians, however, have never heard of this condition, because it is not taught in medical school. As a result, physicians don't test for it or treat it. The only form of adrenal fatigue recognized by most physicians is adrenal fatigue in its most severe form, called *Addison's disease.*

Addison's disease was named after Sir Thomas Addison, who first described the disease in 1855. The disease is a profound chronic adrenal failure—the adrenal glands simply do not function. This failure is generally caused by an autoimmune disease or occasionally by infection. It is sometimes called chronic adrenal insufficiency or "hypocortisolism." Symptoms of Addison's disease include low blood sugar, nausea, loss of appetite, low blood pressure, weight loss, and muscle weakness. Those afflicted typically have lightheadedness or dizziness upon standing and hypoglycemia (low blood sugar). They also generally have hyperpigmentation of the mucous membranes, lips, skin folds, and pressure points. President John F. Kennedy suffered from Addison's disease. The condition is rare—only about four people in every one hundred thousand individuals will develop it.

While Addison's disease is rare, "low" adrenal function is much more widespread.

One of the reasons that only a few endocrinologists recognize adrenal fatigue as a medical condition is because the standard blood tests for adrenal gland function are designed to detect only the most extreme forms of adrenal failure. Patients who are in "adrenal fatigue," as opposed to "adrenal failure," almost always register normal adrenal hormone levels on standard blood tests. Adrenal salivary hormone tests are necessary to accurately identify "adrenal fatigue."

Most of adrenal fatigue is caused by excessive long-term stress.

A SHORT COURSE ON THE ADRENAL GLANDS

I certainly don't want to bore you with medical details, but I do believe it is important for you to understand how the adrenal glands work. Here is a very brief "short course" about what happens to your body when you are under stress.

The adrenal glands are two small glands, each approximately the size of a large grape. One gland sits atop each of the kidneys. The main purpose of the adrenal glands is to enable the body to cope with stress.

Each adrenal gland has two parts. The inner part, called the medulla, mediates the "fight-or-flight" response. It secretes epinephrine and norepinephrine, which modulate the sympathetic nervous system. When an alarm reaction occurs in our bodies, the adrenal medulla secretes these potent hormones. Blood pressure, heart rate, and respiratory rate all increase. Blood sugar and fats are dumped into the bloodstream. Blood is shunted away from the digestive organs and diverted to the brain and muscles. The body is prepared to "run" or "fight."

The other part of the adrenal gland—the outer portion—called the cortex actually makes up about 80 percent of the gland. It produces many different hormones, but they generally fall into three classes: glucocorticoids, androgens, and mineralocorticoids.

Glucocorticoids

The most important glucocorticoid hormone is cortisol. It is the primary stress relief hormone. One of the functions of cortisol is to raise blood sugar levels.

The typical American diet is high in processed carbohydrates and sugars, so most people already have a flood of "sugar" pouring into their bloodstreams. Insulin, a hormone that lowers the blood sugar level, becomes elevated in the bloodstream when sugary foods and processed carbohydrate intake is high. Adequate amounts of cortisol are very important to keep sugar levels high enough to produce energy. Otherwise, the insulin would compensate for the increase of blood sugar, and not enough blood sugar would be available to help a person flee or fight.

If stress is chronic—the adrenal glands eventually get "tired" of producing so much cortisol. Adrenal fatigue sets in. It can eventually lead to severe adrenal exhaustion or burnout, at which point the output of cortisol is greatly reduced and a person typically develops low blood sugar, or hypoglycemia, as a physical condition.

Cortisol is also a powerful anti-inflammatory hormone. Inflammation is simply the swelling, redness, and pain that generally accompany such physical ailments as a sore throat, a sprained ankle, or an insect sting.

We now know that many diseases are associated with excessive inflammation. They include osteoarthritis, rheumatoid arthritis, lupus, most autoimmune diseases, asthma, allergies, heart disease, Alzheimer's disease, inflammatory bowel disease, ulcers, and most forms of cancer. If cortisol is very low, it cannot provide anti-inflammatory compounds that are part of the body's overall anti-inflammatory response. In treating inflammation, patients are often given hydrocortisone cream for insect bites and sunburns, or steroid medication, such as prednisone, for severe allergies, asthma, and arthritis. These cortisone-based medications are intended to fight inflammation. Inflammation and hypoglycemia are related to low cortisol levels.

Cortisol levels that are too high are related to a suppression of the immune system. Too much cortisol can suppress the work of the natural killer cells that are our frontline defense against viruses, bacteria, and even cancer cells. Elevated cortisol levels decrease the effectiveness of white blood cells, macrophages, monocytes, and mast cells.

Attaining and then maintaining just the right cortisol level in the bloodstream is a major challenge! Too little cortisol, and the body becomes subject to inflammation and hypoglycemia. Too much cortisol, and the body becomes subject to a higher risk of developing high blood pressure, type 2 diabetes, obesity, autoimmune diseases, and lower immunity to viruses, bacteria, and even cancer.

Mineralocorticoids

Another class of hormones produced by the adrenal cortex is the mineralocorticoids. The primary mineralocorticoid is aldosterone. Its main function is to increase sodium retention by the kidneys, and thereby, help regulate blood pressure. Excessive stress, however, generally leads to an increased secretion of aldosterone. This causes sodium to be retained in the bloodstream, and this can lead to hypertension or edema. It can also cause an increased loss of two very important minerals: magnesium and potassium.

If adrenal exhaustion occurs, the glands may produce inadequate amounts of aldosterone. This allows sodium and chloride to spill into the urine, which may lead to dehydration. When aldosterone levels are very low, patients often develop a non-pitting edema of their extremities, yet they are dehydrated even though they still have "swelling" that indicates a major retention of fluid. If these patients are placed on diuretics to reduce the edema, they can become even more dehydrated. Overall, mineralocorticoids help maintain the mineral and electrolyte balance in the body.

Androgens

The adrenal cortex also produces male and female hormones in both men and women. The adrenal cortex produces large amounts of the hormone DHEA, which is the most abundant steroid hormone produced in the body. DHEA is a mild androgen or male hormone. It is used to make both the hormones estrogen and testosterone. Another hormone produced by the adrenal glands is pregnenolone. It can be used to produce either DHEA or progesterone.

Normally the adrenal glands produce only very small amounts of these sex hormones. Too many of the hormones can cause masculine tendencies in women—such as facial hair, acne, a deeper voice, hair on the chest, and loss of scalp hair—and feminine tendencies in men.

As a person ages, levels of DHEA decline. DHEA and other hormone levels also decline in times of prolonged stress. People with severe adrenal fatigue or adrenal exhaustion generally have very low production of sex hormones and extremely low levels of DHEA.

DHEA and the sex hormones not only relate to sex drive, but also to a person's muscle mass and a person's overall sense of well-being. People who are low in these hormones often develop depression, muscle aches and pains, and a variety of other ailments.

I often tell my patients that when they have a headache, they do not have a "Tylenol deficiency." When they have heartburn, they do not have a "Tums" or "Prilosec deficiency." We need to start treating root causes for disease, not just the symptoms. The metaphor I like to use is that of a person driving a car when suddenly an indicator light begins to flash on the dashboard. It indicates the person should have the engine checked. A person would be very silly to drive to the mechanic, tell him about the warning light, and then ask the mechanic to pull out the fuse so that the indicator light goes off. The engine needs to be fixed!

When certain symptoms in your body indicate adrenal fatigue, instead of rushing to the doctor and having him treat a particular symptom, ask for an adrenal salivary hormone test to see if you have adrenal fatigue. Ask that your adrenal-gland problem be addressed.

THE SYMPTOMS OF ADRENAL FATIGUE

I have a Jet Ski, and I enjoy jet skiing through the chain of lakes in Central Florida. On occasion, my Jet Ski runs out of fuel and stops abruptly. At that point, I am able to switch over to a "reserve tank," which holds another gallon of fuel, usually just enough to get me safely back to shore. The adrenal glands serve as the body's "reserve tank."

One of the most common symptoms that I find in people with adrenal fatigue is a "low energy level." Patients usually complain of feeling tired all the time and of barely having enough energy to make it through a normal day. They commonly fall asleep during movies. One patient complained that he could fall asleep waiting for a red light to change! When I had severe adrenal fatigue, it was not uncommon for me to fall asleep during a movie within ten to fifteen minutes after the movie began. I usually missed half the movie before I awoke. My adrenal fatigue got so bad that I was unable to drive for an hour without fearing I might fall asleep at the wheel.

Patients with adrenal fatigue generally have problems getting up in the morning. Their lack of energy seems to peak in the early morning, and again in the afternoon between three and five o'clock. Even when a person seems to get a good night's sleep, he awakens feeling fatigued.

Some people become so lethargic that the simplest chores become a major challenge. They also have a reduced ability to withstand emotional pressure. Even minor things that would not normally bother them can be the source of major irritation or frustration.

Those with adrenal fatigue often "need" a cup of coffee or other stimulant to get going in the morning—one cup of coffee is rarely adequate, and typically these individuals use coffee, cola drinks, or tea throughout the day just to keep their energy level up. They often crave salty foods because they are losing sodium in the urine (as a result of inadequate aldosterone). Salty foods, unfortunately, are often potato chips, corn chips, pretzels, salted and buttered popcorn, processed meats, dill pickles, salsa, or salted nuts—the vast majority of which are loaded with highly processed carbohydrates, food additives, and the wrong kinds of fats. These generally lead to weight gain, blood sugar swings, mood swings, and even more stress.

Individuals with adrenal fatigue often have a reduced sex drive. Women often suffer from increased symptoms of PMS: irritability, bloating, fatigue, mood swings, menstrual cramps, and heavy periods. They may feel dizzy or lightheaded when they stand up quickly. They may also experience thinning hair or unexplained hair loss.

They often are not very productive on the job because they have difficulty staying focused on a task or take longer to complete a task. They may have difficulty in making decisions, become forgetful or absentminded, or lose their train of thought easily. I have seen this occur in patients in their early thirties, with symptoms so severe they thought they were developing Alzheimer's disease. Once their adrenal fatigue was treated, however, they generally regained their memory as well as their ability to focus and concentrate.

Many people with adrenal fatigue develop mild depression and seem to lose their joy. They often take longer to recover from injuries or illnesses. They are prone to gain weight and to suffer from hypoglycemia.

Certainly none of these symptoms or conditions by itself would warrant a diagnosis of adrenal fatigue. But if a number of these symptoms are present, salivary adrenal hormones should be tested.

WHAT LEADS TO ADRENAL FATIGUE?

I recently examined a twenty-year-old male who is a biology major at a large university. He desires to go to medical school one day, but last semester he made two Cs in spite of studying diligently. He came to my office mildly depressed, with weight gain in the abdominal area. He was experiencing symptoms of hypoglycemia, was lightheaded when he stood up suddenly, and was extremely fatigued, especially upon awakening. He craved coffee and salty foods and admitted when I questioned him that he was grumpy and irritable much of the time. Everything he told me pointed to adrenal fatigue.

I have found that many university students, and especially those who are aiming for professional careers that require graduate school, are prone to adrenal fatigue. They are burning the candle at both ends by studying day and night and not getting adequate sleep. Certain professions are extremely prone to adrenal fatigue—physicians (especially those on call), school teachers, police officers, middle managers, firefighters, and any profession that involves alternating shift work are among those most likely to experience adrenal fatigue. In addition, people who are beginning new businesses, experiencing excessive work pressures, frequent deadlines, demanding bosses, chronic fear of job termination, or an unhappy work environment are predisposed to adrenal fatigue. So are people who have developed a habit of all work and little (or no) play.

Traumatic events such as a divorce, marital separation, bankruptcy, loss of a job, death of a family member or close friend, a major accident, a major injury, a major illness, a major move, or a major surgery can lead to adrenal fatigue.

Lifestyle choices can also lead to adrenal fatigue, as can excessive exercise, poor diet, lack of sleep, and excessive use of coffee and other stimulants.

Emotional and mental stress can cause adrenal fatigue. Anger, hostility, depression, guilt, fear, anxiety, bitterness, unforgiveness, grief, being critical or perfectionistic, feeling rejected, or simply not loving and accepting one's self can all lead to adrenal fatigue.

SIMPLE TESTS TO SCREEN FOR ADRENAL FATIGUE

There are several simple tests that you can perform that are commonly correlated with adrenal fatigue. They include Ragland's Sign, Rostoff's Sign, and Sergent's White Line Test.

Ragland's Sign

This test has been performed for more than seventy-five years. Essentially, blood pressure is checked in three positions by any medical personnel, such as a nurse, doctor, or medical assistant: sitting, then lying, and then standing. A patient's blood pressure is first taken with the person sitting. Then the patient lies on his back, relaxes for about two minutes, and the blood pressure is taken again. Finally, with the blood pressure cuff still on the person's arm, the patient is instructed to stand up quickly and very straight. Blood pressure should be taken immediately. Many times a patient with adrenal fatigue will feel lightheaded or dizzy, and some may even pass out. It's good to have a chair behind the person and an assistant present to help a patient who becomes lightheaded.

Normally a patient's systolic blood pressure will increase 4 to 10 mmHg in going from a lying down to a standing position. If the person has adrenal fatigue, the systolic blood pressure will usually stay the same or drop. The fall is often between 5 to 10 mmHG, but in some cases, it may be as much as thirty to forty points. This drop in blood pressure is known as the "Ragland effect."[1]

Rostoff's Sign

Another simple adrenal test is Rostoff's Sign, which is also called an iris contraction test. This test was initially described by Dr. C. F. Arroyo in 1924. A person can do this test on himself. You will need a flashlight or penlight, a mirror, a watch with a second hand, and a completely dark room. To conduct the test, sit in a chair with a mirror in front of you, and shine the penlight or flashlight across one eye from the side of your head and not directly into the eye. Keep the light shining into that eye, and watch the pupil with the other eye. As soon as the light is shined into the eye, the pupil should contract or become much smaller. If it does not contract or does not remain contracted after initially getting smaller, and begins to dilate (become larger) even with the light still shining, the person may have adrenal fatigue. Dilation occurs within two minutes and can last for thirty to forty-five seconds before the pupil recovers and contracts again. The person should record how long the pupil stays dilated.

This simple little test is one I teach my patients so they can track their progress from month to month as they recover from adrenal fatigue. As the adrenal glands become restored, the iris will hold its contraction longer, and eventually it will not dilate.[2]

Sergent's White Line Test

This test was initially described by a French physician named Emile Sergent in 1917. In order to perform this test, simply take the dull end of a ballpoint pen and make a mark approximately six inches long by stroking the skin of the abdomen. A normal test is when the mark made by the pen is white at first and then turns red within a few seconds. If a person has low adrenal function, the line will stay white for approximately two minutes, and it will become wider. This latter result occurs in approximately 40 percent of individuals with low adrenal function, so the test is not as predictive as Ragland's Sign or Rostoff's Sign.

THREE STAGES OF ADRENAL FATIGUE OR ADRENAL EXHAUSTION

Rather than talk about the three stages of stress identified by Hans Selye, I use three stages of adrenal exhaustion. Their classifications are described below.[3] They are similar to Selye's classifications, but they have significant differences.

Stage 1

This is defined as a prolonged, increased excitatory stimulus to the adrenals having resulted in a prolonged, increased cortisol output, usually with a corresponding prolonged decrease in DHEA. The continued demand for increased cortisol production necessitates an ongoing release of ACTH by the pituitary. The adrenals can eventually experience difficulty in meeting the demand placed upon them. Other pathways must compensate to facilitate the production of sufficient cortisol. One compensation is to shunt or "steal" pregnenolone from the DHEA/sex hormone pathway to the progesterone/cortisol pathway. Total cortisol levels are elevated in Stage 1.

Stage 2

This is a transitional phase. It signifies a continuing decline in cortisol output from levels above normal to those below normal, although ACTH stimulation remains high or even increases. There is a gradual change from increased to decreased stimulation. Any one or more of the morning, noon, or afternoon cortisol values are low or borderline low, but the nighttime cortisol level is usually normal. The decreasing cortisol output is a marker of midstage adrenal exhaustion. DHEA is usually low or borderline low.

Stage 3

This stage is marked by the failure of the adrenals to produce enough cortisol to reach normal levels. DHEA levels are also low. The result is a hypothalamic-pituitary-adrenal axis "crash," in which nighttime cortisol levels also drop. There are usually severe imbalances in other hormone systems.

ADDRESSING ADRENAL EXHAUSTION

There are a number of supplements on the market today that can help address adrenal exhaustion. Some have not yet been subjected to long-term clinical studies; others are well documented in scientific literature. Since these products deal with adjustments to hormones, I strongly recommend that you use products prescribed by a physician knowledgeable in hormone use and, more specifically, knowledgeable about your hormone deficiency and needs. *Do not use over-the-counter products.* They vary widely in quality and amounts of active ingredients. It is imperative that you are under the care of a knowledgeable physician to monitor your condition.

Vitamins and minerals for adrenal fatigue

A multivitamin and mineral supplement is critically important to restoring function. Particularly important nutrients include the B vitamins, especially B_5 or pantothenic acid.

Vitamin B$_5$ plays a very important role in the production of adrenal hormones. It also has a main role in both cellular metabolism and maintaining adequate adrenal cortical function. Adequate amounts of vitamin C are also important and are actually more concentrated in the adrenal glands than anywhere else in the body.

Low magnesium levels are very common in individuals with adrenal fatigue. Approximately three-fourths of the U.S. population does not consume adequate amounts of magnesium in their diets. Increased stress as well as adrenal fatigue causes our bodies to have an increased need for magnesium. For more information on the vitamins and minerals needed to treat adrenal fatigue and excessive stress, refer to chapter fifteen.

DHEA

DHEA is involved in many processes in the human body. It promotes the growth and repair of protein tissue, especially muscle, and it acts to regulate cortisol, negating many of the harmful effects of ongoing excessive cortisol. When demands for cortisol are increased for a prolonged time, DHEA levels decline and the DHEA no longer is able to balance the negative effects of excess cortisol. A depressed level of DHEA may serve as an early warning sign of adrenal exhaustion.

After age twenty-five, DHEA levels begin to decline. By the time a person is sixty years old, he has only about a quarter of the DHEA he had when he was twenty. By the time he is eighty, he has only about 20 percent of what he had when he was sixty![4]

One major study on DHEA monitored DHEA levels in men between the ages of fifty and seventy-nine over a period of twelve years. They found a 48 percent reduction in cardiovascular disease and a 36 percent reduction in mortality from any cause for the group of men that were given DHEA supplements. DHEA has also been shown to be an effective anti-obesity agent.[5]

Low DHEA levels have been associated with autoimmune diseases such as rheumatoid arthritis, lupus, and multiple sclerosis. Low DHEA levels are typically found in patients with diabetes, heart disease, cancer, Alzheimer's disease, and most other degenerative diseases.[6]

DHEA levels can fluctuate a great deal during any given day. DHEA is stored in the body in a reservoir of DHEA-sulfate, which remains generally constant from day to day. DHEA-S (sulfate) levels can be checked by salivary hormone testing or by a blood test. I recommend pharmaceutical-grade DHEA to patients who are low in DHEA. I generally start with 10 mg two to three times a day in sublingual application for men, and 5 mg two to three times a day in sublingual application for women. DHEA products are sold over-the-counter, but since DHEA is a hormone, it should be used with caution. As I said earlier, a high dosage of DHEA can cause hair loss, unwanted growth of hair in women, acne, and a deeper voice.

Before starting DHEA therapy, men should have their PSA level checked, as well as have a digital rectal exam. Men with prostate cancer or significant benign prostatic hypertrophy should avoid DHEA supplements. Women who have had or who have an estrogen-dependent cancer such as breast or ovarian cancer should consult their physician prior to taking DHEA supplements.

Pregnenolone

If DHEA is considered the "mother" hormone, then pregnenolone is the "grandmother" hormone. It is a natural hormone discovered in the 1940s—and is made largely from cholesterol, which is used, in turn, to make DHEA. When the body is under stress, pregnenolone is used to produce more cortisol.

For years, researchers focused more on cortisol than on pregnenolone. The attention is now turning to pregnenolone. Studies in laboratory animals have shown that pregnenolone is one of the most effective and powerful memory boosters. It increases the level of the neurotransmitter acetylcholine in the hippocampus and other memory areas of the brain. It may help prevent memory loss or even dementia. It is known as the "hormone balancer" since it has the ability to increase levels of steroid hormones that are deficient in the body and can decrease excessive levels of circulating hormones. Long-term deficiencies of this hormone usually lead to a decrease in both glucocorticoids and mineralocorticoids, including cortisol and aldosterone.

Supplementation of pregnenolone can be beneficial for many people who are under severe stress, but it does rarely have side effects that can include insomnia, acne, irritability, headaches, loss of scalp hair, and overstimulation of the nervous system. High doses can cause heart palpitations. Patients with estrogen-dependent cancers should take pregnenolone only under the supervision of a physician. I generally recommend 5 to 15 mg in sublingual application, and in divided doses.

Natural progesterone

As women age, the ovaries gradually produce less and less progesterone, and eventually the production ceases around menopause. In women suffering from severe adrenal fatigue, cortisol levels are typically low, as are progesterone levels. Some women benefit tremendously from natural progesterone supplementation using transdermal creams. Prior to suggesting this, however, I insist that a woman have a salivary test for female hormones. If levels are low, I recommend a pharmaceutical-grade progesterone cream since many over-the-counter products are not consistent. In menstruating females, I generally prescribe natural progesterone cream for the last two weeks of a menstrual cycle, and for postmenopausal women, I recommend use of the cream for three weeks in a month.

Natural progesterone cream is very different from Provera, a popular synthetic version of progesterone. Side effects from Provera include blood clots, depression, nausea, insomnia, breast cancer, fluid retention, breast tenderness, as well as other symptoms. I have not found any of these side effects in my patients who use natural progesterone cream.

Adrenal glandular supplements

The ancient Egyptians used glandular therapy thousands of years ago on the premise that "like heals like." Glandular therapy in the form of desiccated thyroid glands has been used since the 1880s to help individuals with goiters and low thyroid function. Armour Thyroid is still quite popular even today in treating patients with hypothyroidism or low thyroid function. It is a desiccated, or heat-dried, thyroid glandular product. Adrenal glandular supplements contain protomorphogens or extracts of tissues from the adrenal glands of pigs or cattle. These can be taken orally to support human adrenal function. Each organ of the body has a unique mix of vitamins, minerals, and hormones. Glandular substances in pigs and cattle have an "adrenal mix" close to that of the human adrenal glands. Some doctors of natural medicine have used adrenal glandular supplements with their patients for decades and report very positive results.

Natural hydrocortisone supplementation

When hydrocortisone or cortisol are severely deficient, hydrocortisone supplementation may be beneficial. I do not recommend pharmacologic doses of prednisone, but rather physiologic doses of hydrocortisone for those patients with severe adrenal fatigue. Prior to supplementation, a person's adrenal function must be tested by salivary cortisol tests. If cortisol levels are extremely low, I very rarely recommend supplementation with natural hydrocortisone or cortisone-acetate in doses of 2.5 to 5 mg two to four times a day. This supplementation needs to be under the guidance of a physician. For physicians interested in learning safe uses of cortisol, I recommend endocrinologist Dr. William Jeffries' book *Safe Uses of Cortisol*.[7]

Licorice root

Licorice root has been used in food and medicinal remedies for thousands of years. It is now primarily used in treating adrenal exhaustion. It has been shown to help endurance, energy, and vitality. Licorice root contains glycyrrhizin, which has a structure very similar to cortisone.

Licorice root has a compound that is approximately fifty times sweeter than sugar. It is available in capsules, liquid herbal extracts, and as a dried root from which a tea can be made. Licorice candy, by the way, usually has an excessive amount of sugar and licorice flavoring, but not any actual licorice.

In my practice, I check the adrenal salivary hormone levels of patients, and if cortisol levels are low during the day, I recommend starting with approximately five drops of licorice root extract, which is about 50 mg of licorice. This supplement should be used during the day, not before bedtime. Those with severe adrenal fatigue may need three to four separate doses of licorice root extract during a day, and may need up to 10 drops per dose. Individuals with hypertension should not use this supplement.

A SUMMARY OF TREATMENT FOR ADRENAL EXHAUSTION

In treating adrenal exhaustion, it is important to determine what stage of adrenal exhaustion a person is in. This should be done by taking an adrenal salivary hormone test.

Get eight to ten hours of sleep a night, and try to go to bed by ten o'clock each evening.

Avoid drinking caffeine—including coffee, caffeinated sodas and tea, and other stimulants.

Follow a well-balanced diet with the right proportion of lean, organic, nonprocessed proteins to unprocessed carbohydrates and good fats. Keep your blood sugar stable by eating at least every three to four hours and having a healthy snack between meals. Never skip meals.

Laugh! Ten belly laughs a day are recommended!

If you are suffering from severe adrenal fatigue, do light exercises such as stretching or slow walks as tolerated every other day, and don't overexert yourself.

Drink at least two quarts of filtered water a day.

Based upon your salivary adrenal hormone test results, you may need supplements of multivitamins, minerals, DHEA, and pregnenolone. You may also need natural hormone replacement in the form of natural progesterone, estrogen, or testosterone, as well as adrenal glandular supplements or licorice root. See Appendix D for more information on supplements.

Work with your health-care professional to get your adrenal system back on track. Once you overcome adrenal exhaustion, you are well on your way to a "stress less" life and to experiencing a peace that passes all understanding.

2 0

The Peace That Passes Understanding

Icannot begin to tell you how many patients I have seen over the decades who do not love God, do not love others, and do not love themselves. The sickest people I have encountered—those who were ill not only in their bodies but also in their emotions— were those who were harboring long-term resentment, bitterness, anger, and even hatred against another person, against God, or against themselves. They suffered tremendously—from major depression to anorexia nervosa and bulimia...from cancer and autoimmune disorders to diseases marked by severe inflammation and pain...from allergies to chronic anxiety.

Some who claim to love themselves do so in an entirely self-focused, selfish way. They have little regard for helping others or for being generous toward those in need.

I have come to believe with a very strong conviction that the ultimate prescription for overcoming stress is this:

- Love God.
- Love other people.
- Love yourself.

Rarely do I treat patients for stress who genuinely love the Lord, are active in serving others, and who have a personal confidence and love for themselves that is rooted in knowing they have been forgiven by God and are presently "God's work in progress." People who are quick to thank and praise the Lord, quick to confess their sins and receive forgiveness for them, and quick to reach out to other people and to see even strangers as potential allies rather than potential enemies are rarely "stressed out."

Jesus taught His disciples to feed the hungry, give drink to the thirsty, clothe the naked, and befriend strangers—and to reach out to those who might be considered "the least of these." (See Matthew 25:31–46.)

"UNTO THE LEAST OF THESE"

Mother Teresa was a great example of a woman who did just this. For seventeen years, Mother Teresa taught at St. Mary's High School for Girls in Calcutta, India, where she saw tremendous suffering outside the walls of her convent and school. In 1950 she requested permission from the Vatican to start her own order, which later became known as the Missionaries of Charity. Their mission was to care for the "least of these" people. Mother Teresa received the Nobel Peace Prize in 1979, and she said in her acceptance speech:

> I am grateful to receive [the Nobel Peace Prize] in the name of the hungry, the naked, the homeless, of the crippled, of the blind, of the lepers, of all those people who feel unwanted, unloved, uncared for throughout society, people that have become a burden to the society and are shunned by everyone.[1]

As part of her Nobel lecture the next day, Mother Teresa told this experience:

> One evening we went out, and we picked up four people from the street. And one of them was in a most terrible condition. And I told the sisters, "You take care of the other three, I will take care

of this one that looks worse." So I did for her all that my love could do. I put her in bed and there was such a beautiful smile on her face. She took hold of my hand as she said one word only: "Thank you"—and she died.…

And she died with a smile on her face. [Just] as that man whom we picked up from the drain, half-eaten with worms, and we brought him to the home. [And he said], "I have lived like an animal in the street, but I am going to die like an angel, loved and cared for." And it was so wonderful to see the greatness of that man who could speak like that, who could die like that without blaming anybody, without cursing anybody, without comparing anything.[2]

Toward the end of her lecture, Mother Teresa gave this charge to the audience:

Let us keep that joy of loving Jesus in our hearts. And share that joy with all that we come in touch with. And that radiating joy is real, for we have no reason not to be happy because we have Christ with us. Christ in our hearts, Christ in the poor that we meet, Christ in the smile that we give and the smile we receive.[3]

At the time of her death, Mother Teresa's Missionaries of Charity had more than 4,000 nuns and more than 100,000 volunteers. They operated out of 610 missions in 120 nations. Their work included orphanages, hospices, and homes for those with leprosy, TB, and HIV/AIDS. They ran soup kitchens, schools, and centers for children and family counseling. The order today has grown to more than 4,500 nuns who are at work in 133 nations—and the order continues to grow in numbers and influence.

These are among my favorite quotes from Mother Teresa:

If now we have no peace, it is because we have forgotten how to see God in one another.[4]

The dying, the crippled, the mental, the unwanted, the unloved—they are Jesus in disguise.[5]

It is not how much we do, but how much love we put in the doing. It is not how much we give, but how much love we put in the giving.[6]

We can do no great things, only small things with great love.[7]

Speak tenderly to them. Let there be kindness in your face, in your eyes, in your smile, in the warmth of your greeting. Always have a cheerful smile. Don't only give your care, but give your heart as well.[8]

Mother Teresa recognized Jesus Christ as the Prince of Peace. She preached that Jesus died on the cross for all people the world over. Jesus loved to the point of laying down His life for our sins so that we might experience forgiveness of sins now and eternal life after we die. He calls us to love others with a selfless love.

CHANGE YOUR PERCEPTIONS

In the vast majority of my patients, I have found that stress levels change dramatically when a patient changes his perceptions. When a person is able to change the way he "sees" a potentially stressful situation, he wins the battle against stress.

Perhaps the most potent way a person can change his or her perspective is to choose to perceive, interpret, and process information according to the Owner's manual about how we are to think as human beings. That manual is the Word of God, the Holy Bible. Our Creator made us to process information "His way," and when we choose to do so, not only do we see things with greater clarity, truth, and a positive outlook, but also we experience a deep and abiding peace.

What the world perceives as valuable—fame and fortune—is not the same as God's perception. Most people desire to be recognized as someone important, distinguished, and served by others. Two of Jesus' disciples, James and John, wanted recognition and positions of prominence in glory. When the other ten disciples heard this, they were not just displeased with James and John, but they were greatly displeased and upset. Jesus then simply taught them, "Whoever desires to become great among you shall be your servant. And whoever of you desires to be first shall be slave of all. For even the Son of Man did not come to be served, but to serve and to give His life a ransom for many" (Mark 10:43–45). If we seek His kingdom first, then all of the rest will follow. (See Matthew 6:33.)

To seek the kingdom of God is to seek to know how the kingdom of God functions—we must understand God's principles and commandments, and the way to gain that understanding is to read and study the Bible. To seek His righteousness is to seek to be in "right" relationship with God. The way we do that is to confess our sins, receive God's forgiveness, and walk in a close reliance upon Him daily, talking to Him often about what we encounter, experience, need, perceive, and enter into as relationships and commitments. We must make God's opinion central and first in our lives.

I find that many people are very careful about what they feed their children, pets, and themselves. They are concerned about what type of fuel they put in their cars. They are not, however, very careful about what they feed their minds and souls. I encourage many of my patients to go on a media fast—turning off the television and radio for a while, and choosing instead to read the Bible and other wholesome books, and perhaps to listen to teaching tapes or tapes of the Scriptures. Begin to memorize positive, faith-building passages of the Bible. I have seen countless patients do this to great benefit—their frustration level decreases dramatically, and simultaneously, their health level improves!

What is the right "perspective" to have? I believe it is this:

- See life as an adventure—exciting and worth living—rather than a "struggle."

- See life as a wonderful opportunity to encounter other people and share the love of God with them.

- See life as unfolding according to God's plan—see it unfolding in a way that will result in your earthly blessing and eternal good. The apostle Paul wrote, "Forgetting those things which are behind and reaching forward to those things which are ahead, I press toward the goal for the prize of the upward call of God in Christ Jesus" (Phil. 3:13–14).

Your perception about life can dramatically change your stress level and help you to stress less.

OUR PRINCE OF PEACE LOVES US SO WE CAN LOVE OTHERS!

The Old Testament prophet Isaiah gave this prophecy about Jesus: "For unto us a Child is born, unto us a Son is given; and the government will be upon His shoulder. And His name will be called Wonderful, Counselor, Mighty God, Everlasting Father, Prince of Peace" (Isa. 9:6). Jesus came to be our source of peace. As our source of peace, Jesus told us how we can experience *His* peace—it happens as we receive God's love and then choose to pass that love on to others.

One day a religious lawyer asked Jesus to identify the greatest commandment in the Law of Moses. Jesus said, "Thou shalt love the Lord thy God with all thy heart, and with all thy soul, and with all thy mind. This is the first and great commandment. And the second is like unto it, Thou shalt love thy neighbour as thyself. On these two commandments hang all the law and the prophets" (Matt. 22:37–40, KJV). Jesus pointed to a love of God that includes our entire being—the conscious mind and the unconscious mind, the will, and the emotions. He pointed to a love of other people and to a love of self.

How can we receive God's love, which enables us to love others? The first step is to accept Jesus as our Savior and Lord, and then ask Him daily to direct our lives.

The late Dr. Bill Bright, founder of Campus Crusade for Christ and a wonderful friend of mine, wrote the foreword to my book *Deadly Emotions.* Through his organization, more than 150 million people have given their hearts and lives to Jesus Christ through the years. Dr. Bright told me that when he was just a young man, he wrote out a contract saying, "From this day forward, I am a slave of Jesus Christ." He then signed his name at the bottom of the contract. Dr. Bright had a tremendous purpose for his life; it was a purpose that gave him satisfaction and fulfillment. Even as he was dying, he had a great inner calm because he knew without a shadow of doubt that Jesus was his Savior and heaven was his future home. Dr. Bright taught millions of people to pray this simple prayer, and I encourage you to pray it today:

> Lord Jesus, I need You. Thank You for dying on the cross for my sins. I open the door of my life and receive You as my Savior and Lord. Thank You for forgiving my sins and giving me eternal life. Take control of the throne of my life. Make me the kind of person You want me to be.

I have no doubt that if you pray this prayer with sincere humility, God will hear and answer your prayer, and you will stand in right relationship with Him—forgiven and cleansed of all your sin. The Bible promises, "If we confess our sins, He is faithful and just to forgive us our sins and to cleanse us from all unrighteousness" (1 John 1:9). (See Appendix A.)

Knowing Jesus as your Savior is the key to peace. It is the foundation stone on which to begin the transformation of your life through the renewal of your mind.

Ask the Lord to show you how you can apply the truth of His Word as you read the four Gospels: Matthew, Mark, Luke, and John. Read the other books of the New Testament, always asking the Lord, "How can I live this out? How can I do what Your Word tells me to do?"

Start attending church every week. Become part of a church that teaches the Bible, and begin to make friends with the people in that church. Study God's Word with them on a regular basis.

Begin to read books that will challenge you to grow in your faith and to help you develop the perspective on life that God desires for you to have. I especially recommend these four books:

- The Holy Bible
- *The Purpose-Driven Life* by Rick Warren
- *The Battlefield of the Mind* by Joyce Meyer
- *The Bondage Breaker* by Neil T. Anderson

The Bible tells us to pursue two things: "peace with all people" and "holiness" (Heb. 12:14). I believe that as you do this, you will experience a peace that passes all understanding. The door on stress will be slammed shut, and contentment will flood your soul.

God's desire for you is not that you live a stressful, frantic, overburdened, striving life. His desire for you is love, joy, and peace. Choose to do things God's way, and God will give you not only the desires of your heart, but also the desire of His heart.

Appendix A

Salvation Prayer

God desires to heal you of stress. His Word is full of promises that confirm His love for you and His desire to give you His abundant life. His desire includes more than physical health for you; He wants to make you whole in your mind and spirit as well as through a personal relationship with His Son, Jesus Christ.

If you haven't met my best friend, Jesus, I would like to take this opportunity to introduce Him to you. It's very simple.

If you are ready to let Him come into your heart and become your best friend, just bow your head and sincerely pray this prayer from your heart:

> *Lord Jesus, I want to know You as my Savior and Lord. I believe You are the Son of God and that You died for my sins. I also believe that You were raised from the dead and now sit at the right hand of the Father praying for me. I ask You to forgive me for my sins and change my heart so that I can be Your child and live with You eternally. Thank You for Your peace. Help me to walk with You so that I can begin to know You as my best friend and my Lord. Amen.*

If you have prayed this prayer, we rejoice with you in your decision and your new relationship with Jesus.

Below are the very popular "Four Spiritual Laws," which have been in circulation by Campus Crusade for Christ for decades:[1]

Law 1

- God loves you and offers a wonderful *plan* for your life.

- *God's love*: "God so loved the world that he gave his one and only Son, that whoever believes in him shall not perish but have eternal life" (John 3:16, NIV).

Law 2

- Man is sinful and separated from God. Therefore, he cannot know and experience God's love and plan for his life.

- *Man is sinful*: "All have sinned and fall short of the glory of God" (Rom. 3:23).

- *Man is separated*: "The wages of sin is death" (Rom. 6:23). Death in this verse refers to spiritual separation from God.

Law 3

- Jesus Christ is God's *only* provision for man's sin. Because Jesus died for your sins on the cross, you can know and experience God's love and plan for your life.

- *He died in our place:* "God demonstrates His own love toward us, in that while we were still sinners, Christ died for us" (Rom. 5:8).

- *He is the only way to God:* "Jesus said to him, 'I am the way, the truth, and the life. No one comes to the Father except through Me" (John 14:6).

Law 4

- We must individually receive Jesus Christ as Savior and Lord; then we can know and experience God's love and plan for our lives.

- *We must receive Christ*: "As many as received Him, to them He gave the right to become children of God, to those who believe in His name" (John 1:12).

- *We receive Christ through personal invitation:* Jesus said, "Behold, I stand at the door and knock. If anyone hears My voice and opens the door, I will come to him" (Rev. 3:20).

Appendix B

Positive Affirmations

I am beautiful, capable, and lovable. I am valuable. I have complete faith and trust in Jesus Christ. All of my needs are met. God shall supply all of my needs according to His riches and glory in Christ Jesus. I love myself unconditionally and nurture myself in every way. I trust my conscience, which is led by the Holy Spirit. I follow my conscience and choose to walk in the Spirit and not in the flesh.

I am a beautiful child of God. I am filled with love. I love people and radiate love, warmth, and friendship to all. I am healed of all my childhood wounds, and I am moving toward greater peace and happiness every day. I hold no account of wrong done to me.

I am diligent, faithful, and have a spirit of excellence. Whatever I put my hand to will prosper. I am the head and not the tail. God always causes me to triumph. I am unique and the apple of God's eye. The Greater One, Jesus, lives in me. I can be intimate with myself and others. I can love myself, and I can love others. I choose to love everyone with whom I come in contact. Love is patient; therefore, I am patient. Love is kind; therefore, I am kind. Love does not envy; therefore, I am content. Love does not exalt itself and is not proud; therefore, I am meek and humble. Love is not rude; therefore, I am courteous. Love is not selfish; therefore, I am giving. Love is not provoked; therefore, I am forgiving. Love thinks no evil. My thoughts are true, honest, just, pure, loving, and of good report. Love does not rejoice in iniquity but rejoices in the truth; therefore, I rejoice in the truth. Love bears all things, believes all things in God's Word, hopes all things, and endures all things. Love never fails; therefore, I will not fail.

Everything that happens to me I create consciously or unconsciously. I have made a decision not to judge anyone, including myself. Jesus said, "Judge not, and ye shall not be judged. Condemn not, and ye shall not be condemned. Forgive, and you will be forgiven." I choose to forgive, and I will be forgiven. I choose to forgive everyone from whom I feel less than unconditional love. I choose to walk in unconditional love toward all men. I choose to see the best in everyone. I am open to new beliefs. I accept and love my parents.

I create my own happiness. I am appreciated, and I appreciate others. I make decisions with confidence. I let go of things I cannot control. I have the courage to change the things I should change. I have the serenity to accept the things I cannot change, and I have the wisdom to know the difference. I allow myself to play and have fun. I have no need to control people or situations. I release all need to control. I am controlled by the Holy Spirit.

All my needs, desires, and goals are met. Whatever I can conceive and believe, I can achieve. All things are possible to me because I believe. My capabilities and potential are unlimited. I express my potential more and more each day. I see problems as exciting challenges that cause me to grow stronger and stronger in faith. I vividly visualize myself as the person I want to be, and I am enthusiastically achieving my goals.

My mind is creative, and my thoughts are illuminated by the light and wisdom of God. I think the thoughts of God. Ideas are now coming to me that will help me to achieve whatever God wants in my life. I thankfully and gratefully accept these ideas and enthusiastically and immediately act on them. I radiate with power and enthusiasm. I am always positive and filled with self-confidence. I always think before I act. I control my thoughts at all times.

I have all the abilities I need to succeed. I love challenges and learn from every situation in my life. I live every day with power and passion. I feel strong, excited, passionate, and powerful. I feel tremendous confidence that I can do anything. All of my relationships are based on integrity and respect.

I awaken each day feeling healthy and alive with energy. I feel more energized throughout the day. I am bursting with energy, health, and vitality. Every pressure and tension I feel is simply a signal to relax, release, and let go. I always have more than enough energy to do all I want to do. I surrender my life to Jesus Christ. I have a wonderful, fulfilling relationship with Jesus. Jesus guides my life. I can always trust the guidance of the Holy Spirit. I feel God's presence in everything I do.

Appendix C

Scriptural Affirmations

Therefore, having been justified by faith, we have peace with God through our Lord Jesus Christ.

—Romans 5:1

There is therefore now no condemnation to those who are in Christ Jesus, who do not walk according to the flesh, but according to the Spirit.

—Romans 8:1

Now we have received, not the spirit of the world, but the Spirit who is from God, that we might know the things that have been freely given to us by God.

—1 Corinthians 2:12

For "who has known the mind of the Lord that he may instruct Him?" But we have the mind of Christ.

—1 Corinthians 2:16

Or do you not know that your body is the temple of the Holy Spirit who is in you, whom you have from God, and you are not your own? For you were bought at a price; therefore glorify God in your body and in your spirit, which are God's.

—1 Corinthians 6:19–20

Now He who establishes us with you in Christ and has anointed us is God.

—2 Corinthians 1:21

For the love of Christ compels us, because we judge thus: that if One died for all, then all died; and He died for all, that those who live should live no longer for themselves, but for Him who died for them and rose again.

—2 Corinthians 5:14–15

For He made Him who knew no sin to be sin for us, that we might become the righteousness of God in Him.

—2 Corinthians 5:21

I have been crucified with Christ; it is no longer I who live, but Christ lives in me; and the life which I now live in the flesh I live by faith in the Son of God, who loved me and gave Himself for me.

—GALATIANS 2:20

Blessed be the God and Father of our Lord Jesus Christ, who has blessed us with every spiritual blessing in the heavenly places in Christ.

—EPHESIANS 1:3

The God of our Lord Jesus Christ, the Father of glory, may give to you the spirit of wisdom and revelation in the knowledge of Him.

—EPHESIANS 1:17

Even when we were dead in trespasses, made us alive together with Christ (by grace you have been saved), and raised us up together, and made us sit together in the heavenly places in Christ Jesus.

—EPHESIANS 2:5–6

For through Him we both have access by one Spirit to the Father.

—EPHESIANS 2:18

He has delivered us from the power of darkness and conveyed us into the kingdom of the Son of His love, in whom we have redemption through His blood, the forgiveness of sins.

—COLOSSIANS 1:13–14

To them God willed to make known what are the riches of the glory of this mystery among the Gentiles: which is Christ in you, the hope of glory.

—COLOSSIANS 1:27

And you are complete in Him, who is the head of all principality and power.

—COLOSSIANS 2:10

Buried with Him in baptism, in which you also were raised with Him through faith in the working of God, who raised Him from the dead. And you, being dead in your trespasses and the uncircumcision of your flesh, He has made alive together with Him, having forgiven you all trespasses.

—COLOSSIANS 2:12–13

If then you were raised with Christ, seek those things which are above, where Christ is, sitting at the right hand of God. Set your mind on things above, not on things on the earth. For you died, and your life is hidden with Christ in God. When Christ who is our life appears, then you also will appear with Him in glory.

—COLOSSIANS 3:1–4

Let us therefore come boldly to the throne of grace, that we may obtain mercy and find grace to help in time of need.

—HEBREWS 4:16

By which have been given to us exceedingly great and precious promises, that through these you may be partakers of the divine nature, having escaped the corruption that is in the world through lust.

—2 PETER 1:4

Appendix D

Product Information

LABORATORY COMPANIES

BioHealth Diagnostics, Inc.
Phone: (800) 570-2000
Web sites: www.biodia.com (practitioner resource); www.biohealthinfo.com (patient resource)
E-mail: info@biodia.com

Physicians may order: Profile 201 Adrenal Stress Kit

Bowen Research & Training Institute
Phone: (727) 937-9077
Web site: www.bowen.org

ELISA/ACT test
Phone: (800) 553-5472
Your physician may order test kits.

NeuroScience
Phone: (888) 342-7272
Web site: www.neuroscienceinc.com

Your physician may order test kits and supplements.

SpectraCell
Phone: (800) 227-5227
Web Site: www.spectracell.com

For physicians only

ZRT Laboratory
Phone: (503) 466-2445
Web site: www.salivatest.com

Both physicians and patients can order.

MINISTRIES

Hillsong Church
Web site: www.hillsong.com
Praise and worship music

Dennis Swanberg (Christian comedian)
Web site: www.dennisswanberg.com

Jesse DuPlantis Ministries
Phone: (985) 764-2000
Web site: www.jdm.org
A Merry Heart Doeth Good Like a Medicine (CD)

Joel Osteen Ministries
Lakewood Church
Phone: (888) 870-7322
Web site: www.lakewood.cc

John Hagee Ministries
Phone: (210) 494-3900
Web site: www.jhm.org
The Seven Secrets: Unlocking Genuine Greatness

Joyce Meyer Ministries
Phone: (636) 349-0303
Web site: www.joycemeyer.org
Beauty for Ashes; Forgiving Your Abuser; The Battlefield of the Mind

Neil T. Anderson
Freedom in Christ Ministries
Phone: (865) 342-4000
Web site: www.ficm.org
The Bondage Breaker

Rick Warren
Phone: (866) 829-0300
Web site: www.purposedrivenlife.com
E-mail: info@purposedrivenlife.com
The Purpose-Driven Life

VITAMIN SUPPLEMENT COMPANIES

Please provide the "code number" provided or mention Dr. Colbert as the referring physician for the companies listed below:

BioHealth Diagnostics, Inc.

Phone: (800) 570-2000
Web sites: www.biodia.com (practitioner resource); www.biohealthinfo.com (patient resource)
E-mail: info@biodia.com

To order Pregnenolone (sublingual), DHEA (sublingual), Licorice Root Extract (sublingual), Support Minerals (sublingual), Support Adrenals (sublingual).

Divine Health Nutritional Products

Phone: (407) 331-7007
Web site: www.drcolbert.com

Divine Health Chelated Magnesium; Divine Health 5-HTP; Divine Health Buffered Vitamin C; Divine Health Omega 3 Fatty Acids; Divine Health Relora Plus; Divine Health Multivitamin for Stress; What Would Jesus Eat?; What Would Jesus Eat? Cookbook

Douglas Laboratories

Phone: (800) 245-4440
Web site: www.douglaslabs.com

Ayur-Aswaganda (Ashwaganda); Eleutherococcus Senticosus (Siberian Ginseng); Korean Ginseng Max-V. Please provide identification code 34563012.

Integrative Therapeutics

Phone: (800) 931-1709
Web site: www.integrativeinc.com

L-theanine; Ginseng Phytosome (Korean Ginseng). Please provide identification code PCP 5266.

Moducare

Phone: (800) 776-1981 (physicians only)
Web site: www.moducare.com

Check your local health food store.

Natur-Leaf

Life Line, Inc.
Phone: (888) 532-7845

NutriWest

Phone: (800) 451-5620
Web site: www.nutri-westfl.com

Natural Change Progesterone Cream; DSF Formula (Adrenal Glandular)

Ortho Molecular, Inc.

Phone: (800) 332-2351
Web site: www.orthomolecularproducts.com

Siberian Ginseng; Licorice Root; Korean Ginseng. Please provide program # COLB10 when ordering product.

Brekhman Elixir (Prime One)

Phone: (866) 297-3934

Trivita, "The Healthy Living Company"

Phone: (800) 991-7116
Web site: www.trivita.com

Sublingual B_{12}

Vital Nutrients

Phone: (888) 328-9992
Fax: (888) 328-9993
Web site: www.vitalnutrients.net

Adrenal Support (Adrenal Glandular)

Xymogen

Phone: (800) 647-6100
Fax: (407) 445-0204
Web site: www.xymogen.com

Progensa (progesterone cream); Viriligen a/k/a Epimedium (Horny Goat Weed)

INFORMATION WEB SITES AND EDUCATIONAL PRODUCTS

American Institute of Stress
Web site: www.stress.org

HeartMath
Phone: (800) 450-9111
Web site: www.heartmath.com

Freeze-Frame computer program with heart variability monitor

Holosync
Centerpointe Research Institute
Phone: (800) 945-2741
Web site: www.holosync.com

Or go to http://www.drcolbert.com /partners.html and click on "Instant Meditation"

National Sleep Foundation
Web site: www.sleepfoundation.org

The National Sleep Foundation is a nonprofit organization dedicated to improving public health and safety by achieving public understanding of sleep and sleep disorders and by supporting public education, sleep-related research, and advocacy.

The American Academy of Pediatrics
Web site: www.aap.org

The National Domestic Violence Hotline
Phone: (800) 799-SAFE (7233)

Thought Field Therapy
Phone: (800) 359-CURE
Web site: www.selfhelpuniv.com

Tapping the Healer Within

Notes

CHAPTER 2: ONE NATION, UNDER STRESS

1. D. Wayne, "Reactions to Stress," Identifying Stress, Health-Net & Stress Management, February 1998, in Vincent M. Newfield, "Defeating Deadly Emotions," Enjoying Everyday Life, April 2004, http://www.thehealingdoctor.com/articles.htm (accessed March 22, 2005).

2. Dave Tuttle, "Cortisol: Keeping a Dangerous Hormone in Check," *Life Extension*, July 2004, 61.

3. Albert Ellis, *A New Guide to Rational Living* (New York: Institute for Rational-Emotive Therapy, 1975).

4. Cary Cooper and Roy Payne, eds., *Causes, Coping and Consequences of Stress at Work* (New York: John Wiley and Sons, 1988). Stephen G. Minter, "Easing the Stress," Safety Zones, Occupational Hazards, April 9, 2003, http://www.occupationalhazards.com/articles/index.php?id=6893 (accessed February 3, 2005).

5. H. J. Eysenck, et al., "Personality Type, Smoking Habit and Their Interaction as Predictors of Cancer and Coronary Disease," *Personality and Individual Difference* 9(2) (1988): 479–495; H. Eysenck, British Journal of Medical Psychology 61 (pt. 1) (1988).

6. T. G. Allison, "Medical and Economic Costs of Psychologic Distress in Patients With Coronary Artery Disease," *Mayo Clinic Proceedings* 70(8) (1995): 734–742.

7. Eysenck, et al., "Personality Type, Smoking Habit and Their Interaction as Predictors of Cancer and Coronary Disease." Eysenck, *British Journal of Medical Psychology* 61.

8. J. A. Blumenthal, et al., "Stress Management and Exercise Training in Cardiac Patients With Myocardial Ischemia: Effects on Prognosis and Evaluation of Mechanisms," *Archives of Internal Medicine* 157 (October 27, 1997), referenced in "Learning How to Manage Stress May Reduce Further Cardiac Problems in Heart Patients," Research/Clinical News, Psychiatric News, http://www.psych.org/pnews/97-12-19/heart.html (accessed February 3, 2005).

CHAPTER 3: FIGHT, FLEE...OR STEW IN YOUR OWN JUICES

1. L. D. Kubzansky, et al., "Is Worrying Bad for Your Heart? A Prospective Study of Worry and Coronary Heart Disease in the Normative Aging Study," *Circulation* 94 (1997): 818-824.

2. H. Dreher, *The Immune Power Personality* (New York: Dutton, 1995), 15.

3. Mike Mitka, et al., "Metabolic Syndrome Recasts Old Cardiac, Diabetes Risk Factors as a 'New' Entity," *Journal of American Medical Association* 291 (2004): 2062–2063.

4. M. Starkman, et al., "Hippocampal Formation Volume, Memory Dysfunction, and Cortisol Levels in Patients With Cushing Syndrome," *Biological Psychiatry* 32 (1992): 756.

5. P. M. Plotsky, et al., "PsychoNeural Endocrinology of Depression: Hypothalamic-Pituitary-Adrenal Axis," *Psychoneurology* 21(2) (1998): 293–306.

6. S. Kennedy, J. K. Kiecolt-Glaser, and R. Glaser, "Immunological Consequences

of Acute and Chronic Stressors: Mediating Role of Interpersonal Stressors," *British Journal of Medical Psychology* 61 (1988): 77–85.

7. News Release, United States Department of Agriculture, Release No. 0012.05, "New Dietary Guidelines Will Help Americans Make Better Food Choices, Live Healthier Lives," January 12, 2005, http://www.usda.gov/wps/portal/!ut/p/_s.7_0_A/7_0_1OB?contentidonly=true&contentid=2005/01/0012.xml (accessed March 4, 2005).

8. "The Dietary Approach to High Blood Pressure," PDRHealth, http://www.pdrhealth.com/content/nutrition_health/chapters/fgnt12.shtml (accessed March 4, 2005).

9. "Osteoporosis: A Lifespan Approach for Prevention, Filling and Maintaining the Bone Bank," Combined Sections Meeting 2003, Tampa, FL, February 12–16, 2003, http://www.geriatricspt.org/csm2003/4520.pdf.

10. James L. Wilson, *Adrenal Fatigue: The 21st-Century Stress Hormone* (Santa Rosa, CA: Smart Publications, 2002).

CHAPTER 4: MENTAL AND EMOTIONAL HABITS PREPROGRAM US FOR STRESS

1. "Psychiatric Effects of Media Violence," American Psychiatric Association, http://www.psych.org/public_info/media_violence.cfm (accessed February 3, 2005).

2. Ibid.

3. Barbara Frazier, "The Impact of TV Violence on Children and Adolescents," The Successful Parent, http://www.thesuccessfulparent.com/articles/tv.htm (accessed February 3, 2005).

4. C. D. Jenkins, "Psychological and Social Precursors of Coronary Artery Disease," *New England Journal of Medicine* 284 (1971): 244–255.

CHAPTER 5: ADDRESSING DISTORTIONAL THOUGHT PATTERNS

1. "Biography of Dr. Aaron T. Beck," *Beck Institute of Cognitive Therapy and Research*, http://www.beckinstitute.org/Library/InfoManage/Guide.asp?FolderID=222&SessionID={569A20BA-1521-44C3-9B4C-10699D23F659} (accessed April 9, 2005).

2. David D. Burns, MD, *Feeling Good*: The New Mood Therapy (New York: Harper Collins, 1980).

3. Burns, *Feeling Good*, 42–43, copyright © 1980 David D. Burns, MD. Used by permission.

4. Ellis, *A New Guide to Rational Living*.

5. Roger Callahan, *Tapping the Healer Within* (New York: Contemporary Books, 2001).

CHAPTER 6: REDUCE YOUR FRUSTRATION FACTORS

1. R. B. Williams, et al., "Psychosocial Risk Factors for Cardiovascular Disease: More Than One Culprit at Work," *Journal of the American Medical Association* 290 (October 22, 2003): 2190–2192.

2. Paul Pearsall, *Toxic Success* (Makawao, Hawaii: Inner Ocean Publishing, 2002).

3. Thomas H. Davenport and John C. Peck, *The Attention Economy* (Boston, MA: Harvard Business School Press, 2001), in Pearsall, Toxic Success, 68;

4. Dave Ramsey, *The Total Money Makeover* (Nashville, TN: Thomas Nelson, Inc., 2003), 19.

5. Ramsey, *The Total Money Makeover*, 23.

6. Pearsall, *Toxic Success*, 68. Also, Divorce Rates, http://www.divorcereform.org/rates.html (accessed March 4, 2005).

7. "Facts and Figures About Our TV Habit," TV Turnoff Network, http://www.tvturnoff.org/images/facts&figs/factsheets/FactsFigs.pdf (accessed March 4, 2005).

8. Doc Childre and Deborah Rozman, PhD, *Overcoming Emotional Chaos* (San Diego, CA: Jodere Group, Inc., 2002), 226.

9. Stephen R. Covey, *The 7 Habits of Highly Effective People* (New York: Simon and Schuster, 1989).

10. Viktor E. Frankl, *Man's Search for Meaning* (New York: Simon and Schuster, 1963), 104–105.

CHAPTER 7: DEALING WITH THE INEVITABLE OFFENSES

1. Redford Williams, *Anger Kills* (New York: HarperTorch, 1998).

2. Lijing L.Yan, et al., "Psychosocial Factors and Risk of Hypertension," *Journal of the American Medical Association* 290 (October 22, 2003): 2138–2148.

3. J. C. Barefoot, et al., "Hostility, CHD Incidence. and Total Mortality—a 25-Year Follow up Study of 255 Physicians," *Psychosomatic Medicine* 45 (1983): 59–63.

4. The Cost of Frivolous Litigation, House Rpt. 108–682—Lawsuit Abuse Reduction Act of 2004.

CHAPTER 8: WIPING OUT WORRY

1. Rick Warren, *The Purpose-Driven Life* (Grand Rapids, MI: Zondervan, 2002).

2. Motivation Quotes About Life, Museum Marketing Tips, http://www.museummarketingtips.com/quotes/quotes_life.html (accessed February 11, 2005).

3. Joel Osteen Ministries, Lakewood Church, Houston, TX, audiocassette #221, http://www.lakewood.cc/index.htm.

4. Doc Childre and Howard Martin, *The HeartMath Solution* (San Francisco, CA: HarperSanFrancisco, 2000).

5. David L. Rambo, "Come Apart Before You Fall Apart," March 1993, in Swenson, *The Overload Syndrome*, 181.

CHAPTER 9: THE POWER OF ATTITUDE TO CREATE OR RELIEVE STRESS

1. John Hagee, *The Seven Secrets* (Lake Mary, FL: Charisma House, 2004), 31.

2. Childre and Martin, *The HeartMath Solution*.

3. Doc Childre, *Freeze-Frame* (Boulder Creek, CA: HeartMath, 1998).

4. Abraham Maslow, et al. *Abraham Maslow: A Memorial Volume* (Monterey, CA: Brooks/Cole, 1972).

5. M. E. McCullough, et al., "The Grateful Disposition: A Conceptual and Empirical Topography," *Journal of Personality and Social Psychology* 82 (2002): 112–127.

CHAPTER 10: LEARN TO BE ASSERTIVE

1. J. Grant Howard, *Balance Life's Demands* (Portland, OR: Multnomah Press, 1983), 144.

2. "I Have a Dream," speech by Dr. Martin Luther King Jr., given on the steps of the Lincoln Memorial, Washington DC, on August 28, 1963. Text for the speech can be viewed at http://www.mecca.org/~crights/dream.html (accessed February 11, 2005).

3. Wikipedia, the Free Encyclopedia, s.v. "Pareto principle," http://en.wikipedia.org/wiki/Pareto_principle (accessed February 9, 2005).

CHAPTER 12: BUILDING "MARGIN" INTO YOUR LIFE

1. John de Graff, *Afluenza: The All-Consuming Epidemic* (San Francisco, CA: Berrett-Koehler, 2001).

2. Meyer Friedman and Ray Rosenman, *Type A Behavior and Your Heart* (New York: Knopf, 1974). See also Ray H. Rosenman, et al., "Coronary Heart Disease in the Western Collaborative Group Study, Final Follow-Up and Follow-Up Experience of 8½ Years," *Journal of the American Medical Association* 233 (1975): 872-977.

3. F. W. Boreham, "The Mistress of the Margin," *Mushrooms on the Moor* (New York: Abingdon, 1915), 259.

4. Leo Tolstoy, translated by Ronald Wilks, *"How Much Land Does a Man Need" and Other Stories* (New York: Penguin Books, 1993).

5. Richard A. Swenson, *The Overload Syndrome* (Colorado Springs, CO: NavPress, 1998).

6. Ibid., 155.

CHAPTER 13: SLEEP—GOD'S "STRESS BUSTER"

1. "Less Fun, Less Sleep, More Work: An American Portrait," Press Release, March 27, 2001, National Sleep Foundation, http://www.sleepfoundation.org/PressArchives/lessfun_lesssleep.cfm (accessed February 11, 2005).

2. National Sleep Foundation, 2001 Sleep in America Poll, quoted in "Sleep Facts and Stats," http://www.sleepfoundation.org/NSAW/pk_sleepfacts.cfm (accessed January 27, 2005).

3. W. E. Waters, et al., "Attention, Stress and Negative Emotion and Persistent Sleep Onset and Sleep Maintenance Insomnia," *Sleep* 16(2) (1993): 128–136.

4. K. Spiegel, R. Leproult, and E. Van Cauter, "Impact of Sleep Debt on Metabolic and Endocrine Function," *Lancet* 354 (October 23, 1999): 1435–1439, referenced in "Backgrounder: Why Sleep Matters," www.sleepfoundation.org/NSAW/pk_background.cfm (accessed February 10, 2005).

5. A. A. Kuo, "Does Sleep Deprivation Impair Cognitive and Motor Performance as Much as Alcohol Intoxication?" *Western Journal of Medicine* 3(174) (March 1, 2001): 180, referenced in "Backgrounder: Why Sleep Matters," www.sleepfoundation.org/NSAW/pk_background.cfm (accessed February 10, 2005).

6. Shawn M. Talbott, PhD, *The Cortisol Connection* (Alameda, CA: Hunter House 2002), 52–54.

7. "Less Fun, Less Sleep, More Work: An American Portrait," Press Release, March 27, 2001, National Sleep Foundation, http://www.sleepfoundation.org/PressArchives/lessfun_lesssleep.cfm (accessed February 10, 2005).

8. "Caffeine Content of Food and Drugs," Center for Science in the Public Interest, http://www.cspinet.org/new/cafchart.htm (accessed February 10, 2005) and "The Caffeine Corner: Products Ranked by Amount," Nutrition Action Health Letter, Center for Science in the Public Interest, http://www.cspinet.org/nah/caffeine/caffeine_corner.htm (accessed February 10, 2005).

CHAPTER 14: A DIET TO REDUCE STRESS

1. R. Pasquali, et al., "Hypothalamic-Pituitary-Adrenal Axis Activity and Its Relationship to the Autonomic Nervous System in Women with Visceral and Subcutaneous Obesity: Effects of the Corticotrophin-Releasing Factors-Arginine-Vasopressin Test and of Stress," *Metabolism* 45 (1996): 351–356.

2. Barry Sears, *Omega Rx Zone* (New York: Harper Collins, 2002).

3. Russell Blaylock, *Excitotoxins: The Taste That Kills* (Santa Fe, NM: Health Press, 1997), 180.

4. Ibid.

Notes

CHAPTER 15: NUTRIENTS FOR COPING WITH STRESS

1. Robert H. Fletcher and Kathleen M. Fairfield, "Vitamins for Chronic Disease Prevention in Adults (Multivitamin Recommendation)," *Journal of the American Medical Association* 287 (2002): 3127–3129.

2. L. Smidt, et al., "Influence of Thiamin Supplementation on the Health and General Wellbeing of an Elderly Irish Population with Marginal Thiamin Deficiency," *Journal of Gerontology* 46 (1991): M16–22.

3. "Riboflavin in Adrenal Cortex," *Nutritional Review* 31(1973): 96–97.

4. S. M. Madigan, et al., "Riboflavin and Vitamin B_6 Intakes and Status and Biochemical Response to Riboflavin Supplementation in Free Living Elderly People," *American Journal of Clinical Nutrition* 69 (1999): 389–395.

5. L. J. Machlin, "New Views on the Function and Health Effects of Vitamins," *Nutrition* 10(6) (1994): 562.

6. A. Fidanza, "Therapeutic Action of Pantothenic Acid," *International Journal of Vitamin and Nutrition Res Suppl* 24 (1983): 53–67.

7. A. H. Merrill, et al., "Diseases Associated With Defects in Vitamin B_6 Metabolism or Utilization," *Ann Rev Nutrition* 7 (1987): 137–156.

8. R. Carmel, "Subtle Cobalamine Deficiency," *Annals of Internal Medicine* 124 (1996): 338–340.

9. "Getting Enough B_{12}?" Tufts E-news, September 10, 2001, http://enews.tufts.edu/stories/091001GettingEnoughB12.htm (accessed February 11, 2005).

10. S. P. Stabler, et al., "Vitamin B_{12} Deficiency in the Elderly: Current Dilemmas," *American Journal of Clinical Nutrition* 66 (1997): 741–749.

11. R. M. Russell, "A Minimum of 13,500 Deaths Annual From Coronary Artery Disease Could Be Prevented by Increasing Folate Intake to Reduce Homocysteine Levels," *Journal of the American Medical Association* 275 (1996): 1828–1829.

12. M. Fava, et al., "Folate, Vitamin B_{12}, and Homocysteine in Major Depressive Disorder," *American Journal of Psychiatry* 153(2) (1997): 426–428.

13. A. Odumosu, "Ascorbic Acid and Cortisol Metabolism and Hypovitaminosis, see guinea pigs," *International Journal of Vitamin and Nutritional Research* 55 (1982): 176–185.

14. S. P. Campbell, "Vitamin C Lowers Stress Hormone in Rats," *Science News* 156(10) (1999): 158.

15. "Magnesium and Aging," LamMD.com, An Insider's Guide to Natural Medicine, http://www.drlam.com/A3R_brief_in_doc_format/1999-No3-MagnesiumandAging.cfm (accessed February 11, 2005).

16. H. Ising, et al., "Increased Noise Trauma in Guinea Pigs Through Magnesium Deficiency," *Archives of Otorhinolaryngology* 236 (1982): 139–146.

17. H. Kuribara, W. B. Stavinoha, and Y. Maruyama, "Honokiol, a Putative Anxiolytic Agent Extracted From Magnolia Bark, Has No Diazepam-like Side Effects in Mice," *Journal of Pharmacy and Pharmacology* 51(1) (1999): 97–103.

18. H. Juribara, et al., "The Anxiolytic Effect of Two Oriental Herbal Drugs in Japan Attributed to Honokiol From Magnolia Bark," *Journal of Pharmacy and Pharmacology* 52(11) (2000): 1425–1429.

19. Y. C. Lo, et al., "Magnolol and Honokiol Isolated From Magnolia Officinalis Protect Rat Heart Mitochondria Against Lipid Peroxidation," *Biochemical Pharmacology* 47(3) (1994): 549–553.

20. R. R. Engel, et al., "Double-Blind Crossover Study of PS Versus Placebo in Patients With Early Dementia of the Alzheimer Type," *European Neuropyschopharmacology* 2 (1999): 1149–1155.

21. P. Monteleone, et al., "Blunting by Chronic PS Administration of the Stress Induced Activation of the Hypothalamo-Pituitary-Adrenal Axis in Healthy Men," *European Journal of Clinical Pharmacology* 42(4) (1992): 385–388.

22. N. Beckham, *Journal of Complementary Medicine* (February 2, 1996), quoted in "Our Phytosterols," Integra Nutrition Inc., http://www.integranutrition.com/phytosterol-sheet.html (accessed March 11, 2005).

23. P. J. Bouic, et al., "The Effects of B-Sitosterol (BSS) and B-Sitosterol Glucoside (BSSG) Mixture on Selected Immune Parameters of Marathon Runners: Inhibition of Post Marathon Immune Suppression and Inflammation," *International Journal of Sports Medicine* 20 (1999): 258–261.

24. "A Retrospective Analysis of Prime One and Its Active Ingredients," A Review of the Clinical Trials and Evaluations of Prime One, Volume One, Number One, February 19, 2002, page 1, published by Advantage Marketing Systems, Inc.

25. V. Darbinyan, et al. "Rhodiola Rosea and Stress-Induced Fatigue—a Double-Blind Crossover Study of a Standardized Extract SHR-5 With a Repeated Low-Dose Regimen on the Mental Performance of Healthy Physicians During Night Duty," *Phytomedicine* 7(5) (2000): 365–371.

26. A. A. Spasod, et al., "A Double-Blind Placebo-Controlled Pilot Study of the Stimulating and Adaptagenic Effect of Rhodiola Rosea SHR Extract on the Fatigue of Students Caused by Stress During an Examination, With a Repeated Low-Dose Regimen," *Phytomedicine* 7(2) (2000): 85–89.

27. N. R. Farnswoth, A. D. Kinghorn, and D. P. Waller, "Siberian Ginseng (Eleuthrococcus senticosus): Current status of an adaptogen," *Economic Medicinal Plant Research* 1 (1985): 156–215.

28. I. Yaychuk-Arabei, "Ancient Herb for Modern Lifestyles: Ginseng," *Health Naturally*, December/January 1998, 7–8.

29. K. Asano, et al., "Effect of Eutherococcus Senticoccus Extract on Human Working Capacity," *Planta Medica* 37 (1986): 175–177.

30. Ashwagandha, "The Gods Make Love: The Great Hot Plant," Medicine Hunter, http://www.medicinehunter.com/ashwagandha.htm (accessed February 11, 2005).

31. T. Wu, et al., "Experimental Study on Antagonizing Action of Herba Epimedii on Side Effects Induced by Glucocorticoids," *Zhongguo Zhong Yao Za Zhi* 12 (1996): 748–751, 763.

32. A. K. Kuang, et al., "Effects of Yang-Restoring Herb Medicines on Levels of Plasma Corticosterone, Testosterone and Triiodothyronine," *Zhong Xi Yi Jie He Za Zhi* 12 (1989): 737–738, 710.

33. "A Retrospective Analysis of Prime One and Its Active Ingredients," A Review of the Clinical Trials and Evaluations of Prime One, Volume One, Number One, February 19, 2002, page 1, published by Advantage Marketing Systems, Inc.

34. W. Poelding, et al., "A Functional-Dimensional Approach to Depression: Serotonin Deficiency as a Target Syndrome in a Comparison of 5-hydroxytryptophan and Fluvoxamine," *Psychopathology* 24 (1991): 53–81.

35. T. Kakuda, et al., "Inhibiting Effects of Theanine on Caffeine Stimulation Evaluated by EEG in the Rat," *Biosci Biotechno Biochem* 64 (2000): 287–293; also, R. Mason, "200 mg of Zen; L-theanine Boosts Alpha Waves, Promotes Alert Relaxation," Alternative and Complementary Therapies, April 7, 2001, 91–95.

CHAPTER 16: EXERCISES THAT RELIEVE STRESS

1. James Blumenthal, "Effects of Exercise Training in Older Patients With Major Depression," *Archives of Internal Medicine* 159 (1999): 2349–2356.

2. P. D. Thompson, "Cardiovascular Complications of Vigorous Physical Activity,"

Archives of Internal Medicine 156 (1996): 2297–2302.

3. "Hatha Yoga and Its Effects," SelfGrowth.com, http://www.selfgrowth.com/articles/Various1.html (accessed March 11, 2005).

4. Stress Management, "Medical Research on Effects of Sahaja Yoga on Hypertension," Sahaja Yoga India, http://www.sahajayoga.org.in/StressMgmt.asp (accessed February 14, 2005).

5. Marian S. Garfinkel, et al., "Yoga-Based Intervention for Carpal Tunnel Syndrome," *Journal of the American Medical Association* 280 (November 11, 1998): 1601–1603.

6. Judith Horstman, "Tai Chi," *Arthritis Today*, http://www.arthritis.org/resources/arthritistoday/2000_archives/2000_07_08_taichi.asp (accessed February 14, 2005). Jacqueline Stenson, "Tai Chi Improves Lung Function in Older People," Medical Tribune News Service (1995). Also, D. D. Brown, et al., "Cardiovascular and Ventilatory Responses During Formalized Tai Chi Chuan Exercise," Research Quartery for Exercise and Sport 60 (1989): 246–250.

7. P. Jin, "Changes in Heart Rate, Noradrenaline, Cortisol and Mood during Tai Chi," *Journal of Psychosomatic Research* 33 (1989): 197–206.

8. Shawn Talbott, PhD, "Look to the Salmon: Controlling Your Cortisol Levels," Xtri.com, Real Triathlon, http://www.xtri.com/article.asp?id=845&offset=0 (accessed February 14, 2005).

9. D. J. Brillon, et al., "Effect of Cortisol on the Energy Expenditure and Amino Acid Metabolism in Humans," *American Journal of Physiology* 268 (1995): E501–513.

CHAPTER 17: CULTIVATING HAPPINESS AND JOY AS A LIFESTYLE

1. Rich Bayer, PhD, "Benefits of Happiness," Upper Bay Counseling and Support Services, Inc., http://www.upperbay.org/benefits_of_happiness.htm (accessed April 11, 2005).

2. *Merriam-Webster's Collegiate Dictionary* (Springfield, MA: Merriam-Webster, Inc., 2003), s.v. "happiness."

3. Ibid., s.v. "happy."

4. Martin Seligman, *Authentic Happiness* (N.p.: Free Press, 2002), quoted in Wikipedia Free Encyclopedia, s.v. "happiness," retrieved from http://www.answers.com/topic/happiness (accessed April 11, 2005).

5. *Merriam-Webster's Collegiate Dictionary*, s.v. "joy."

6. "In the Psalms, the psalmist rejoices over God's righteousness (71:14-16), salvation (21:1; 71:23), mercy (31:7), creation (148:5), Word (119:14,162), and faithfulness (33:1-6). God's characteristics as well as His acts are the cause of rejoicing. The joy required of the righteous person (Ps 150; Phil 4:4) is produced by the Spirit of God (Gal 5:22). This kind of joy looks beyond the present to our future salvation (Rom 5:2; 8:18; 1 Peter 1:4,6) and to our sovereign God, who works out all things for our ultimate good, which is Christlikeness (Rom 8:28-30). This kind of joy is distinct from mere happiness. Joy like this is possible, even in the midst of sorrow (1 Cor 12:26; 2 Cor 6:10; 7:4)." [From *Nelson's Illustrated Bible Dictionary* (Nashville, TN: Thomas Nelson Publishers, 1986), s.v. "joy," accessed through PC Study Bible 3.0, (Seattle, WA: Biblesoft Electronic Database, 1994).]

7. Humor and Laughter: Health Benefits and Online Sources, http://www.helpguide.org/aging/humor_laughter_health.htm (accessed April 9, 2005).

8. Bayer, "Benefits of Happiness," http://www.upperbay.org/benefits_of_happiness.htm (accessed April 11, 2005).

9. Ibid.

10. Ibid.

11. Ibid.

12. Lynn Shaw, "A Prescription to Laugh: Healing Through Humor and Laughter," The Herbs Place, http://www.theherbsplace.com/AHM/ahmlaughprescription.html (accessed April 11, 2005).

13. Ibid.

14. Ibid.

15. Ibid.

16. "Humor and Laughter: Health Benefits and Online Sources," Helpguide.com, http://www.helpguide.org/aging/humor_laughter_health.htm (accessed April 11, 2005).

17. Ibid.

18. Ibid.

19. "Science of Laughter," Discovery Health, http://www.discoveryhealth.co.uk/naturalhealth/nh_story.asp?storyid=102437&feature=tv (accessed April 11, 2005).

20. Kimberly Bailey, "What's In a Smile?" Science Has Shown That Smiling Really IS Good for You, About.com, http://bipolar.about.com/cs/humor/a/000802smile.htm (accessed April 11, 2005).

21. "One Smile Can Make You Feel a Million Dollars," World of Psychology, Blog Archive, http://psychcentral.com/blog/archives/2005/03/07/one-smile-can-make-you-feel-a-million-dollars (accessed April 11, 2005).

22. Bailey, "What's In a Smile?"

CHAPTER 18: LEARNING TO RELAX

1. "The Relaxation Response: Elicitation of the Relaxation Response FAQs," Mind/Body Medical Institute, http://www.mbmi.org/pages/mbb_rr3.asp (accessed April 13, 2005).

2. "Mindfulness," Mind/Body Medical Institute, http://www.mbmi.org/pages/wi_ms1aa.asp (accessed April 13, 2005).

3. Ibid.

4. Thich Nhat Hanh, *The Miracle of Mindfulness* (Boston: Beacon Press, 1987), 20.

5. John Glenn Paton and Van A. Christy, *Foundations in Singing*, seventh edition (New York: McGraw-Hill Higher Education, 2002), 8.

6. Ibid., 9.

7. Ibid., 11.

8. Ibid., 14.

9. Herbert Benson, MD, *Relaxation Response* (New York: William Morrow and Co., 1976).

10. Warren, *The Purpose-Driven Life*.

11. Jeffrey Cram, PhD and D. P. Wirth, "The Psychophysiology of Non-Traditional Prayer," *International Journal of Psychosomatics* 41 (1994): http://www.semg.org/education/articles/article4.htm (accessed April 13, 2005).

12. Ibid.

13. Ibid.

14. Childre, *Freeze-Frame*.

15. This title is still in print: Edmund Jacobson, *Progressive Relaxation*, 3rd rev. ed. (Chicago, IL: University of Chicago Press, 1974)

16. "Progressive Relaxation," http://www.mindspring.com/~yepstein/progrel.htm (accessed April 13, 2005).

17. Robert Woolfolk and Frank Richardson, *Stress, Sanity, and Survival* (New

York: Signet Books, 1979).

18. Wolfgang Linden, *Autogenic Training: A Clinical Guide* (N.p.: Guilford Press, 1990). Martha Davis, PhD, Elizabeth Robbins Eshelman, MSW, and Matthew McKay, PhD, The Relaxation and Stress Reduction Workbook (Oakland, CA: New Harbinger Publications, Inc., 1995).

19. "Techniques: Everything You Wanted to Know About Massage," About Massage.Com, http://www.aboutmassage.com/techniques.htm (accessed April 13, 2005).

20. Ibid.

CHAPTER 19: ADRENAL FATIGUE AND BURNOUT

1. H. R. Harrower, "Hypoadrenia Ordinarily Spells Hypotension," *Endocrine Diagnostic Charts* (Glendale, CA: Harrower Laboratory, 1929), 79.

2. "DHEA (Dehydroepiandrosterone)," RemedyFind, http://remedyfind.com/rm-401-DHEA.asp (accessed March 11, 2005).

3. Dr. William Timmins, *Foundational Health Program Interpretive Guide*, 2004 edition (San Diego, CA: BioHealth Diagnostics).

4. Bonne, et al., *Journal of Steroid Biochemistry and Molecular Biology* 20 (1984): 13.

5. E. Barrett-Connor, et al., "A Prospective Study of Dehydroepiandrosterone Sulfate, Mortality, and Cardiovascular Disease," *New England Journal of Medicine* 315 (December 11, 1986): 1519–1524.

6. Timmons, *Foundational Health Program Interpretive Guide.*

7. W. Jefferies, *Safe Uses of Cortisol* (Springfield, IL: Thomas, 1996).

CHAPTER 20: THE PEACE THAT PASSES UNDERSTANDING

1. Mother Teresa, excerpt from the Nobel Peace Prize acceptance speech, The Nobel Prize Internet Archive, http://www.nobelprizes.com (accessed February 15, 2005).

2. Mother Teresa, Nobel Lecture, 11 December 1979, http://nobelprize.org/peace/laureates/1979/teresa-lecture.html (accessed February 15, 2005).

3. Ibid.

4. Mother Teresa: Letters, message that Mother Teresa addressed to the Albanian people, April 28, 1997, http://www.tisv.be/mt/en/let.htm (accessed February 15, 2005).

5. Edward W. Desmond, "A Pencil in the Hand of God," a *Time* interview with Mother Teresa, Time, December 4, 1989, http://www.time.com/time/reports/motherteresa/t891204.html (accessed February 15, 2005).

6. 32 Quotations From Mother Teresa, Workstations at Maryland, University of Maryland at College Park, http://www.wam.umd.edu/~stwright/rel/xty/MotherTeresa.html (accessed February 15, 2005).

7. Ibid.

8. Ibid.

APPENDIX A: SALVATION PRAYER

1. Adapted from Bill Bright, "Four Spiritual Laws" (Orlando, FL: Newlife Publications, 1994). Used by permission.

Are you sick and tired of being *sick* and *tired*?

If you enjoyed *Stress Less* by Dr. Don Colbert, you may be interested in the Bible Cure books, *Walking in Divine Health, Toxic Relief, What You Don't Know May Be Killing You, Fasting Made Easy, Deadly Emotions,* and *What Would Jesus Eat?*

Choose from 30 health topics of The Bible Cure series, which have sold more than 2.5 million copies. Available at $6.99 each, these books are trusted resources combining biblical healing and modern health.

More Than 2.5 Million SOLD

THE BIBLE CURE FOR ASTHMA
Ancient Truths, Natural Remedies and the Latest Findings for Your Health Today

THE BIBLE CURE FOR HIGH CHOLESTEROL
Ancient Truths, Natural Remedies and the Latest Findings for Your Health Today

THE BIBLE CURE FOR AUTOIMMUNE DISEASES
Ancient Truths, Natural Remedies and the Latest Findings for Your Health Today
DON COLBERT, MD

THE BIBLE CURE FOR COLDS, FLU AND SINUS INFECTIONS
Ancient Truths, Natural Remedies and the Latest Findings for Your Health Today
DON COLBERT, MD

THE BIBLE CURE FOR OVERCOMING CANDIDA
Ancient Truths, Natural Remedies and the Latest Findings for Your Health Today
DON COLBERT, MD

Don Colbert, MD

For more information
Call 407-331-7007
Or visit www.drcolbert.com

SILOAM®
A STRANG COMPANY
Solutions for healthy living!

5142

Strang Communications, the publisher of both Charisma House and *Charisma* magazine, wants to give you 3 FREE ISSUES to our award-winning magazine.

Since its inception in 1975, *Charisma* magazine has helped thousands of Christians stay connected with what God is doing worldwide.

Within its pages you will discover in-depth reports and the latest news from a Christian perspective, biblical health tips, global events in the body of Christ, personality profiles, and so much more. Join the family of *Charisma* readers who enjoy feeding their spirit each month with miracle-filled testimonies and inspiring articles that bring clarity, provoke prayer, and demand answers.

To claim your **3 free issues** of *Charisma,* send your name and address to: Charisma 3 Free Issue Offer, 600 Rinehart Road, Lake Mary, FL 32746. Or you may call 1-800-829-3346 and ask for Offer # 93FREE. This offer is only valid in the USA.

---

www.charismamag.com

3581